Leith's Cookery Course 3

PRUDENCE LEITH founded Leith's Good Food, a City party-catering business which delivers all over London, in 1964; Leith's Restaurant, considered one of the top ten in London today, in 1969; and Leith's School of Food and Wine, Notting Hill Gate, in 1975.

Born in South Africa in 1940, she became addicted to cooking while in Paris, and trained at the Cordon Bleu school in London. She began her catering career from a bed-sitter in Earls Court, travelling about on the Tube with peach flans and cucumber soup. She has published three previous cookbooks and is cookery correspondent of the *Sunday Express*. Married to Rayne Kruger (writer and fellow-Director of the Leith's Group), she has two children and divides her time between her restaurant, school, catering business and Leith's Farm in Oxfordshire.

CAROLINE WALDEGRAVE, now Principal of Leith's School of Food and Wine, joined Leith's Good Food as a cook in 1971 after training at the Cordon Bleu school in London. She has studied food and cooking in America and is a qualified instructor in wine. She was born in 1952 and is married to William Waldegrave MP.

Leith's Cookery Course

Leith's Cookery Course consists of three books based, respectively, on the beginners', intermediate and advanced courses at Leith's School of Food and Wine.

Book 1 combines factual information about food and detailed instruction of kitchen techniques with step by step French and English recipes designed for the beginner.

Book 2 assumes basic knowledge and cooking experience on the part of the reader. The recipes build up to give the accomplished learner some mastery of French, English and many other *cuisines*.

Book 3 is for the dedicated amateur, or the professional cook: its recipes enable the reader to produce classic *haute cuisine* dishes with confidence.

Leith's Cookery Course 3

PRUDENCE LEITH
and
CAROLINE WALDEGRAVE

FONTANA PAPERBACKS

First published by Fontana Paperbacks 1980
Copyright © Leith's Farm Ltd 1980
Filmset in 'Monophoto' Times by
Northumberland Press Ltd, Gateshead, Tyne and Wear
and printed in Great Britain by
Richard Clay (The Chaucer Press) Ltd, Bungay, Suffolk

To the staff, past
and present, of the
Leith's Group

Contents

Acknowledgements 9

Introduction 11

1. About Cooking 13

   Conversion tables 13; Glossary of cooking terms 17; Classic
   garnishes 25; Traditional British accompaniments 28; Methods
   of cooking 28; Baking breads, cakes, pastries etc. 37; Savoury
   sauces 54; Fish 60; Meat 65; Poultry 77; Ice cream 86; Catering
   quantities 89

2. First Courses 96

   Soups 96; Pâtés and terrines 101; Other first courses and pasta
   105; Fruit and vegetable starters 118; Eggs, savoury soufflés and
   mousses 125; Salads 129

3. Vegetables and Rice 132

4. Fish 140

5. Meat 170

   Beef 170; Lamb 179; Pork and ham 186; Veal 191; Offal 197

6. Poultry and Game 201

   Chicken and turkey 201; Duck and goose 216; Game 223

7. Savoury Stocks, Butters and Sauces 229

   Stocks 229; Butters 235; Sauces 237

8. Puddings and Desserts 247

   Baked puddings and pancakes 247; Meringues 250; Fruit puddings and desserts 255; Custards, creams, mousses and soufflés
   261; Dessert jellies 270; Ice creams and bombes 277

9. **Pasta, Pastries, Batters and Breads** 285

Pasta 285; Pastry 286; Pastries 296; Batters 314; Breads 316

10. **Sweet Sauces, Fillings, Cakes and Icings** 320

Sweet sauces 320; Icings and confectionery 324; Biscuits and cakes 333

Index 345

ACKNOWLEDGEMENTS

We would like to thank, first and foremost, the staff and students of Leith's School of Food and Wine for testing, re-testing and perfecting the recipes, with special thanks to Sally Procter.

We also pay grateful tribute to most of the good cookery writers of today, especially to Rosemary Hume, Elizabeth David, Jane Grigson, Delia Smith, Katie Stewart, Robin Howe and Margaret Costa, whose recipes we have unashamedly pinched for use in the School, and used for inspiration and reference for this book.

For painstaking work in compiling the book, and for constant good temper, we would like to thank Polly Tyrer, Seemah Joshua, Margaret Cain and June Avis; and for recipe ideas and general helpfulness Jean Reynaud and Chef Max Markarian of Leith's Restaurant, and the staff of Leith's Good Food (Caterers).

In addition our thanks are due to Colin Cullimore, CBE, Managing Director of J. H. Dewhurst Ltd, for his help on the meat chapters, and to the White Fish Authority and the Herring Industry Board for helping on the fish chapters.

Finally, we would like to thank Myra Street for editing this book.

P.L.
C.W.

Note: Purists will complain about the hotch-potch of English and French culinary terms used in these books. We are unrepentant: French words are now so much part of the cook's vocabulary that they cannot be substituted. 'Sauté potatoes', for example, is precise and unambiguous. 'Fried potatoes' could mean chips, 'pommes sautées' could mean apples, and 'pommes de terre sautées' is too long and pompous. French words, we contend, are part of the international language of the kitchen.

P.L.
C.W.

INTRODUCTION

LEITH'S COOKERY COURSE consists of three books. *Book 1* contains the chapter 'All about Cooking' which I hope answers every question that the cook, beginner or professional, is ever likely to ask – from how to grease a cake tin to how to carve smoked salmon, skin an eel or bone a turkey. The recipes in *Book 1* range from the very simple – poached eggs, rice pudding and macaroni cheese, for example – to the more complicated roast pheasant with sauerkraut or Chinese cabbage and apple salad; but all make use of the basic skills that are fundamental to good cooking.

Book 2 builds on those skills: the recipes become more advanced and there is special emphasis on yeast cookery, soufflé making, and *cuisines* other than French and British. It should, I think, provide a challenge to the interested cook and be a useful manual for the experienced one.

Book 3 is unashamedly written for the dedicated cook or enthusiastic amateur. It is not for the bachelor in a bed-sitter or the overworked Mum on a tight budget. It is, rather, for those who want to practise the art – as well as the science – of cooking, and who long occasionally to produce food as perfect as in the best restaurants.

Once the basic cooking methods have been mastered, advanced cookery is much like simple cookery: the techniques and ingredients are merely used in ever more interesting combinations. Someone who can make shortcrust pastry, custard, choux paste and caramel, and can whip cream, can also make that amazing pyramid of a French wedding cake, Gateau St Honoré. However, many keen enthusiasts, having realized this, start too soon to be 'creative', wrongly imagining that if one glass of sherry in a dish is good, four must be four times better; that if a recipe calls for a pinch of fresh thyme, two tablespoons of dried herbs must be an improvement.

11

My advice, especially to beginners, is to stick like a limpet to the recipe, and not hesitate to weigh and measure quantities. After a while you begin to tell by the look, texture or taste if the quantities are right; but I've been cooking all my grown-up life and I still weigh the beef to work out the roasting time, look up quantities for unfamiliar cakes, measure every ingredient for choux pastry.

When planning a menu, the rule is to keep it simple. If the main course needs last-minute work, choose a starter and pudding that can be done in advance. Try to balance the texture, colour and taste of the meal: avoid three white courses (vichyssoise, chicken with rice, and syllabub, for example); avoid cream or alcohol in all the courses; try to include something crisp and crunchy if the main part of the meal is soft and smooth. Serve vegetables that provide contrast in colour and texture – not cabbage with sprouts, for example.

The sight of food should make the mouth water, and induce feelings of positive greed and hunger. I think this is best achieved not by cutting radishes into roses or tomatoes into waterlilies, but by presenting food simply and freshly, with perhaps a sprig of watercress to set off the colour, or surrounded by simple fried croutons, or dusted with finely chopped herbs.

This does not mean that food should ever be sloppily served, or presented in a way which suggests anything other than care and calm organization. The cherished vision of great chefs gripped with rage and hurling knives is a myth. By and large, knife-hurlers make bad chefs, and the qualities required to earn a reputation for culinary genius are more mundane: a quiet temperament, a logical mind, a love of order – and of food. Another prerequisite is clear information and a set of interesting, reliable recipes that whet the appetite and challenge the cook to attempt new dishes. I hope that this is what the three books in *Leith's Cookery Course* provide.

P.L.

1
About Cooking

CONVERSION TABLES

The tables below are approximate, and do not conform in all respects to the official conversions, but we have found them convenient for cooking.

WEIGHTS

Imperial	Metric
$\frac{1}{4}$oz	$7\frac{1}{2}$–8g
$\frac{1}{2}$oz	15g
$\frac{3}{4}$oz	20g
1oz	30g
2oz	55g
3oz	85g
4oz ($\frac{1}{4}$lb)	110g
5oz	140g
6oz	170g
7oz	200g
8oz ($\frac{1}{2}$lb)	225g
9oz	255g
10oz	285g
11oz	310g
12oz ($\frac{3}{4}$lb)	340g
13oz	370g
14oz	400g
15oz	425g
16oz (1lb)	450g

Imperial	Metric
1¼lb	560g
1½lb	675g
2lb	900g
3lb	1·35 kilos
4lb	1·8 kilos
5lb	2·3 kilos
6lb	2·7 kilos
7lb	3·2 kilos
8lb	3·4 kilos
9lb	4·0 kilos
10lb	4·5 kilos

LIQUID MEASURES

	ml	fl.oz
1¾ pints	1000 (1 litre)	35
1 pint	570	20
¾ pint	425	15
½ pint	290	10
⅓ pint	190	6·6
¼pint (1 gill)	150	5
	56	2
2 scant tablespoons	28	1
1 teaspoon	5	

WINE QUANTITIES

	ml	fl.oz
Average wine bottle	730	25¾
1 glass wine	100	3½
1 glass port or sherry	70	2½
1 glass liqueur	45	1½

LENGTHS

Imperial	Metric
½in	1cm
1in	2½cm
2in	5cm
6in	15cm
12in	30cm

APPROXIMATE AMERICAN/EUROPEAN CONVERSIONS

Commodity	USA	Metric	Imperial
Flour	1 cup	140g	5oz
Caster and granulated sugar	1 cup	225g	8oz
Caster and granulated sugar	2 level tablespoons	30g	1oz
Brown sugar	1 cup	170g	6oz
Butter/margarine/lard	1 cup	225g	8oz
Sultanas/raisins	1 cup	200g	7oz
Currants	1 cup	140g	5oz
Ground almonds	1 cup	110g	4oz
Golden syrup	1 cup	340g	12oz
Uncooked rice	1 cup	200g	7oz

Note: In American recipes, when quantities are stated as spoons, 'level' spoons are meant. English recipes (and those in this book) call for rounded spoons except where stated otherwise. This means that 2 American tablespoons equal 1 English tablespoon.

USEFUL MEASUREMENTS

1 American cup	225ml/8 fl.oz
1 egg	56ml/2 fl.oz
1 egg white	28ml/1 fl.oz
1 rounded tablespoon flour	30g/1oz
1 rounded tablespoon cornflour	30g/1oz
1 rounded tablespoon sugar	30g/1oz
2 rounded tablespoons breadcrumbs	30g/1oz
2 level teaspoons gelatine	8g/$\frac{1}{4}$oz

30g/1oz granular (packet) aspic sets 570ml (1 pint) liquid. 15g/$\frac{1}{2}$oz powdered gelatine, or 4 leaves, will set 570ml (1 pint) liquid. (However, in hot weather, or if the liquid is very acid, like lemon juice, or if the jelly contains solid pieces of fruit or meat and is to be turned out of the dish or mould, 20g/$\frac{3}{4}$oz should be used.)

OVEN TEMPERATURES

°C	°F	Gas mark
70	150	$\frac{1}{4}$
80	175	$\frac{1}{4}$
100	200	$\frac{1}{2}$
110	225	$\frac{1}{2}$
130	250	1
140	275	1
150	300	2
170	325	3
180	350	4
190	375	5
200	400	6
220	425	7
230	450	8
240	475	8
250	500	9
270	525	9
290	550	9

GLOSSARY OF COOKING TERMS

Abats: French for offal (hearts, livers, brains, tripe etc.). Americans call them 'variety meats'.

Bain-marie: A baking tin half-filled with hot water in which terrines, custards etc. stand while cooking. The food is protected from direct fierce heat and cooks in a gentle, steamy atmosphere. Also a large container which will hold a number of pans standing in hot water, used to keep soups, sauces etc. hot without further cooking.

Bard: To tie bacon or pork fat over a joint of meat, game bird or poultry, to be roasted. This helps to prevent the flesh from drying out.

Baste: To spoon over liquid (sometimes stock, sometimes fat) during cooking to prevent drying out.

Beignets: Fritters.

Beurre manié: Butter and flour in equal quantities worked together to a soft paste, and used as a liaison or thickening for liquids. Small pieces are whisked into boiling liquid. As the butter melts it disperses the flour evenly through the liquid, so thickening it without causing lumps.

Beurre noisette: Browned butter – see *Noisette* (a).

Bisque: Shellfish soup, smooth and thickened.

Blanch: Originally, to whiten by boiling, e.g. briefly to boil sweetbreads or brains to remove traces of blood, or to boil almonds to make the brown skin easy to remove, leaving the nuts white. Now commonly used to mean parboiling (as in blanching vegetables when they are parboiled prior to freezing, or precooked so that they have only to be reheated before serving).

17

Bouchées: Small puff pastry cases like miniature vol-au-vents.

Bouillon: Broth or uncleared stock.

Bouquet garni: Parsley stalks, small bay leaf, fresh thyme, celery stalk, sometimes with a blade of mace, tied together with string and used to flavour stews etc. Removed before serving.

Braise: To bake or stew slowly on a bed of vegetables in a covered pan.

Canapé: A small bread or biscuit base, sometimes fried, spread or covered with savoury paste, egg etc., used for cocktail titbits or as an accompaniment to meat dishes. Sometimes used to denote the base only, as in *champignons sur canapé.*

Caramel: Sugar cooked to a toffee.

Chateaubriand: Roast fillet steak, for two people or more.

Clarified butter: Butter that has been separated from milk particles and other impurities which cause it to look cloudy when melted, and to burn easily when heated. It is usually clarified by first heating until foaming, then skimming; or (which is easier) straining through a double thickness of muslin, a coffee filter paper, or 2 J-cloths.

Court bouillon: Liquid used for cooking fish (see page 233).

Crêpes: Thin French pancakes.

Croquettes: Paste of mashed potato and possibly poultry, fish or meat, formed into small balls or patties, coated in egg and bread-crumbs and deep fried.

Croûte: Literally crust. Sometimes a pastry case, as in fillet of beef *en croûte,* sometimes toasted or fried bread, as in Scotch woodcock or scrambled eggs on toast.

Croutons: Small evenly sized cubes of fried bread used as a soup garnish, and occasionally in other dishes.

Dariole: Small castle-shaped mould used for moulding rice salads and sometimes for cooking cake mixtures.

Déglacer: To loosen and liquefy the fat, sediment and browned juices stuck at the bottom of a frying pan or saucepan by adding liquid (usually stock, water or wine) and stirring while boiling.

Deglaze: See *Déglacer.*

Dégorger: To extract the juices from meat, fish or vegetables, generally by salting then soaking or washing. Usually done to remove indigestible or strong-tasting juices.

Dépouiller: To skim off the scum from a sauce or stock: a splash of cold stock is added to the boiling liquid. This helps to bring scum and fat to the surface, which can then be more easily skimmed.

Dropping consistency: The consistency where a mixture will drop reluctantly from a spoon, neither pouring off nor obstinately adhering.

Duxelle: Finely chopped raw mushrooms, sometimes with chopped shallots or chopped ham, often used as a stuffing.

Eggwash: Beaten raw egg, sometimes with salt, used for glazing pastry to give it a shine when baked.

Entrecôte: Sirloin steak.

Entrée: Traditionally a dish served before the main course, but usually served as a main course today.

Entremets: Dessert or sweet course, excluding pastry sweets.

Escalope: A thin slice of meat, sometimes beaten out flat to make it thinner and larger.

Farce: Stuffing.

Fécule: Farinaceous thickening, usually arrowroot or cornflour.

Flamber: To set alcohol alight. Usually to burn off the alcohol, but frequently simply for dramatic effect. (Past tense flambé or flambée.) English: to flame.

Flame: See *Flamber.*

Fleurons: Crescents of puff pastry, generally used to garnish fish or poultry.

Fold: To mix with a gentle lifting motion, rather than to stir vigorously. The aim is to avoid beating out air while mixing.

Frappé: Iced, or set in a bed of crushed ice.

Fricassé: White stew made with cooked or raw poultry, meat or rabbit and a velouté sauce, sometimes thickened with cream and egg yolks.

Fumet: Strong flavoured liquor used for flavouring sauces. Usually the liquid in which fish has been poached, or the liquid that has run from fish during baking. Sometimes used of meat or truffle-flavoured liquors.

Glace de viande: Reduced brown stock, very strong in flavour, used for adding body and colour to sauces.

Glaze: To cover with a thin layer of shiny jellied meat juices (for roast turkey), melted jam (for fruit flans) or syrup (for rum baba).

God's gravy: Jus de viande or roasting juices, unthickened, served as sauce.

Gratiner: To brown under a grill after the surface of the dish has been sprinkled with breadcrumbs and butter and, sometimes, cheese. Dishes finished like this are sometimes called *gratinée* or *au gratin.*

Hard ball: Term used in sugar boiling. As *soft ball* (see below), but further heated and reduced until the sugar forms hard balls.

Hors d'oeuvre: Usually simply means the first course. Sometimes used to denote a variety or selection of many savoury titbits served with drinks, or as a mixed first course (*hors d'oeuvres variés*).

Infuse: To steep or heat gently to extract flavour, as when infusing milk with onion slices.

Julienne: Vegetables or citrus rind cut in thin matchstick shapes or very fine shreds.

Jus or *jus de viande:* God's gravy, i.e. juices that occur naturally in cooking, not a made-up sauce. Also juice.

Jus lié: Thickened gravy.

Knock down or *knock back:* To punch or knead out the air in risen dough so that it resumes its pre-risen bulk.

Knock up: To separate slightly the layers of raw puff pastry with the blade of a knife to facilitate rising during cooking.

Lard: To thread strips of bacon fat (or sometimes anchovy) through meat to give it flavour, and in the case of fat, to make up any deficiency in very lean meat

Lardons: Small strips or cubes of pork fat or bacon generally used as a garnish.

Leavening or *leavening agent:* Ingredient used to make mixtures rise during cooking, e.g. yeast, baking powder, whisked egg whites.

Liaison: Ingredients for binding together and thickening sauce, soup or other liquid, e.g. roux, beurre manié, egg yolk and cream, blood.

Macedoine: Small diced mixed vegetables, usually containing some root vegetables. Sometimes used of fruit meaning a fruit salad.

Macerate: To soak food in a syrup or liquid to allow flavours to mix.

Mandolin: Frame of metal or wood with adjustable blades set in it for finely slicing cucumbers, potatoes etc.

Marinade (verb): To soak meat, fish or vegetables before cooking in acidulated liquid containing flavourings and herbs. This gives flavour and tenderizes the meat.

Marinade (noun): The liquid described above. Usually contains oil, onion, bay leaf and vinegar or wine.

Marmite: French word for a covered earthenware soup container in which the soup is both cooked and served.

Médallions: Small rounds of meat, evenly cut. Also small round biscuits. Occasionally used of vegetables if cut in flat round discs.

21

Mirepoix: The bed of braising vegetables described under Braise.

Moule-à-manqué: French cake tin with sloping sides. The resulting cake has a wider base than top, and is about 3cm/1½in high.

Napper: To coat, mask or cover, e.g. éclairs *nappées* with hot chocolate sauce.

Needleshreds: Fine, evenly cut shreds of citrus rind (French *julienne*) generally used as a garnish.

Noisette (a): Literally 'nut'. Usually means nut-brown as in beurre noisette, i.e. butter browned over heat to a nut colour. Also hazelnut.

Noisette (b): Boneless rack of lamb rolled and tied, cut into neat rounds.

Panade or *Panada:* Very thick mixture used as a base for soufflés or fish cakes etc., usually made from milk and flour.

Papillote: A wrapping of paper in which fish or meat is cooked to contain the aroma and flavour. The dish is brought to the table still wrapped up. Foil is sometimes used, but as it does not puff up dramatically, it is less satisfactory.

Parboil: To half-boil or partially soften by boiling.

Parisienne (usually *pommes Parisiennes*): Potato (sometimes with other ingredients) scooped into small balls with a melon baller and, usually, fried.

Pass: To strain or push through a sieve.

Pâte: The basic mixture or paste, often used of uncooked pastry, dough, uncooked meringue etc.

Pâté: A savoury paste or liver, pork, game etc.

Pâtisserie: Sweet cakes and pastries. Or cake shop.

Paupiette: Beef (or pork or veal) olive, i.e. a thin layer of meat, spread with a soft farce, rolled up, tied with string and cooked slowly.

Poussin: Baby chicken.

Praline: Almonds cooked in sugar until the mixture caramelizes, cooled and crushed to a powder. Used for flavouring desserts and ice cream.

Prove: To put dough or yeasted mixture to rise before baking.

Purée: Liquidized, sieved or finely mashed fruit or vegetables.

Quenelles: A fine minced fish or meat mixture formed into small portions and poached. Served in a sauce, or as a garnish to other dishes.

Rechauffée: A reheated dish made with previously cooked food.

Reduce: To reduce the amount of liquid by rapid boiling, causing evaporation and a consequent strengthening of flavour in the remaining liquid.

Refresh: To hold boiled green vegetables under a cold tap, or to dunk them immediately in cold water to prevent their further cooking in their own steam, and to set the colour.

Relax or *rest:* Of pastry: to set aside in a cool place to allow the gluten (which will have expanded during rolling) to contract. This lessens the danger of shrinking in the oven.
Of batters: to set aside to allow the starch cells to swell, giving a lighter result when cooked.

Render: To melt solid fat (e.g. beef, pork) slowly in oven.

Rouille: Garlic and oil emulsion used as flavouring.

Roux: A basic liaison or thickening for a sauce or soup. Melted butter to which flour has been added.

Salamander: A hot oven or grill used for browning or glazing the tops of cooked dishes, or a hot iron or poker for branding the top with lines or a criss-cross pattern.

Salmis: A game stew sometimes made with cooked game, or partially roasted game.

Sauter: Method of frying in a deep-frying pan or sautoir. The food is continually tossed or shaken so that it browns quickly and evenly.

Sautoir: Deep-frying pan with a lid used for recipes that require fast frying and then slower cooking (with the lid on).

Scald: Of milk: to heat until on the point of boiling, when some movement can be seen at the edges of the pan but there is no over-all bubbling.
Of muslin, cloths etc.: to dunk in clean boiling water, generally to sterilize.

Seal or *seize:* To brown meat rapidly (usually in fat), forming a dryish skin to trap juices inside.

To season: Of food: to flavour, generally with salt and pepper.
Of iron frying pans, girdles etc.: to prepare new equipment for use by placing over high heat, generally coated with oil and sprinkled with salt. This prevents subsequent rusting and sticking.

Slake: To mix flour, arrowroot, cornflour or custard powder to a thin paste with a small quantity of cold water.

Soft Ball: The term used to describe sugar syrup reduced by boiling to sufficient thickness to form soft balls when dropped into cold water and rubbed between finger and thumb.

Suprême: Choice piece of poultry (usually from the breast).

Sweat: To cook gently (usually in butter or oil, but sometimes in the food's own juices) without frying or browning.

Tammy: A fine muslin cloth through which sauces are sometimes forced. After this treatment they look beautifully smooth and shiny. Tammy cloths have recently been replaced by blenders or liquidizers which give much the same effect.

Tammy strainer: A fine mesh strainer, conical in shape, used to produce the effect described under *Tammy*.

To the thread: Of sugar boiling. Term used to denote degree of thickness achieved when reducing syrup, i.e. the syrup will form threads if tested between finger and thumb. Short thread: about 1cm/½in; long thread: 5cm/2in or more.

Timbale: A dish which has been cooked in a castle-shaped mould, or a dish served piled up high.

Tournedos: Fillet steak. Usually refers to a one-portion piece of grilled fillet.

To turn vegetables: To shape carrots or turnips to a small olive shape. To cut mushrooms into a decorative spiral pattern.

To turn olives: To remove the olive stone with a spiral cutting movement.

Velouté: See under Sauces, page 56.

Vol-au-vent: A large pastry case made from puff pastry with high raised sides and a deep hollow centre into which is put chicken, fish etc.

Well: A hollow or dip made in a pile or bowlful of flour, exposing the table top or bottom of the bowl, into which other ingredients are placed prior to mixing.

Zest: The thin coloured skin of an orange or lemon, used to give flavour. It is very thinly pared without any of the bitter white pith.

CLASSIC GARNISHES

Anglaise: Braised vegetables such as carrots, turnips and quartered celery hearts (used to garnish boiled salted beef).

Aurore: A flame-coloured sauce obtained by adding fresh tomato purée to a bechamel sauce; used for eggs, vegetables and fish. Means 'dawn'.

Bolognaise: A rich sauce made from chicken livers or minced beef flavoured with mushrooms and tomatoes. Usually served with pasta.

Bonne femme: To cook in a simple way. Usually, of chicken, sautéed and served with white wine gravy, bacon cubes, button onions and garnished with croquette potatoes. Of soup, simple purée of vegetables with stock. Of fish, white wine sauce, usually with mushrooms; and served with buttered mashed potatoes.

Boulangère: Potatoes and onions sliced and cooked in the oven in stock. Often served with mutton.

Bouquetière: Groups of very small carrots, turnips, French beans, cauliflower florets, button onions, asparagus tips etc. Sometimes served with a thin demi-glaçe or gravy. Usually accompanies beef or lamb entrées.

Bourgeoise: Fried diced bacon, glazed carrots and button onions. Sometimes red wine is used in the sauce. Used for beef and liver dishes.

Bourguignonne: Button mushrooms and small onions in a sauce made with red wine (Burgundy). Used for beef and egg dishes.

Bretonne: Haricot beans whole or in a purée. Sometimes a purée of root vegetables. Usually served with a gigot (leg) of lamb.

Chasseur: Sautéed mushrooms added to a sauté of chicken or veal.

Clamart: Garnish of artichoke hearts filled with buttered petits pois. Sometimes a purée of peas, or simply buttered peas.

Doria: A garnish of cucumber, usually fried in butter.

DuBarry: Denotes the use of cauliflower: potage DuBarry is cauliflower soup. Also, cooked cauliflower florets masked with Mornay sauce and browned under the grill, used for meat entrées.

Flamande: Red cabbage and glazed small onions used with pork and beef.

Florentine: Spinach in purée, or leaf spinach. Also a sixteenth-century name for a pie.

Indienne: Flavoured with curry.

Joinville: Slices of truffle, crayfish tails and mushrooms with a lobster sauce, used for fish dishes.

Lyonnaise: Denotes the use of onions as garnish – the onions are frequently sliced and fried.

Meunière: Of fish, lightly dusted with flour, then fried and served with beurre noisette and lemon juice; also frequently (but not classically) chopped parsley.

Milanese: With a tomato sauce, sometimes including shredded ham, tongue and mushrooms. Frequently served with pasta.

Minute: Food quickly cooked, either fried or grilled. Usually applied to a thin entrecôte steak.

Mornay: With a cheese sauce.

Nantua: With a lobster sauce.

Napolitana: A tomato sauce and Parmesan cheese (for pasta). May also mean a three-coloured ice cream.

Nicoise: Name given to many dishes consisting of ingredients common in the South of France, e.g. tomatoes, olives, garlic, fish, olive oil.

Normande: Garnish of mussels, shrimps, oysters and mushrooms. Or creamy sauce containing cider or calvados, and sometimes apples.

Parmentier: Denotes the use of potato as a base or garnish.

Paysanne: Literally, peasant. Usually denotes the use of carrots and turnips sliced across in rounds.

Portuguaise: Denotes the use of tomatoes or tomato purée.

Princesse: Denotes the use of asparagus (usually on breast of chicken).

Printanière: Early spring vegetables cooked and used as a garnish, usually in separate groups.

Provençale: Denotes the use of garlic, and sometimes tomatoes and/or olives.

St Germain: Denotes the use of peas, sometimes with pommes Parisienne. Also the name of a cream of pea soup.

Soubise: Onion purée, frequently mixed with a béchamel sauce.

Vichy: Garnish of small glazed carrots.

TRADITIONAL BRITISH ACCOMPANIMENTS

Roast lamb: Mint sauce or redcurrant jelly, onion sauce or gravy.

Roast beef: Horseradish, very thin gravy, Yorkshire pudding, mustard.

Roast chicken: Bacon rolls, sausages, bread sauce, gravy.

Roast turkey: Cranberry sauce, bread sauce, sausages, bacon, stuffings, gravy, sprouts or chestnuts.

Ham: Cumberland sauce or parsley sauce, mustard.

Game: Game chips, fried breadcrumbs, bread sauce, redcurrant jelly, unthickened 'God's gravy'.

Roast pork and goose: Apple sauce or gooseberry sauce, gravy.

METHODS OF COOKING

The tougher the food, or the larger its volume, the slower it must be cooked.

The quick methods of cooking – frying, deep frying (the quickest) and grilling – are suitable therefore for small pieces of tender meat, whereas the slower methods – braising, stewing etc. – are best for tough ones.

GRILLING

Brushing the grilling meat with butter or oil is done for two reasons – to stop it sticking to the pan or grill and to give flavour. The speed with which the food is cooked is the essential factor in keeping it moist. An outside cooked surface is quickly formed, which prevents the juices inside the meat running out. If the grill is not hot enough, the outer seal will not be formed and the inner juices will escape, giving a dried-up result. With practice it is possible to tell by pressure of the fingers if the food is cooked, but if you don't trust your 'feel' you will have to cut one piece open and look.

Heat

The grill must be really hot. Always pre-heat the grill well in advance.

Preparation of the food

The meat or fish should be brushed with oil or butter and seasoned with pepper. Never season foods for grilling with salt as this draws out the juices and renders the meat dry and tough.

Distance from the heat

The grill pan should be held at about 7·5cm/3in from the grill itself so that the meat can be 'sealed' immediately. The pan can be lowered for any further cooking that may be necessary. Thick pieces of meat are cooked further away from the heat for longer. Thin pieces are cooked close to the heat, faster.

Turning the food over

This should be done with a pair of tongs or with two spoons but not with a fork, which would pierce the meat and allow the juices to run out.

Serving

Grilled foods should be served at once. They dry out and toughen if kept hot.

FRYING

(*a*) SHALLOW FRYING

The principle of shallow frying is similar to that of grilling (see above). The essential difference is that whereas in grilling the fat drops off the meat, in frying it stays in the pan and can sometimes be served with the dish. Fat used for shallow frying should never be more than half the depth of the food.

Rules for shallow frying

1. Never add too many pieces of food to a frying pan at once as this reduces the temperature of the fat and the food will stew rather than fry.
2. Always fry first the side of the chop, steak, fish etc. which is to be uppermost; being fried in clean fat generally makes it look better.

(*b*) DEEP FRYING

Most foods to be deep fried are given a protective coating of beaten egg, or a batter, or egg and breadcrumbs. This is done for five reasons:

1. The frying fat is at an extremely high temperature (about 185°C/360°F), which would burn the outside of some foods before the middle was cooked. The insulating coating allows the food inside to cook evenly.

    Some foods, such as potato crisps, do not need any coating because they are in and out of the hot fat too fast to burn. All they have to do is brown and then they are done. Other unprotected foods (such as the larger potato chips) are generally given a first frying at a non-burning lower temperature to ensure that the insides are cooked before the foods are browned in the very hot fat.

2. The heat of the fat would make uncooked moist food (like fish fillets or pineapple rings) splutter and splash dangerously, and the hot fat would bubble over the edge of the pan, possibly causing a fire.
3. As the fat is to be used again it must be prevented from absorbing the taste and smell of foods, especially of fish. The neutral egg batter or egg and crumb layer in contact with the fat is tasteless and odourless.
4. Many foods, such as cheese or cooking apple, become liquid on being cooked. The crisp batter then becomes a container for the runny inside.
5. The crisp coating provides a pleasing contrast with the moist food inside, which is the chief attraction of deep-fried food.

After use the fat should be cooled, then strained through muslin to remove food particles. When it has become at all dark it should be replaced, rather than topped up.

Fats suitable for deep frying are almost-tasteless vegetable oils and lard as these can be heated without burning to the required 170–185°C/330–360°F. The lower temperature (which will produce a gentle fizzing if a piece of bread is dropped in) is suitable for the first frying of potato chips and for deep-fried choux pastry dishes such as beignets soufflés.

The higher temperature (when tested with a piece of bread the fat will fizz vigorously and the bread will begin to brown) is suitable for rissoles, croquettes, fruit fritters and the second frying of potatoes.

Deep-frying technique

When cooking a large amount of food in a fryer, fry only a small amount at a time – little enough not to lower the temperature of the fat significantly. If the fat has cooled too much, the batter or outer layer of the food will not instantly form an impervious crisp crust, but will become soggy and allow the fat to enter the food, producing a greasy unattractive dish. Once the food is cooked, lift it immediately out of the fat and drain it on absorbent paper. Crumpled brown paper, kitchen paper, or even dry-inked newspaper will do.

If you cannot serve the food immediately (which would be best) do not cover it with a lid. If you do, steam trapped inside will make the food soggy. Spread the cooked food in one layer only (if piled up the bottom pieces will become soggy) on a hot dish and put it in the warm oven, with the door ajar to allow free circulation of air.

Add a sprinkling of salt to the food (if savoury) or caster sugar (if sweet) just before serving.

Safety precautions when deep frying

Because of the great heat of the liquid fat the deep fryer is potentially the most dangerous object in the kitchen. The following points should be observed for safety's sake:

1. The fat or oil should not be too deep. When a basket of food is lowered into hot fat it will bubble up briefly, and if it should spill over (especially on to a naked gas flame beneath) fire could result.
2. Make sure that food is properly coated in batter or egg and breadcrumbs, or is really dry. Dry off potato chips in a tea-towel before frying. Wet food causes the fat to splash and splutter.
3. If the fat rises up dangerously, remove the food immediately and cool the fat slightly (or remove some of the food from the basket) before trying again.
4. Never go away and leave a heating fryer. Deep fat or oil does not boil; it simply explodes into flame. But if you are in the room, before it reaches that stage you will have seen and smelt it smoking.
5. Never attempt to move over-hot or burning fat. The danger is that you will spill it on your arm, or on to the flame beneath. Just turn off the source of heat and leave it where it is. Have the lid of the pan close at hand so that if the fat does catch fire, you can quench the flames calmly by shutting off their oxygen supply with the lid. Failing that, drop a thick woollen (not nylon) blanket or coat over the whole burning pot. Better a singed blanket than a burnt kitchen!
6. If the fat is obviously too hot, but not on fire, it will cool without danger if you turn off its source of heat. The cooling process can be hurried by putting a raw potato (dry) or a

large piece of bread into the fat. This will cool the fat as it browns.

BROILING

Broiling is an American word usually used to mean grilling, but sometimes roasting.

ROASTING

Roasting is the most satisfactory way of cooking large pieces of fairly tender, or very tender, meat. The extremely fast frying, grilling or deep frying would char the outside while the middle is still raw. However the same principles apply, i.e. the meat is first 'sealed' (the outer surface is cooked very fast either in a frying pan or in a very hot oven) so that the juices of the meat are locked in. The temperature is then lowered (or the meat is put into a cooler oven) until the required degree of roasting has been reached. With a small piece of meat it is not necessary to lower the oven temperature as the cooking time will be short, so the outside cannot over-cook.

The roasting meat is generally basted during cooking. Melted fat (perhaps butter) and/or juices or stock are regularly ladled over the roasting meat. This is done to add flavour and to keep the outer skin from drying to a very hard and inedible layer.

When meat was roasted on a turning spit the dripping fat was caught in a tray beneath the turning meat, and spooned back over the top of it. Spit roasting is considered better than oven roasting simply because as the meat turns, the fat runs automatically over the surface, even without the help of the additional basting. With oven roasting, the top of the meat is bound to be dryer than the bottom as the juices run down both inside and outside the meat. For this reason it is a good idea to start roasting a turkey or chicken upside down in the roasting pan to enable some of the juices to run into the breast, before turning it right side up to brown.

Roasting in a bag, in foil, or in a clay brick pot, are all attempts to keep the meat moist. They share the disadvantage that, because the meat is cooked in a closed steamy atmosphere, they do not have a crisp brown skin. But the oven is kept clean.

BAKING

Baking differs from modern roasting only in that with roasting, fat is generally basted over the food whereas baked food is left undisturbed. But they both entail putting food into a hot closed oven to cook. Baking, because of the perfectly controlled, all-over even heat, is most suitable for cakes and breads, where exact temperatures are vital. It is also an excellent method for the slow cooking of tough meats, which are usually baked in a closed container and therefore in a moist and steamy atmosphere. For breads, cakes etc. see pages 37–54.

STEAMING

There are two principal methods of steaming: for quickly cooked foods, such as fish, chicken or vegetables, the food is placed in the top of a two-tier steamer and cooked in the direct steam from the boiling water below. This method is frequently used for invalid cookery as no fat or sauce needs to be added to the food, and fatless food is easy to digest. It is a good method of cooking floury potatoes which might break up if boiled. Care should be taken not to overcook food as it may become tasteless with prolonged steaming. The steaming water should be saved for stock. If a two-tier steamer is not available one can be improvised by placing the food in a metal strainer (perhaps loosely lined with foil), and suspending this in a saucepan over boiling water. It may, however, be necessary to cover the saucepan and its lid with a layer of foil to prevent the steam from escaping under the lid which now will not fit properly on account of the strainer.

Foods that require prolonged gentle cooking, such as suet puddings and meat puddings, are steamed but the food itself does not come in contact with the moist steam. The pudding basin containing the food is placed in a large saucepan of boiling water, the water coming to within 5cm/2in of the rim of the pudding basin. The pudding must be carefully wrapped to prevent water getting into it and making it soggy. It is generally covered with a double layer of greaseproof paper which has a folded pleat down the centre, and tied firmly with string. The pleat is to allow the food inside to expand during cooking (even a Christmas pudding will rise slightly) without bursting through its coverings. The whole is then wrapped in foil. A folded cloth or double strip of foil laid under the basin but projecting up the sides of the saucepan will make lifting the pudding out of the boiling water easier. If the cloth used for this purpose is large it can be loosely tied over the top of the basin. It is vital that a well-fitting lid to the saucepan is used: if the steam is allowed to escape too freely the pudding will not cook in the specified time.

The water should be kept boiling vigorously throughout the process, and it is a good plan to have a kettle of steaming water handy to replenish the saucepan as and when necessary. The saucepan should be large enough for steam to surround the pudding easily.

Very large steamers with upper compartments large enough to take a pudding basin are available, but they are cumbersome items for the average kitchen, and a saucepan with a good lid works very well.

STEWING

Stewing is the perfect slow-cooking method for foods in a liquid. If there is any danger of the food breaking up with the agitation of the bubbling water or syrup (as with slices of apple) it is best to stew in the oven where the temperature can be fixed so low that it hardly moves the liquid. Stew pans are always covered to keep in the steam.

STEWING FRUIT

Fruit should never be boiled. It should be very gently poached in a sugar syrup (see page 320). The amount and thickness of the syrup depends on the fruit to be poached. Very juicy fruit (plums, cherries, raspberries, rhubarb) should be cooked in a small quantity of thick syrup while drier fruits (apples and pears) should be poached in a thinner syrup.

It is important to make a syrup rather than simply to put sugar, water and fruit together in a pan. The danger of the latter method is overcooking the fruit before the sugar is dissolved. Besides, heating undissolved sugar often leads to crystallized lumps.

When stewing whole fruits that are liable to discolour, there are several important rules to follow:

1. Peel the fruit with a stainless steel knife.
2. Dunk it, as soon as it is peeled, into the sugar syrup.
3. Allow the sugar syrup to boil once right up over the fruit, before turning down the heat to poach it gently.
4. Poach the fruit for at least 15 minutes in the syrup. This is to allow the sugar syrup (which will prevent discoloration) to penetrate the outer layer of fruit.

POT ROASTING

Pot roasting is not really roasting at all. But the resulting meat has the browned look of a roast. The meat is first browned by frying in the same deep pot that it will stew in. It is then covered and left to stew (in or out of the oven) in its own juice. This is done at a very low temperature. Great care must be taken not to allow the meat to catch at the bottom.

BRAISING

Braised foods (e.g. beef olives) are cooked on a bed of chopped-up root vegetables. Little or no liquid is added and the contents cook slowly in their own juices. The braising vegetables give flavour and moisture to the meat, but may be discarded before the meat is served, or used later in soup. Sometimes they are sieved and used for sauce.

BOILING

True boiling is a method of cooking rarely used except for the quick cooking of fresh vegetables, for rice and pasta, and for boiling puddings in a pudding bowl. It is also used for jam making, when a good rolling boil is essential.

Boiling often entails a considerable loss of nutritive value, as many nutrients are thrown away with the cooking water. The word 'boiled' is often incorrectly applied to dishes like boiled egg custard (which if it was really boiled would be curdled) and boiled salmon, which should be poached, not boiled.

POACHING

For food to be poached it must be submerged, or partly submerged, in a flavoured liquid (e.g. syrup for poached pears, or chicken stock for poached chicken), and it should be cooked so that the liquid barely moves. If it bubbles in only one part of the pan, it is simmering, and if it bubbles everywhere, it is boiling. Truly poached chicken or fish has a juiciness and tenderness not found in boiled food. If the food is cooled in the poaching liquid, so much the better. (Removing it allows it to dry out.) But the poaching pan should be stood in cold water so that the contents cool fast. This is to avoid the danger of food (kept too long in a warm steamy atmosphere) going bad.

BAKING BREADS, CAKES, PASTRIES ETC.

When wheat flour and water are mixed together and cooked, a primitive type of bread – a flat, hard biscuit – is produced.

Examples of this are the unleavened bread of the Israelites, the damper of the Australians and the flapjacks of prospectors and pioneers of America.

Wheat flour has a remarkable ingredient. This is the protein gluten, which, when wet, will stretch and expand, allowing the dough to be kneaded and pulled into a most elastic substance. The strands of dough can stretch without breaking even when expanding gas trapped inside caused the dough to puff up. This means that, provided we can get the dough to rise, the gluten will hold it in its puffed-up shape until it solidifies during baking. This makes a much lighter, less brittle bread and makes possible a hundred different recipes for breads, cakes and puddings which all depend on trapped gas for their lightness and open texture.

RAISING AGENTS

But how to get the gas into the mixture? And what gas will it be?

Air

There are several mechanical methods of incorporating air into a basic mixture, all of which depend on agitating the ingredients, rather like stirring up a bubble bath. These methods include sifting flour, creaming fat and sugar together until light and mousse-like, beating (as for batters) and whisking (as for egg whites). In all these, air is the raising agent.

Steam

Steam is also a raising agent. Some mixtures will rise, even though no effort has been made to beat air into them. These usually contain a high proportion of liquid, like Yorkshire pudding batter or choux pastry. What happens is that, because they are baked in a hot oven, the liquid ingredients quickly reach boiling point, and begin to convert to steam. As the steam rises it takes with it the dough or batter, and puffs it up, and while it is in this puffed-up state, the heat of the oven hardens the dry ingredients of the mixture and the dough becomes solidified with the steam trapped inside. The texture of such a mixture is generally very open and uneven, with large pockets of air.

Bicarbonate of soda

This is another effective raising agent. It is a substance which, when mixed with liquid and heated, will give off half its substance as the gas carbon dioxide (CO_2) which will puff up the mixture as it forms. But the residue of the 'bicarb' will remain in the cooked mixture as carbonate of soda. Unfortunately this carbonate of soda has an unpleasant taste and smell, and a yellow colour. This method of raising is therefore suitable for strong-tasting foods such as gingerbread, chocolate cake, and cakes flavoured with treacle, when the taste of the carbonate of soda will be masked.

The carbon dioxide trapped in the bread or cake will gradually escape and be replaced by air.

The addition of an acid substance (vinegar, sour milk, cream of tartar, tartaric acid, yoghurt, even marmalade or jam) speeds up the liberation of the carbon dioxide from the bicarbonate of soda, and is often included for this reason.

Bicarbonate of soda has a weakening effect on gluten, preventing it from forming a hard, bread-like crust. This makes it suitable for scones and cakes, when yeast (which does not so affect the gluten) would produce too crisp a crust.

A disadvantage of bicarbonate of soda is that it destroys many of the vitamins present in flour.

Baking powder

This is a mixture of bicarbonate of soda and acid powder – and also a filler to absorb any dampness in the air which might allow the two active ingredients to get going before they are thoroughly wet in a dough or cake mixture. A 'delayed reaction' baking powder is available in America which needs heat as well as moisture to start it off, but it is not widely known in Britain.

Self-raising flour

This is a flour (generally 'weak', i.e. low in gluten) already containing a raising agent (usually baking powder).

Yeast

Yeast, when activated, also produces carbon dioxide which will puff up the dough, but yeast cookery is complex enough to need a section of its own. See page 43.

CAKES

(See section on raising agents, page 38.)

THE FOUR BASIC METHODS

Rubbing-in method

The first stage of this method is similar to that for shortcrust pastry (see page 50): the fat is rubbed into the flour with the fingers. The remaining dry ingredients (sugar, peel etc.) are then added, and finally eggs and/or milk are added to give a sloppy 'dropping consistency' mixture.

This method is used in making rock buns and plain fruit cakes.

Melting method

The water, milk, syrup and the fat and any other liquid ingredients are heated together. They are then cooled and poured into a bowl containing all the sieved dry ingredients, usually including bi-carbonate of soda and/or baking powder. The mixture is stirred, not beaten, until it resembles a thick batter.

This method produces very moist cakes, e.g. gingerbread.

Creaming method

The butter or margarine is creamed with a wooden spoon until it is smooth and very light in colour. The sugar is then added by degrees and beaten in the same way until the mixture is pale and fluffy. The eggs are then added, also by degrees, and finally the sifted flour is folded into the mixture, with as little mixing and stirring as possible. Adding the egg slowly, with much beating, and perhaps a spoonful of flour between each addition, is said to help prevent curdling.

This method is used for Victoria sandwich cakes, Dundee and Madeira cakes. Butter gives a better flavour, but margarine is easier to cream.

Whisking method

The simplest whisked cake is a fatless sponge. The sugar and eggs are whisked together until light and thick, and then the flour is folded in. A Genoise 'commune' has just-runny butter folded into it with the flour. The richer Genoise 'fine' cake has a greater proportion of butter to flour, and the eggs are separated. The yolks and sugar are whisked, the butter and flour folded in, and lastly the whisked egg whites.

But in all the whisked cakes the whisked-in air is the raising agent, and throughout the process, every effort is made to keep in as much air as possible.

The sugar and eggs (or yolks only) are whisked in a bowl set over a pan of near-simmering water. It is important that the base of the bowl does not touch the surface of the water as the heat at the bottom of the bowl would then be too great and the eggs would scramble. The gentle heat helps to melt the sugar and speeds up the whisking process. The mixture has been sufficiently whisked when it is very pale in colour, and leaves a ribbon-like trail on the surface when the whisk is lifted. When the flour is folded in, great care should be taken to fold rather than stir or beat, as the aim is to incorporate the flour without losing any of the beaten-in air. The correct movement is more of lifting the mixture and cutting into it, than stirring.

Butter, which should be just runny but not hot, should be poured round the edge of the bowl. If it is poured on top of the whisked cake mixture, it will push out some of the air. Folding in should be gentle and not over-done.

The cakes are cooked when the impression left by a finger on the surface of the cake will disappear. The sponge will be slightly springy. Cakes should be cooled for a few minutes in the tin, then turned out on to a cake rack.

Whisked sponges are used for many gateaux and composite cakes. They are sometimes simply filled with jam or cream, or eaten plain, perhaps dusted with icing sugar.

PREPARING A CAKE TIN

All tins should be greased before use. This is to prevent the cake mixture sticking or burning at the edges or bottom. Lard or oil are the most suitable fats. If using oil, always turn the tin upside down after greasing to allow any excess oil to drain away. Use a paint brush to get a thin layer.

Buns

The tins need no preparation other than greasing.

Cakes made by melting or creaming methods

Grease the tin, then line the base with greaseproof paper, cut exactly to size, and brush out with more melted lard or oil.

Cakes made by whisking method

As above, but dust with caster sugar and flour after lining and greasing.

Fruit cakes

Grease tin, then line sides and base with greaseproof paper as follows:-
1. Cut two pieces of greaseproof paper to fit the base of the cake tin.
2. Cut another piece long enough to go right round the sides of the tin and to overlap slightly. It should be 1cm/½in deeper than the height of the cake tin.
3. Fold one long edge of this strip over 1cm/½in all along its length.
4. Cut 1cm/½in snips at right angles to the edge and about 1cm/½in apart, all the way along the folded side. The snips should just reach the fold.
5. Grease the tin, place one of the paper bases in the bottom and grease again.
6. Fit the long strip inside the cake tin with the folded cut edge

on the bottom (the flanges will overlap slightly), and the main uncut part lining the sides of the tin. Press well into the corners.

7. Grease again and lay the second base on top of the first.
8. Brush out with more melted lard and dust with flour.

COOKING WITH YEAST

Yeast baking, one of the most addictive and satisfying forms of cookery, needs a book to itself. One of the best is *Beard on Bread* by James Beard. Another is Elizabeth David's *English Bread and Yeast Cookery*.

WHEAT FLOUR

Wheat flour (rather than cornflour, potato flour, rice flour, rye flour etc.) is most commonly used because of its high gluten content. Gluten is the protein that allows the dough to become elastic. The more gluten in the flour, the more it will be able to rise, the strands of dough stretching without breaking as the loaf fills with gas.

White flour

Made from ears of wheat that have had their outer casing of bran and inner centre of wheatgerm removed, white flour is very fine and can be bought bleached or unbleached. Obviously the more refining and processing that the flour goes through, the less flavour and vitamins it will have. For this reason white flours generally have some of the B vitamins returned to them before packaging.

Strong flour

This flour is made from hard wheat. The best hard wheat comes from North America and has an exceptionally high gluten content. This makes it highly suitable for use in bread-making, giving a well-risen light loaf. It is the flour most commonly used by professional bakers.

Plain household flour

This is a general all-purpose flour suitable for cakes and breads but more often used for the former as it does not have the high gluten content of strong flour. It is generally made from soft wheat of the kind grown in Europe. Bread produced with household flour will not have quite the lightness of that produced with strong flour.

Self-raising flour

Usually 'weak' i.e. made from soft wheat, this is flour to which a raising agent (generally baking powder) has been added. It is not used in yeast cookery.

Wholemeal flour (or wholewheat flour)

This is flour milled from the whole grain, including bran and wheatgerm. As most of the B vitamins in wheat reside in the wheatgerm, and bran provides roughage for the digestive system, bread made from wholewheat is much better for you. But it undoubtedly produces a heavier loaf, and because of the presence of wheatgerm, the bread does not keep as well as the white variety. A mixture of wholewheat and white flour is a good compromise.

Stoneground flour

Produced by the ancient method of milling between stone rollers, this flour is said to be a less 'messed about' and processed flour than that made by modern milling methods. It is certainly a slightly coarser, heavier flour, and, even in the white version, is heavier than factory milled flour. It needs more yeast to make it rise

Brown flour

This is brown but not necessarily because of the inclusion of wheatgerm and bran. It may simply be dyed flour, so look for the word 'wholewheat' or 'wholemeal' on the packet. Dyed brown flour is lighter than wholewheat and usually sold as 'wheatmeal'.

Bran

Bran can be bought on its own in health food shops, to give a coarseness and colour to the bread, but provides neither flavour nor nutrition. It does provide roughage for the digestive system, however.

To conclude: strong, unbleached white flour is best for white loaves and a mixture of this and wholewheat flour is best for brown bread.

LEAVENING

Raising agents other than yeast have been discussed previously, but yeast is the most usual agent for bread.

Yeast is a one-celled plant of the fungus family. Its main advantage from a cook's point of view is that, given the right humid conditions, it can reproduce amazingly fast, giving off carbon dioxide (CO_2) gas as it does so. If yeast cells are incorporated into a mixture for baking, the carbon dioxide produced as the organisms grow will puff up the dough or batter, giving a light and aerated result. Yeast can be bought in two forms:

Compressed or fresh yeast

This is generally considered the most satisfactory kind of yeast, less likely to produce a loaf smelling and tasting beery or over-yeasty. But it is becoming very difficult to obtain, especially in small quantities. However, if you buy a pound at a time it can be frozen successfully. Freeze it in small pieces so that you can thaw them as you need them. Use as soon as the yeast has defrosted. Fresh yeast will keep in the refrigerator wrapped in plastic for a fortnight or so.

Dried yeast (*often called 'active' dried yeast*)

This is bought in granular form. You need half, or less than half, the weight specified for fresh yeast. It will keep fresh for six months in a cool dry place. To avoid the 'beery' taste referred to earlier, under- rather than over-estimate the amount of yeast needed, and allow rising and proving to take a good long time.

OTHER INGREDIENTS

Sugar (or molasses)

Generally included in a bread recipe to give the yeast something to feed on while busily multiplying. It does, of course, also add a touch of sweetness to the dough, but this is incidental.

Fat

Some breads call for fat, usually butter, which gives a richness to the bread, and a good flavour.

Liquid

Water is usually called for, but sometimes other liquids, such as beer or milk, are used. Milk gives a golden coloured crust.

MIXING AND SPONGING

The basic aim while preparing the dough for the oven is to create the right conditions for the yeast to grow, and the maximum elasticity in the bread to contain the gas released by the yeast. In the first stage – mixing and sponging – we are creating the incubating conditions for the yeast:

The ingredients and bowl should be warm: not so hot that the yeast cells will be killed, and not so cold that they will be discouraged from multiplying. The yeast is usually creamed with a little sugar (upon which it feeds) and mixed with a spoonful of warm (i.e. about 40°C/100°F) liquid. When the yeast looks frothy you know it is on its way. This is called 'sponging'. It is done to check that the yeast cells are alive before mixing in all the flour.

If nothing happens (although you have the yeast in a warm kitchen) in 15 minutes, the yeast is probably dead, and there is nothing for it but to begin again with fresh yeast.

Some recipes require the yeast mixture and all the liquid to be beaten to a batter with a small proportion of the flour, and then 'sponged'. The rest of the flour is then added, and the mixing completed.

KNEADING

Once the dough is mixed it should be kneaded. This is to distribute the yeast cells evenly and to promote the elasticity of the dough. The length of time for kneading varies according to the type of flour and the skill of the kneader, but 10 minutes should do it. The dough should be elastic and satiny-smooth.

Kneading techniques vary, the most common method being to push the lump of dough down and away with the heel of one hand, then to pull it back with the fingers, slap it on the tabletop and repeat the process, turning the dough slightly with each movement.

RISING

The dough is now formed into a ball and put into a warm, lightly oiled bowl. It is a good idea to roll the ball of dough over in the greasy bowl to coat it on all sides. This will prevent hardening and cracking. Cover the bowl with a piece of oiled polythene or a damp cloth. Put the bowl in a warm (about 32°C/90°F) draught-free place and leave it alone for at least one hour. The slower the dough rises the better. Over-risen bread has a coarse texture and beery smell. When it has doubled in bulk, remove it.

KNOCKING DOWN (or knocking back)

This is exactly what the name implies: the air is punched out of the risen dough and it is knocked back to its original size. Then it is kneaded again and shaped (into a round, oblong, plaited or what-have-you loaf) and put into the loaf tin or on to a baking sheet. Again, cover it with oiled polythene.

PROVING

This is the second rising of the dough. It is done when the loaf has doubled in bulk and looks the size and shape you hope the finished bread will be. This rising can be done in a slightly warmer place, for a shorter time – say at 40°C/100°F for 20 minutes. This is because as the dough has now had further kneading it is even more elastic and will rise more easily – rather as a balloon is easier to blow up the second time you do it.

BAKING

The bread will, inevitably, continue to rise for a short time when put in the oven. This is partly due to the rising steam, and partly to the continued growth of the yeast as more warmth is applied. But once the temperature of the dough reaches 60°C/140°F the yeast will be killed and the heat of the oven will cook the dough into a rigid shape. This final rising in the oven is called 'oven spring' and usually causes the top crust to be pushed up away from the body of the loaf, causing larger holes just under the crust. There is nothing wrong with it, but obviously too much oven-spring would have the crust separated entirely from the loaf. Some breads, such as rye bread (which develops a hard and un-yielding crust) is docked half way through baking. This means simply that the top crust is sliced off to allow the gases to escape, and a new crust forms.

To avoid too much oven-spring, bread is baked at a fairly high temperature so that yeast is killed as quickly as possible. Too cool an oven will not kill the yeast cells quickly and they will continue to grow, giving an over-risen, unevenly textured loaf.

The loaf is done when it sounds hollow when tapped. Tap the top first, and if satisfied that it sounds hollow, turn the loaf out (your hand covered with a cloth) and tap the underside. If it feels heavy and solid return it to the oven. Test again in six or seven minutes.

COOLING

Large breads should be cooled out of their tins to allow the steam to escape, thus further lightening the bread. After two hours a loaf will slice easily. If the bread is to be stored in a bread tin or plastic bag (in a refrigerator or freezer) it should be stone-cold before storing. A lukewarm loaf, put into an airtight place, will go soggy, if not mouldy.

GLAZING

Coating the top of the loaf, towards the end of cooking, will give different effects according to the glaze used:

Brushing with *water* ensures a crisp crust.
Milk gives a good pale gold colour and a crisp crust.
Egg yolks and cream produce a dark golden top.
Melted *butter* gives a softer crust.
Melted *apricot jam* gives a sweet sticky shine to sweeter breads.

PASTRIES

In almost all cases 'short' (i.e. crisp, crumbly, but neither brittle nor hard) pastry is the aim. The degree of shortness of pastry comes from the amount and type of fat incorporated in it, and the way in which the paste (uncooked pastry) is handled.

Fats

Butter gives a crisp and short crust, with very good flavour.
Margarine gives a result similar to butter, slightly less rich.
Lard gives a soft, very short but rather tasteless pastry.
Cooking fat gives a crisper crust than lard, also short, but also lacking in flavour.
Suet is only used in suet crust pastry. It produces a soft, rather heavy pastry. To combat this doughiness a raising agent is usually added to the flour.

Flours

Plain household flour is the flour most commonly used, but wholemeal flour and self-raising are used sometimes. Wholemeal flour produces a delicious nutty-flavoured crust, but is inclined to be heavy. For this reason it is sometimes used in conjunction (half and half) with white flour. Self-raising flour produces a thicker, softer, more cakey crust. It is sometimes used to lighten what might be a heavyish pastry (e.g. cheese pastry or suet crust).

Water

As a general rule, the less of this the better. Any child who has mixed flour and water to make a paste knows that the baked result is not unlike concrete. But some crispness and firmness is desirable and the inclusion of a little water ensures this.

Pastry is made in so many different ways that it is difficult to give general rules for success. So to take the broad categories one by one:

SHORTCRUST PASTRY

In this method of pastry-making fat is rubbed into the flour with the fingertips, and then any other ingredients (egg yolks, liquid etc.) are added.

Keep everything as cool as possible: if the fat is allowed to melt, the finished pastry may be tough. Cut the fat, which should be cool and firm rather than softened, into tiny pieces using a small knife and floured fingers (the flouring prevents the fat from sticking to your warm fingers and starting to melt). Add *chilled* water. Roll on a cold surface. Handle the pastry as little as possible.

When rubbing in the fat, handle it lightly so that it doesn't stick to your fingers. Keep your hands well floured to facilitate this. Pick up a few small pieces of fat, and plenty of flour between the fingertips and thumb of each hand. Hold your hands a good 23cm/9in above the bowl and gently and quickly rub the fat pieces into the flour, squashing the fat lightly as you do so. Then immediately drop the lot, from that height, into the bowl (dropping from a height both aerates and cools the mixture). Do not mash each lump of fat – the less thoroughly you do the rubbing in, the better. Keep shaking the bowl so that the big unrubbed pieces of fat come to the top. When the mixture looks like very coarse (by no means 'fine', as many recipes will say) breadcrumbs, stop.

Add only enough liquid to get the pastry to hold together. Rich pastries (with a high proportion of fat) need little if any water added. Although rather moist pastry is easier to handle and roll out, the resulting crust is tough and may well shrink out of shape as the water evaporates in the oven. The drier and more difficult-to-handle pastry will give a crisp 'short' crust.

Do not add too much flour during rolling as the proportion of flour to other ingredients will be altered and the pastry may become heavy.

Allow the pastry to 'relax' in a cool place before baking. This period (10 minutes will do) allows the gluten in the flour to contract, making the pastry less elastic. This will produce a lighter pastry, less likely to shrink.

Always wrap or cover pastry left to relax – especially if there is more rolling to come. The dry atmosphere of a refrigerator dries out the outside of pastry, causing it to crack and flake and making it difficult to handle.

SUET CRUST

The method for suet crust is similar to that for shortcrust, but the suet is generally chopped or shredded into the flour. As self-raising flour (or plain flour and baking powder) is used in order to produce a less doughy pastry, it is important to cook the pastry as soon as possible after making, so that the raising agent is working as the pastry cooks, rather than already spent before the pastry starts to cook. (The raising agent causes the dough to puff up and rise slightly and as the paste hardens during cooking the air will be trapped, and the pastry be light and slightly cakey.)

FLAKY PASTRY (and Puff Pastries)

The first stage in making these pastries is similar to the method used for shortcrust pastry, although the consistency is softer and less 'short'. After this more fat, either in a solid block or small pieces, is incorporated into the paste, which is then rolled, folded and re-rolled several times. This quickly creates layers of pastry which, when baked, will rise in light thin leaves. Pastry folded in three (and rolled out) six times will have 729 layers.

The whole aim at this stage is to create the layers without allowing the fat to melt. This requires quick short strokes with the rolling pin rather than steady long ones. The short strokes allow the bubbles of air in the pastry to move about without being forced out, while the fat is gradually and evenly incorporated in the paste. If there is any danger of the fat breaking through the pastry or becoming warm and sticky, wrap the paste and chill it, then proceed. It sounds a complicated business, but is a lot easier done than said.

Pastry rises evenly to a crisp crust in a damp atmosphere, and for this reason pastries like these, that are expected to rise in the oven, are generally baked at a high temperature in an oven with a roasting tin full of water at the bottom of it, or on a wet baking sheet.

PÂTE SUCRÉE, ALMOND PASTRY AND PÂTE À PATÉ

These pastries and others like them are made by working the egg yolks and fat, and sometimes sugar, together, using the fingertips, until soft and creamy, and then gradually incorporating the flour until a soft, very rich paste is achieved.

The butter and sugar should not be creamed together as for a cake, as this produces too spongy a result.

Use only the fingertips of one hand. Succumbing to the temptation to use both hands, or the whole hand, leads to sticky pastry. The warmth of the fingertips is important for softening the fat, but once that is done the mixing and kneading should be as light and quick as possible. Because of the high proportion of fat, no water is added. A buttery rich pastry results, rather like shortcake. If the pastry is sticky it may need chilling before rolling or pressing to shape. Very soft pastry can be more easily rolled between two sheets of greaseproof paper.

This pastry can be made in a machine, as can many pastries, but it is vital to under- rather than over-mix.

When the pastry is biscuit-coloured and cooked it will still be soft. Do not worry, it will crisp up as it cools. Slide it off the baking sheet (using a palette knife) when cool.

HOT WATER CRUST

For this pastry water and fat are heated together and mixed into the flour.

Because of the high proportion of water, this pastry is

inclined to be hard. Also, as the fat used is generally lard, it can be lacking in flavour, so add a good pinch of salt. Do not allow the water to boil before the fat has melted. If the water reduces by boiling, the proportion of water to flour will not be correct.

Mix the water and melted fat into the flour quickly and keep the pastry in a warm bowl, covered with a hot damp cloth. This prevents the fat becoming set and the pastry flaking and drying out so that it is unmanageable.

CHOUX PASTRY

This pastry, containing eggs and butter, is easy to make but strict adherence to the recipe (page 288) is vital. The following points are particularly important:

1. Measure the ingredients exactly.
2. Do not allow the water to boil until the butter has melted, but when it has, bring it immediately to a full rolling boil.
3. Have the flour ready in a bowl so that the minute your rolling boil is achieved, you can tip the flour in, all in one go.
4. Do not over-beat. Once the mixture is leaving the sides of the pan, stop.
5. Cool before adding the egg – too much heat would scramble the eggs.
6. Do not beat in more egg than is necessary to achieve a dropping consistency. If the mixture is too stiff, the pastry will be stodgy. If it is too sloppy it will rise unevenly into shapeless lumps.
7. Bake on a wet baking sheet – the steam helps the paste to rise.
8. Bake until it is a good even brown, otherwise the inside of the pastry will be uncooked.
9. If the pastry is to be served cold, split the buns/rings, or poke holes in them with a skewer to allow the steam inside to escape. If the steam remains trapped the pastry will be soggy and a little heavy.
10. Serve the pastry on the day it is made, or store frozen. It will not keep well in a tin.

STRUDEL PASTRY

Unlike almost every other pastry, this one benefits from very heavy handling. It is in fact beaten and stretched, thumped and kneaded. This is all to allow the gluten to expand and promote elasticity in the dough. The paste is rolled and stretched on a cloth (the bigger the better) until it is so thin that you should be able to read fine print through it. Keep the paste covered and moist when not in use. When rolled out, brush with butter or oil to prevent cracking and drying.

SAVOURY SAUCES

Larousse defines a sauce as a 'liquid seasoning for food'. A sauce is normally thickened to prevent it running right off the food. There are four basic thickening agents:

Roux

Butter and flour are cooked together before the liquid is added. There are three degrees to which a roux can be cooked:

White: The butter and flour are merely mixed over a gentle heat without browning.
Blond: The roux is allowed to cook to a biscuit colour.
Brown: The roux is cooked until the butter and flour are distinctly brown.

These act as the base for three classic sauces mères (mother sauces) from which there are many derivatives or daughter sauces. See the sauce table.

Cornflour or arrowroot (fécule)

These are 'slaked' (mixed to a paste with cold water, stock or milk), added to hot liquid and allowed to boil for one or two minutes.

Beurre manié

Equal quantities of butter and flour are kneaded to a smooth paste and whisked into a boiling liquid. As the butter melts the flour is evenly distributed throughout the sauce, thickening the liquid without allowing lumps to form.

Egg yolks

These are used in two ways to thicken sauces. Oil or butter beaten into egg yolk will form an emulsion, as in mayonnaise and hollandaise sauces. Egg yolk can also be mixed with cream (or other liquid) to form a liaison. This is then added to a sauce or to milk, and the whole heated without boiling – enough to thicken the yolks without scrambling them. This is the method of thickening used in English custard and in blanquette de veau.

Most classic sauces are derived from basic mother sauces. The following table gives examples of classic daughter sauces and briefly explains how the mother sauce is made. After the table there follows a list of miscellaneous, but nonetheless classic, sauces that do not exactly fit into the mother/daughter pattern.

MOTHER	DAUGHTER	USES
WHITE SAUCE		
Seasoned milk thickened with a white roux.	*Anchovy:* with added anchovy essence.	Fish
Used for vegetables and as a binding for croquettes etc.	*Béchamel:* flavoured with bay leaf, onion, peppercorns.	Eggs, fish, chicken
	Cardinale: béchamel mixed with fish stock and flavoured with truffle essence, lobster butter, cayenne.	Fish
	Crème: with added cream.	Eggs, veal

MOTHER	DAUGHTER	USES
	Egg: with added chopped, hardboiled eggs.	Fish
	Mornay: with added grated cheese.	Fish, eggs, cauliflower
	Soubise: with added cooked, chopped onion.	Mutton, eggs, fish, cauliflower

BLOND SAUCE (Velouté)

MOTHER	DAUGHTER	USES
White stock thickened with a blond roux.	*Aurore:* with added tomato purée.	Eggs, fish, meat, vegetables
Used for eggs, fish, vegetables and white meat.	*Poulette:* with added mushroom essence, lemon juice and chopped parsley.	Carrots, broad and French beans, boiled potatoes, calf's head, veal
	Suprême: made with chicken stock and cream, flavoured with mushroom peelings. Sometimes finished with an egg and cream liaison.	Chicken, vol-au-vents
	Mushroom: sauce suprême, with added mushrooms. Sometimes finished with an egg yolk and cream liaison.	Chicken, sweetbreads

BROWN SAUCES

Sauce espagnole
(also called easy demi-glace sauce)

MOTHER	DAUGHTER	USES
A mirepoix of vegetables is cooked in fat until coloured. Flour is added and cooked until brown and sandy in texture. Brown stock is added with tomatoes and mushroom peelings.	*Chasseur:* espagnole with mushrooms, tomato and white wine, chopped parsley.	Grills, entrées, roasts, rabbit, chicken

MOTHER	DAUGHTER	USES
Used for red meats and game.	*Robert:* chopped onions sweated in butter with added vinegar, white wine and pepper, reduced by half and added to espagnole. Flavoured with mustard.	Pork, kidneys, tongue, ham

Sauce demi-glace

This is a more sophisticated brown sauce, made by simmering equal quantities of espagnole sauce with jellied bone stock. The sauce is then reduced by gentle boiling to half quantity, and is repeatedly skimmed. A good demi-glace looks like a rich syrupy gravy, when hot semi-clear in appearance and setting to a jelly when cold.	*Madeira:* espagnole or demi-glace with Madeira.	Veal, tongue
	Bordelaise: demi-glace with reduced wine, shallots and thyme.	Grilled steaks
	Poivrade: parsley stalks, thyme, crushed pepper corns and bay leaves cooked with a mirepoix which is then marinaded in wine or vinegar and reduced by half. Added to demi-glace and cooked 30 minutes, then strained.	Game
Used for red meats and game.	*Diane:* poivrade with cream.	Grilled steaks
	Reforme: equal quantities of poivrade and demi-glace, garnished with julienne of egg whites, gherkins, truffles and tongue.	Lamb
	Perigueux: demi-glace with truffles or truffle essence.	Red meat, game

57

MOTHER	DAUGHTER	USES

Note: All the brown daughter sauces can be made with either espagnole or demi-glace but the richer ones (madeira, bordelaise, poivrade, diane, reforme and perigueux) should classically by made with a proper demi-glace.

BUTTER SAUCE
(Beurre à l'Anglaise)

MOTHER	DAUGHTER	USES
White roux plus boiling water with added butter beaten in, flavoured with lemon juice.	*Bâtarde:* with added egg yolk.	Cauliflower, veal, eggs etc.
	Câpre (caper): with added capers.	Boiled turbot, cod, mutton
Used for vegetables and fish.	*Fennel:* with added blanched chopped Florence fennel.	Fish

EMULSIONS

Hollandaise sauce

MOTHER	DAUGHTER	USES
This is an emulsion made with egg yolks and butter, flavoured with vinegar, peppercorns and salt.	*Béarnaise:* reduction of chopped shallots, pepper, tarragon, added to hollandaise, served with chopped tarragon and chervil.	Grilled steaks
Used for asparagus, broccoli, eggs etc.	*Choron:* béarnaise with added tomato purée.	Grills, fish and asparagus
	Mousselline: with added whipped cream.	Asparagus, sole, sea kale
	Moutarde: with added mustard.	Herrings, mackerel, poached fish

Mayonnaise

MOTHER	DAUGHTER	USES
An emulsion of egg yolk and oil, seasoned with vinegar, pepper and salt.	*Aioli:* crushed garlic (and sometimes mashed potato) beaten into the emulsion of egg yolk and oil.	Soups, especially provençal fish soups

MOTHER	DAUGHTER	USES
Served cold with cold salads and cold fish, poultry or meat.		Raw vegetables
	Remoulade: with added mustard and sometimes capers, parsley, gherkins, chervil, tarragon and anchovy essence.	Celeriac, celery, salads and herrings
	Tartare: with added chopped hardboiled eggs, capers, gherkins and onions.	Fried fish and shellfish
	Andalouse: with added tomato purée and chopped sweet red peppers.	Salads, chicken and fish

MISCELLANEOUS

CRANBERRY

Cranberries, sugar and water, poached and sieved.

APPLE

Cooking apple, butter and sugar, cooked together to a thick purée and sieved.

BIGARADE

Duck gravy, orange juice and butter, thickened with arrowroot.

BREAD

Milk flavoured with bay leaf, onions and cloves and thickened with breadcrumbs. Seasoned with pepper and salt and enriched with added butter.

CUMBERLAND

Redcurrant jelly and port simmered together and flavoured with orange juice, lemon juice, mustard, cayenne, ginger and chopped cooked shallots. Served cold.

MINT

Vinegar, sugar, salt, pepper, chopped mint, sometimes mixed with small amount of boiling water.

TOMATO

Mirepoix, stock, tomato purée and fresh tomatoes, cooked for 30 minutes and sieved.

FRENCH DRESSING (VINAIGRETTE)

Three to four parts of salad oil to one of vinegar, seasoned with salt and pepper, and sometimes with herbs, mustard, sugar etc.

FISH

The word 'fish' is used to include freshwater and sea fish, but not shellfish.

Freshwater fish are divided into coarse fish, fished mainly for sport with rod and line and generally thrown back live into the rivers, and game fish, which are caught both for sport and commercially. Recently, freshwater fish farms have been set up. Many freshwater fish, such as bass, sturgeon, sea trout and salmon spend most of their adult lives in the sea, swimming back up the rivers to spawn, but they are still classified as freshwater fish despite the fact that most of them are caught by trawl in the sea. Coarse river fish, such as roach, gudgeon and tench are not sold commercially and are seldom eaten except by anglers' families.

Most of our fish come from the sea. As the fishing industry

'modernizes' it is increasingly difficult to get locally caught fish, and in some villages and towns not ten miles from the sea the only fish available is in frozen packets – perhaps a choice of fish fingers, kipper fillets or cod steaks. For the cook this is sad. Fish is a valuable source of protein, vitamin D (in oily fish), calcium and phosphorus (especially found in the edible bones of whitebait, sardines etc.), iodine, fluorine and some of the B vitamins.

Fish contains very little fat. Even oily fish seldom has more than 20 per cent fat content. (A mutton chop will contain 50 per cent fat or more.) This means that fish is easily digestible, and contains fewer calories than its equivalent weight in meat. Fish flesh is so composed (with little connective tissue and little fat) that over-vigorous or over-long cooking will cause dryness and disintegration. For this reason fish is generally grilled or fried fast, or poached gently in barely moving liquid. It cooks a great deal quicker than meat.

Fish, unlike meat, does not improve on keeping. Some *aficionados* say that salmon is best eaten three days after catching, but we feel this is a rationalization of the fact that it used to take three days to bring a salmon down from Scotland to London. Likewise there are some fish chefs and restaurateurs who say that sole is better for a day or two in the chiller, as the flesh is then firmer. But what is undisputed is that any fish (including salmon or sole) eaten within a few hours of catching is remarkably good. Fish as fresh as that should be served as plainly as possible, perhaps with nothing but melted butter and a wedge of lemon.

Fish are either round when seen in section (like a salmon) or flat (like a sole), and are so described.

PREPARATION FOR COOKING

Removing the scales

Large fish have dry scales which should be removed before cooking. To do this, scrape a large knife the wrong way along the fish (from tail to head). This can be a messy business as the scales tend to fly about. But, unless you are buying fish from a wholesale market, the fishmonger will do it for you.

Gutting and cleaning

The fishmonger will probably clean the fish, but if you are to do it yourself you will need a very sharp knife. (Fish skin blunts knives faster than anything else.) If the fish is to be stuffed or filleted it does not matter how big a slit you make to remove the entrails. If it is to be left whole, the shorter the slit the better. Start just below the head and slit through the soft belly skin. After pulling out the innards wash the fish under cold water. If it is large, and of the round type, make sure all the dark blood along the spinal column is removed.

Now carefully cut away the gills. Take care not to cut off the head if you want to serve the fish whole. If you do not, cut off head and tail now. To remove the fins cut the skin round them, take a good grip (if you salt your fingers well it will stop them slipping) and yank sharply towards the head. This will pull the fin bones out with the fin.

Skinning and filleting flat fish

Fish skin is easier to remove after cooking when it comes away easily. But sometimes the fish must be skinned before cooking. Most whole fish are not skinned or filleted before grilling, but sole (and lemon sole, and witch) are skinned on at least the dark side, and sometimes on both sides. To do this make a crosswise slit through the skin at the tail, and push a finger in. You will now be able to run the finger round the edge of the fish loosening the skin. When you have done this on both edges, take a firm grip of the skin at the tail end (salt your fingers to prevent slipping) with one hand, and with the other hold the fish down. Give a quick strong yank, peeling the skin back towards the head. If necessary, do the same to the other side.

Flat fish are generally filleted into four half-fillets. To do this, lay the fish on a board with the tail towards you. Cut through the flesh to the backbone along the length of the fish. Then, with a sharp pliable knife, cut the left-hand fillet away from the bone, keeping the blade almost flat against the bones of the fish. Then swivel the fish round so the head is towards you and cut away the second fillet in the same way. Turn the fish over and repeat the process on the other side. (If you are left-handed, tackle the right-hand fillet first.)

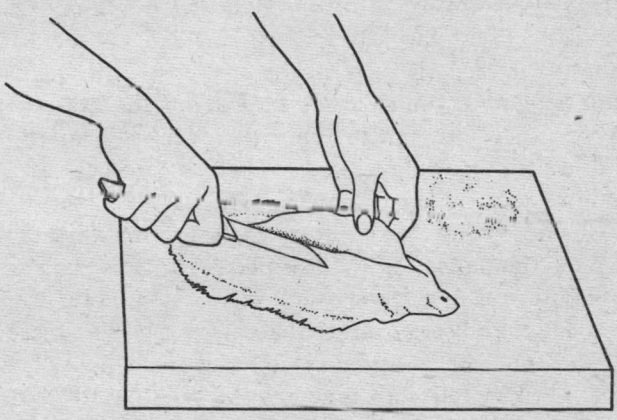

Filleting and skinning round fish

Round fish are filleted before skinning. If they are to be cooked whole, they are cooked with the skin, but this may be carefully peeled off after cooking (e.g. a whole poached salmon). To fillet a round fish lay it on a board and cut through the flesh down to the backbone from the head to the tail. Insert a sharp pliable knife between the flesh and the bones, and slice the fillet away

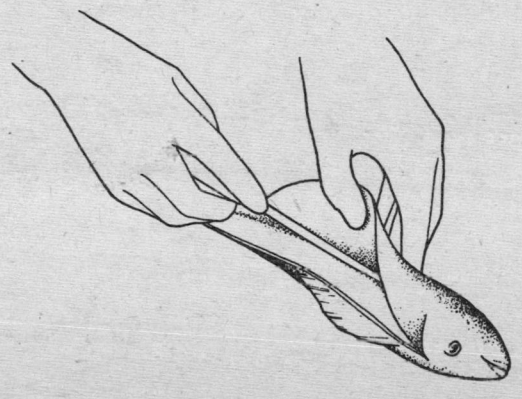

from the bones, working with short strokes from the backbone and from the head end. Remember to keep the knife as flat as possible, and to keep it against the bones. When the fillet is almost off the fish you will need to cut through the belly skin to detach it completely. Very large round fish can be filleted in four, following the flat fish method, or the whole side can be lifted as described here, and then split in two once off the fish.

To skin a fish fillet, put it skin side down on a board. Hold the tip down firmly, using a good pinch of salt to help get a firm grip. With a sharp, heavy, straight knife, cut through the flesh, close to the tip, taking care not to go right through the skin. Hold the knife at rightangles to the fish fillet, with the blade almost upright. With a gentle sawing motion work the flesh from the skin, *pushing* the fillet off rather than cutting it. The reason for keeping the knife almost upright is to lessen the danger of cutting through the skin, but with practice it is possible to flatten the knife slightly, so that the sharp edge is foremost, and simply slide it forward, without the sawing motion.

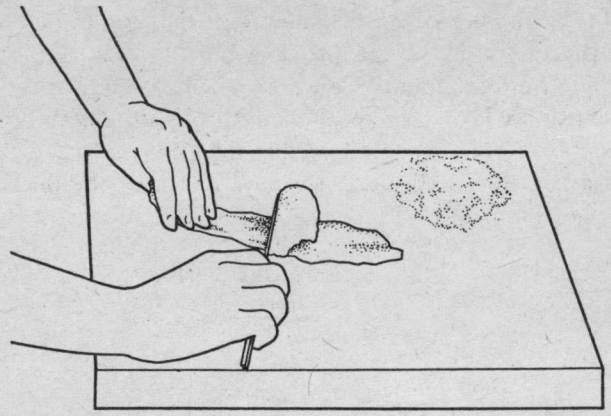

Skinning eel
Cut through the skin round the neck and slit the skin down the length of the body. Hang the eel up by its head – a stout hook

through the eyes is best. Using a cloth to get a good grip, pull hard to peel off the skin from neck to tail.

Stuffing fish

Round fish are more suitable for stuffing whole than flat fish, as there is more space in the body cavity after gutting. Stuffings usually contain breadcrumbs, which swell during cooking, so care should be taken not to overfill the fish. Fish fillets can be sandwiched with stuffing, or rolled up round the mixture. Well-flavoured expensive fish is less often stuffed than the more tasteless varieties, which need the additional flavour of an aromatic filling.

Slicing smoked salmon

Place the side of salmon, skin side down, on a board. Run the tips of the fingers of one hand over the surface of the flesh to locate the ends of the small bones. Pull the bones out with tweezers or pliers. Now slice the flesh in horizontal paper-thin slices, using a long, sharp ham knife. The slices should be long and wide. It is customary to remove the central narrow stripe of brownish flesh, but this is not strictly necessary – it tastes excellent.

If the whole side is not to be sliced, place a piece of plastic wrap on the cut surface of the remaining salmon to prevent drying out.

MEAT

The younger the animal, and the less exercise it has taken, the tenderer will be its meat; but its flavour will be less pronounced. A week-old calf will be tender as margarine, and about as flavourless. An ox that has pulled a cart all its long life will be quite the reverse – good on flavour, but tough as old boots. A relatively young, and therefore tender animal will have white or pale fat, rather than yellow, the meat will be less dark, and the bones more pliable than in an older, tougher animal. So rump steak with a bright red hue and white fat may well be tenderer than the dark flesh and yellow fat of older meat, but it will probably lose on flavour what it gains on texture.

Because tenderness is today rated highly, the most expensive cuts of meat are those from the parts of the animal's body that have had little or no exercise. For example, the leg, neck and shoulder cuts of beef are tougher (and therefore cheaper) than those from rump or loin.

But apart from the age of the animal, there are other factors that affect tenderness. Meat must not be cooked while the muscle fibres are taut due to *rigor mortis* which can last, depending on the temperature in which the carcass is stored, for a day or two. The state of the animal prior to slaughter can also affect the tenderness of the meat – if it is relaxed and peaceable the meat is likely to be more tender. Injections of certain enzymes (proteins that produce changes in the meat without themselves being changed) given to the animal before slaughter will produce the same result artificially.

But the most crucial factor affecting tenderness is the length of time it is stored before cooking. Meat hung in temperatures of 2°C/35°F will, due to enzyme activity, become increasingly tender. Temperatures should not be higher than this, because although the enzyme activity would be greater, the risk of spoilage due to bacterial action would become high. For beef 7 days is the minimum hanging time, 3 weeks or a month being desirable. However, with the commercial demands for quick turnover, the weight-loss during storage and the expense of storing, good hanging is rare these days.

Some enzyme activity continues if the meat is frozen, and the formation, and subsequent melting, of ice-crystals (which, in expanding, bruise the fibres of the meat) means that freezing meat can be said to tenderize it. However the inevitable loss of juices from the meat (and subsequent risk of dryness after cooking) is a disadvantage that outweighs the minimal tenderizing effect.

Hanging is most important in beef, as the animals are comparatively old, perhaps 2 or 3 years, when killed. It is less important for carcasses of young animals such as calves and lambs, as their meat is comparatively tender anyway.

Because, inevitably, some bacterial action (as well as enzyme action) must take place during hanging, the flavour of well-hung meat is stronger, or gamier, than that of under-hung meat. The colour will also deepen and become duller with hanging. But the prime reason for hanging meat is to tenderize it, rather than to increase or change its flavour. This is not so with game, including venison, which is hung as much to produce a gamey flavour as to tenderize the meat.

The last, and probably most important, factor that affects the ultimate tenderness of meat is the method of cooking. Half-cooked or rare meat will be tender simply because its fibres have not been changed by heat, and will still retain the softness of raw meat. But as the heat penetrates the whole piece of meat the fibres of meat set rigidly and the juices cease to run. Once the whole piece of meat is heated thoroughly, all the softness of raw meat is lost, and the meat is at its toughest. This explains the natural reluctance of chefs to serve well-done steaks – it is almost impossible to produce a *tender* well-done grilled steak.

But, paradoxically, further cooking (though not fast grilling or frying) will tenderize that tough steak. This is seen in cooking methods such as braising and stewing, when long slow cooking gradually softens the flesh. A joint from an older animal, which has done much muscular work during its lifetime, and is coarse-grained and fibrous, can be made particularly tender by prolonged gentle cooking. This is because much of the connective tissue present in such a joint, if subjected to a steady temperature of, say, 100°C/200°F, will convert to gelatine, producing a soft, almost sticky tenderness.

Joints with finer graining and little connective tissue, such as rump or sirloin, will never become gelatinous, and are consequently seldom cooked other than by roasting or grilling, when their inherent tenderness (from a life of inaction!) is relied on. But they will never be as tender as the slow-cooked shin or oxtail, which can be cut with a spoon.

It does not matter that few people have any idea which part of the animal their meat comes from. But it is useful to know, if not how to do the butcher's job, at least which cuts are likely to be tender, expensive, good for stewing, or not worth having, and what to look for in a piece of meat.

ROASTING MEAT

1. Weigh the joint and establish length of cooking time (see below).
2. Pre-heat the oven (electric ovens take much longer to heat up than gas ovens).
3. Prepare the joint for roasting (see below).
4. Heat some dripping in a roasting pan and if the meat is lean, brown the joint over direct heat so that it is well coloured. This helps to seal in the juices. Pork and lamb rarely need this but many cuts of beef do.
5. Place the joint in the pan, on a grid if you have one available, as this aids the circulation of hot air; roast for the time calculated.
6. Lean meat needs basting every 20–25 minutes, fatty meats need not be basted.

ROASTING TIMES

Obviously a long thin piece of meat weighing 2·3 kilos/5lb will take less time to cook than a fat round piece of the same weight, so that the times below are meant only as a guide. The essential point is that meat must reach an internal temperature of 60°C/140°F to be rare, 70°C/150°F to be medium pink and 80°C/170°F to be well done. A meat thermometer stuck into the thickest part of the meat, and left there during cooking, eliminates guesswork.

Beef

Beef is generally roasted in the hottest of ovens for 20 minutes to seal the meat (or it may be fried all over in fat before being transferred to the oven). Whatever the method, count the cooking time *after* the sealing has been done, and allow 15 minutes to the pound for rare meat, 20 minutes for medium and 25 for well done, roasting the meat in a pre-heated oven set at 190˚C/375˚F, gas mark 5.

Lamb

Put the lamb into the hottest of ovens, seal for 20 minutes, then allow 20 minutes to the pound at 190°C/375°F, gas mark 5. This will produce very slightly pink lamb. If lamb without a trace of pinkness is wanted allow an extra 20 minutes after the calculated time is up.

Pork

Pork must be well cooked. Allow 40 minutes to the pound at 170°C/325°F, gas mark 3. Sealing is not necessary. If crackling is required roast at 200°C/400°F, gas mark 6 for 25 minutes to the pound, plus 25 minutes over.

Veal

Seal in hot fat over direct heat. Or roast for 20 minutes at maximum temperature. Then allow 25 minutes to the pound at 180°C/350°F, gas mark 4.

Approximate times for cooking steaks

Steaks are grilled according to taste:

Blue	Dark on the outside but almost raw (hot but not cooked) in the middle.
Rare	Dark on the outside but red inside with plenty of red juices running freely.
Medium rare	As rare, but with very little free-flowing juices. Paler centre.
Medium	Pink in the centre but the juices set.
Well done	The centre pale beige but the steak still juicy.

| | Total cooking time per side | |
	Grilled	Fried
Fillet – 2½cm/1in thick		
Blue	2	1½
Rare	2½	2
Medium rare	3	2½
Medium	3½	3
Well done	5	4½
Sirloin – 2½cm/1in thick		
Blue	2½	2
Rare	3	2½
Medium rare	3½	3
Medium	4	3½
Well done	5½	4½
Sirloin – 5cm/2in thick		
Blue	3	2½
Rare	3½	3
Medium rare	4	3½
Medium	5	4
Well done	7	6

Rump

As sirloin, but allow up to 50 per cent longer.

BUTCHERY

Most cuts of meat are available ready prepared from the shop or market. But it is useful to know how to bone and tie certain French and English cuts that a busy butcher may be unwilling to tackle.

Boning

Boning is easier than most people imagine. A short sharp knife is essential. Tunnel boning (where the bone, say from a leg, is extracted from the hole from which it protrudes, without opening out the meat) is more difficult than open boning, when the flesh is split along the bone, the bone worked out and the meat rolled up and tied or sewn. But, whether tunnel boning or open boning, the essential is to work slowly and carefully, keeping the knife as close to the bones as possible, and scraping the meat off the bone rather than cutting it. Any meat extracted inadvertently with the bone can be scraped off and put back into the joint. With most bones it is possible, when tunnel boning, to work from both ends – for example, a leg of mutton can be worked on where the knuckle bone sticks out of the thin end, and the leg bone out of the fillet end.

But in most cases it is simpler to cut neatly through the flesh, along the length of the bone, from the side nearest to the bone, and work the bone out all along its length. After all, some sewing or tying is necessary at the ends of the joints even if tunnel boned, and it is simpler to sew up the length of the joint.

For safety reasons trainee butchers are taught to use the knife in such a way that should it slip it will not hurt them. This means never pulling the knife directly towards the body. In addition the knife is held firmly like a dagger when working, with the point of the knife down (see drawing). But the safest precaution that cooks can take is to see that their knives are sharp. Blunt knives need more pressure to wield, and are therefore more inclined to slip.

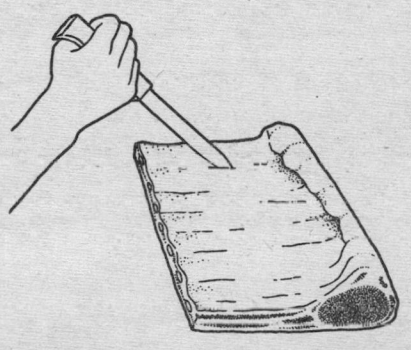

Rolling and tying

Once a joint, such as a loin, is boned, remove most of the fat and lay it, meat side up, on the board. Season it or spread sparingly with stuffing. Roll it up from the thick end and use short pieces of thin cotton (not nylon) string to tie round the meat at 3cm/1½in intervals. These can easily be cut off when serving, or the carver can slice between them when cutting the meat into thick slices.

Sewing up whole joints after stuffing

Use a larding needle or large darning or upholstery needle. Some of these are curved slightly which makes the job easier. Use thin old-fashioned white string, not nylon which will melt under heat. Leave a good few inches of string at the beginning and end, but do not tie elaborate knots which are difficult to undo when dishing the meat. Not-too-tight simple largish stitches are best – the whole length of string can be pulled out in one movement when dishing.

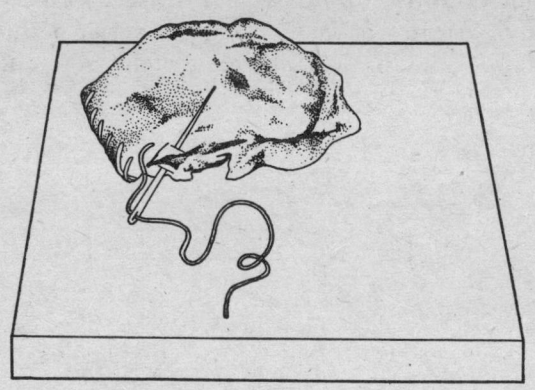

Larding

Some very lean or potentially tough meat is larded before roasting. This promotes tenderness and adds flavour. Most commonly used for slow-roasted dishes like boeuf à la mode or roast veal. A special larding needle is used.

To lard a joint: cut the larding fat (usually rindless back pork fat) into thin strips and put one of them into the tunnel of the needle, clamping down the hinge to hold it in place. The fat should extend a few inches out of the needle. Thread through the meat, twisting the needle gently to prevent the fat pulling off. Once threaded through the meat, release the clamp, and trim the two ends of fat close to the meat. Repeat this all over the lean meat at 2½cm/1in intervals.

BEEF

Steaks for grilling or frying

Cut across the grain of the meat, if possible into thickish slices. Trim neatly, and cut rump slices into two or three individual steaks.

Minute steaks

Cut large thin steaks. Put them between two sheets of paper or polythene and bat gently with a cook's mallet or rolling pin to flatten the meat.

Tournedos steaks

Cut 2cm/1in slices across the trimmed fillet.

For stewing

Remove the gristle, but not *all* the fat (it will add moisture and flavour). Cut into 2½cm/1in cubes, or larger. Too-small pieces are difficult to seal, and may become shreddy and dry during cooking.

For stroganoff

Cut into small strips across the grain of the meat – about the thickness of a pencil.

For roasting

If the meat has no fat on it, tie a piece of pork fat, or fatty bacon, round it. Tie up as described on page 72.

LAMB

Saddle

This consists of both loins of the lamb, left attached at the back-bone, in the same way as a baron of beef.

First remove the skin: with a small sharp knife lift a corner of the skin, hold this firmly with a tea-towel (to get a good grip) and tug sharply to peel off. Trim off any very large pieces of fat from the edges of the saddle, but leave the back fat. Tuck the flaps under the saddle. Cut out the kidneys but keep them (they can be brushed with butter and attached to the end of the saddle with wooden skewers 30 minutes before the end of the roasting time). Using a sharp knife score the back fat all over in a fine criss-cross pattern.

The pelvic or aitch bone, protruding slightly from one end of the saddle, can be removed, or left in place and covered with a ham frill when the saddle is served.

French trimmed best end cutlets (and how to chine)

Skin the best end: lift a corner of the skin from the neck end with a small knife, hold it firmly (using a cloth to get a good grip) and peel it off.

Chine if the butcher has not already done so. This means to saw carefully through the chine bone (or spine) just where it meets the rib bones. Take care not to saw right through into the eye of the meat. Now remove the chine bone completely. Chop off the cutlet bones so that the length of the remaining bones is not more than twice the length of the eye of the meat. Remove the half-moon shaped piece of flexible cartilege found buried between the layers of fat and meat at the thinner end of the best end. This is the tip of the shoulder blade. It is simple to work out with a knife and your fingers.

If thin small cutlets are required cut between each bone as evenly as possible, splitting the rack into six or seven small cutlets. If fatter cutlets are required carefully ease out every other rib bone. Then cut between the remaining bones into thick cutlets. Now trim the fat from the thick end of each cutlet, and scrape the rib bones free of any flesh or skin.

Noisettes

These are boneless cutlets, tied into a neat round shape with string. They are made from the loin or best end. Skin the meat: lift a corner of the skin with a small knife, holding it firmly (using a cloth to get a good grip), and pull it off.

Chine the meat (see page 74). Now remove first the chine bone and then all the rib bones, easing them out with a short sharp knife.

Trim off any excess fat from the meat and roll it up tightly, starting at the meaty thick side and working towards the thin flap. Tie the roll neatly with separate pieces of string placed at 3cm/1½in intervals. Trim the ragged ends of the roll to neaten them. Now slice the roll into pieces, cutting accurately between each string. The average English best end will give four good noisettes. The string from each noisette is removed after cooking.

Crown roast

Two racks (best ends) are needed. For a larger roast use three. The rack is prepared similarly to one destined for cutlets (see above) but the rib bones are left slightly longer, and the rack is not split into cutlets. But it is skinned, chined, the shoulder cartilege is removed, excess fat is cut off and the top inch of the bones are scraped in the same way.

Bend each best end into a semi-circle, with the fatty side of the ribs inside. To facilitate this it may be necessary to cut through the sinew between each cutlet, from the thick end for about 2cm/1in. But take care not to cut into the fleshy eye of the meat. Sew the ends of the racks together to make a circle, with the meaty part forming the base of the crown. Tie a piece of string round the 'waist' of the crown. Traditionally, stuffed; but this can result in undercooked inside fat.

Guard of honour

Prepare two best end racks exactly as for the crown roast. Score the fat in a criss-cross pattern. Hold the two best ends, one in each hand, facing each other with the meaty part of the racks on the board, and the fatty sides on the outside. Jiggle them so the rib bones interlock and cross at the top. Sew or tie the bases together at intervals. Stuff the arch if required.

To score crackling

It is vital that crackling should be scored evenly and thoroughly, each cut (which should penetrate the skin and a little of the fat below it) being even and complete. Unscored crackling is tough and difficult to carve. Make the cuts not more than 1cm/½in apart all over the skin. Score the crackling after boning but before rolling and tying the joint.

PORK AND BACON

Chops

Chops are trimmed of rind, and the fat snipped or cut across (from the outside towards the meat). This is because as the fat shrinks during cooking it tends to curl the chops out of shape.

Gammon steaks or bacon chops

Snip the surrounding fat as described above. Bacon chops (really thick rashers from the prime back) are sometimes cooked with the rind left on. But the snipping is still essential to prevent curling.

American or Chinese spare ribs

These are made from belly of pork (not English spare rib). They can be cut before or after cooking. Simply cut between each belly bone, splitting the meat into long bones.

POULTRY

CLEANING AND DRAWING

Surprisingly, birds keep better, when hanging, with their insides intact. Once eviscerated they must be cooked within a day or two. So when you are ready to cook the bird, take it down, and proceed as follows.

1. Pluck it if you have not already done so.
2. Cut round the feet, at the drumstick joint, but do not cut right through the tendons. Pull the legs off the bird, drawing the tendons out with them. (If the bird is small this is easy enough – just bend the foot back until it snaps, and pull,

perhaps over the edge of a table. Turkeys are more difficult: snap the feet at the drumstick joint by bending them over the end of the table, then hang the bird up by the feet from a stout hook, and pull on the bird. The feet, plus tendons will be left on the hook, the turkey in your arms.) All too often birds are sold with the tendons in the legs, making the drumsticks tough when cooked.

3. Now the head and neck. Lay the bird, breast side down, on a board. Make a slit through the neck skin from the body to the head. Cut off the head and throw it away. Pull back the split neck skin, leaving it attached to the body of the bird (it will come in useful to close the gap if you are stuffing the bird). Cut the neck off as close to the body as you can.

4. Put a finger into the neck hole, to the side of the stump of neck left in the bird, and move the finger right round, loosening the innards from the neck. If you do not do this you will find them difficult to pull out from the other end.

5. With a sharp knife slit the bird open from the vent to the parson's (or pope's) nose, making a hole large enough to get your hand in. Put your hand in, working it so the back of your hand is up against the arch of the breastbone, and carefully loosen the entrails from the sides of the body cavity, all the way round. Pull them out, taking care not to break the gall bladder, the contents of which would embitter any flesh they touch. The first time you do this it is unlikely that you will get everything out in one motion, so check that the lungs and kidneys come too. Have another go if necessary. Once the bird is empty, wipe any traces of blood off with a damp clean cloth. (Covering the gutting hand with a cloth helps extract the intestines intact.)

GIBLETS ETC.

The neck and pinions go into the stockpot. So can the heart and the cleaned gizzard. To clean the gizzard, carefully cut the outside wall along the natural seam so that you can peel it away from the inner bag of grit. Throw the grit bag away, with the intestines, and the gall bladder (be careful not to pierce or break this).

Do not put the liver in the stockpot. It may make the stock bitter. It may be fried and served with the dish, or fried, chopped and added to the sauce, or kept frozen until enough poultry liver has been collected to make pâté. But if the liver is to be used, carefully cut away the discoloured portion of it where it lay against the gall bladder (it will be bitter) and trim off any membranes.

TRUSSING

Trussing is done to keep the bird in a compact neat shape. To truss the bird (usually done after stuffing) sew it up as shown in the following drawings. We feel, however, that trussing large birds is largely unnecessary as the bird is to be carved up anyway, and trussing serves to prevent the inside thigh being cooked by the time the breast is ready. Small birds, especially game birds where underdone thighs are desirable, are trussed, but their feet are left on. Their feet may simply be tied together for neatness sake, and the pinions skewered under the bird. Or they may be trussed in any number of ways, one of which is described below. This is also suitable for large birds such as turkeys and chickens.

Arrange the bird so that the neck flap is folded over the neck hole, and the pinions turned under and tucked in tight. They will, if folded correctly, hold the neck flap in place, but if the bird is well stuffed the neck flap may have to be skewered or sewn in place. Press the legs down and into the bird to force the breast into a plumped up position.

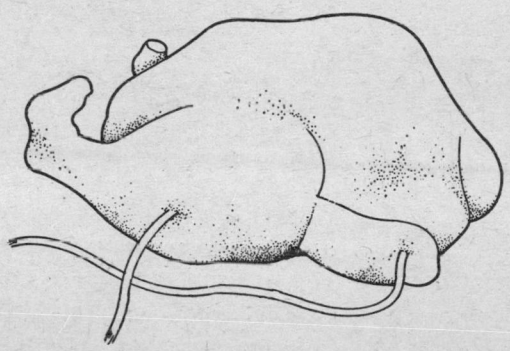

Thread a long trussing needle with thin string and push it through the wing joint, right through the body and out of the other wing joint. Then push it through the body again, this time through the thighs. You should now be back on the side you started. Tie the two ends together in a bow to make later removal quick. Then thread a shorter piece of string through the thin end of the two drumsticks, and tie them together, winding the string round the parson's nose at the same time to close the vent. (Sometimes a small slit is cut in the skin just below the end of the breastbone, and the parson's nose is pushed through it.)

JOINTING

Small birds such as quail are invariably cooked whole, perhaps stuffed, and perhaps boned (see boning, page 83). But medium-sized ones, like chickens and guinea fowl, are often cut into two, four, six or eight pieces.

To split a bird in half simply use a sharp knife to cut right through flesh and bone, just on one side of the breastbone, open

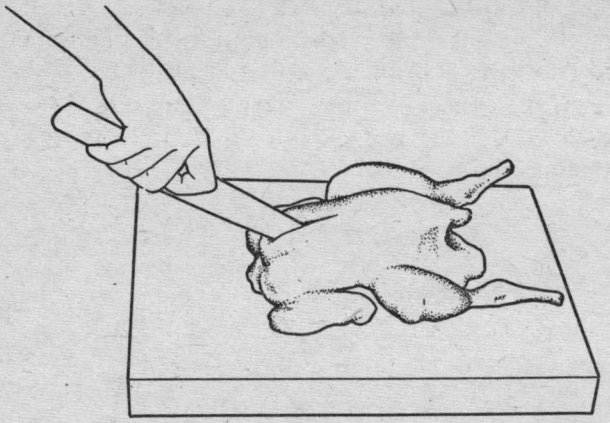

out the bird and cut through the other side, immediately next to the backbone. Then cut the backbone away from the half to which it remains attached.

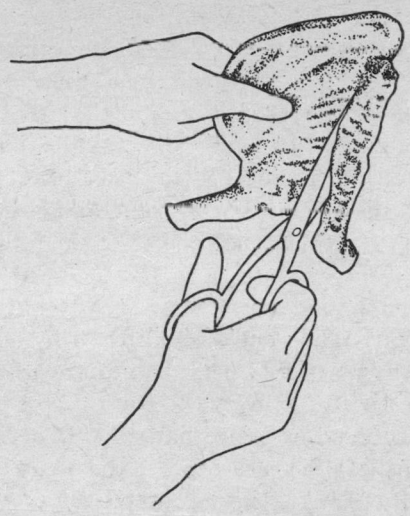

The knobbly end of the drumsticks, and the fleshless tips to the pinions can be cut off before or after cooking. In birds brought whole to the table they are left on.

To joint a bird into four, first pull out any trussing strings, then pull the leg away from the body. With a sharp knife cut through the skin joining the leg to the body, pull the leg away

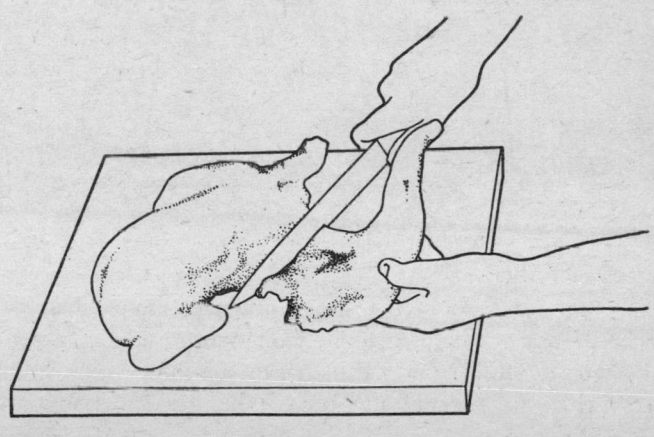

further and cut through more skin to free the leg. Bend the leg outwards and back, forcing the bone to come out of its socket close to the body. Turn the bird over, feel along the backbone to find the oyster (a soft pocket of flesh at the side of the backbone, near the middle). With the tip of the knife, cut this away from the carcass at the side nearest the backbone and farthest from the leg. Then turn the bird over again, and cut through the flesh (the knife going between the end of the thigh bone and the carcass) to take off the leg, bringing the oyster with it.

Then, using poultry shears or a heavy knife, split the carcass along the breastbone. Then cut through the ribs on each side, to take off the fleshy portion of the breast, and with it the wing. Trim the joints neatly to remove scraps of untidy skin.

For six joints, proceed as above but split the legs into thigh portions and drumsticks. The exact join of the bones can be easily felt with a finger if the leg is laid on the board, skin side down.

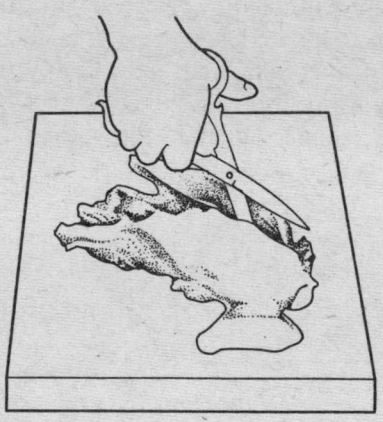

Cut between the bones.

For eight joints, proceed as above and then cut each wing, with a piece of breast attached to it, from the main breast portion. Make the cut almost parallel to the breastbone.

Keep the scraps, backbone, pinions etc. for the stockpot.

BARDING

Poultry liable to dry out during cooking is often barded: lay fatty bacon or rindless back pork fat strips over the body of the bird, and secure or tie in place. The barding is removed during cooking to allow the breast to brown.

BONING AND STUFFING

A short flexible knife is essential. The main point to remember is to keep the boning knife as close to the bone as possible, scraping and easing the flesh away carefully.

Turn the bird breast side down and cut through the skin, along the backbone, from the parson's nose to the neck. Work the skin and flesh away from the bones, peeling back the flesh as you go, gradually exposing the rib cage. When you get to the legs and wings, cut through the tendons close against the carcass at the joints. This will mean the wings and legs stay attached to the skin – not to the carcass. Continue working round the bird, taking special care when boning the breast where the skin and bone are very close.

If the wings and legs are to be boned too, chop off the wing pinions and the knuckle-end of the drumsticks. Working from the thicker end of the joints ease the bones out, scraping the flesh from them carefully. It may be necessary, especially with big birds, to work from the drumstick or the wing tip ends as well, but most of the work should be done from the body side.

Cut off any excess fat, especially from near the parson's nose. When all the bones are out scrape off any flesh still adhering to them and add it to the stuffing.

When stuffing the bird the stuffing is laid down the middle and the sides brought up to enclose it. The bird must then be sewn up if it is to be roasted, and sewn up and/or wrapped in muslin if it is to be poached.

ROASTING TIMES

FOR POULTRY

White poultry, which is cooked through, not left pink, is done when the leg joint will wobble freely, not lifting the whole bird with it, and when the juices run clear, not pink, when the thigh is pierced with a skewer. To calculate cooking times, weigh after stuffing.

Chicken

With the oven set to 220°C/425°F, gas mark 7, allow 15 minutes to the pound. If the juices still run out pink when the flesh is pierced allow a further 15 minutes.

Turkey

Large turkeys should be slow-roasted but smaller birds (under 5·4 kilos/12lb) may be cooked at a higher temperature. Allow 10 minutes to the pound for small birds at 200°C/400°F, gas mark 6.

For larger turkeys use a cooler oven (180°C/350°F, gas mark 4) and allow 15 minutes to the pound, or an even cooler one (170°C/325°F, gas mark 3) and allow 25 minutes to the pound. Keep the breast covered to prevent burning, removing the covering (bacon, foil or what have you) for the last 45 minutes. ·

Thawing and cooking times for turkeys

Although the thawing time in this table can be relied on absolutely, the cooking times are dependent on an accurate oven. For safety's sake, plan the timing so that, if all goes right, the bird will be ready 1 hour before dinner. This will give you leeway if necessary. When the bird is cooked, open the oven door to cool the oven, then put the turkey on a serving dish and put it back in the oven to keep warm.

Thawing in a warm room (over 18°C/65°F) or under warm

water is not recommended, as warmth will encourage the growth of micro-organisms, which might result in food poisoning.

Weight of bird when ready for the oven, regardless of whether it is boned stuffed or empty	Thawing time at room temperature 18°C/65°F	Thawing time in refrigerator 5°C/40°F	Cooking time at 180°C/ 350°F, gas mark 4	Cooking time at 170°C/ 325°F, gas mark 3
	hours	hours	hours	hours
4– 5 kilos/ 8–10lb	20	65	$2\frac{1}{4}$–$2\frac{3}{4}$	4 –$4\frac{1}{2}$
5– 6 kilos/11–13lb	24	70	3 –$3\frac{1}{2}$	5 –$5\frac{1}{2}$
6– 7 kilos/14–16lb	30	75	$3\frac{3}{4}$–$4\frac{1}{4}$	$5\frac{3}{4}$–$6\frac{1}{4}$
8– 9 kilos/17–20lb	40	80	$4\frac{3}{4}$–$5\frac{1}{4}$	$6\frac{1}{2}$–$7\frac{1}{2}$
9–11 kilos/21–24lb	48	96	$5\frac{1}{2}$–$6\frac{1}{2}$	8 –9

FOR GAME BIRDS

	°C	°F	Gas mark	Minutes
Pigeon	200	400	6	25–35
Grouse	190	375	5	25–35
Partridge	190	375	5	20–25
Pheasant	190	375	5	45–60
Snipe	190	375	5	10–12
Wild Duck	200	400	6	30–35
Woodcock	190	375	5	20–30
Quail	180	350	4	20
Teal	210	425	7	20

ICE CREAM

Note: On freezing, ice cream will lose a little colour, sweetness and taste, so this must be compensated for during preparation.

METHODS OF MAKING

HAND-OPERATED CHURN

This is a wooden or heavy plastic bucket with a tightly covered metal container which fits inside. There are paddles reaching into the centre of the container. These are churned by a handle at the side of the bucket. The space between the churn and the bucket is packed with freezing salt and ice. Do not let any of the salt get into the ice cream as this will ruin the taste.

1. Put the churn into the bucket.
2. Surround the metal container with chopped ice and rock salt (1 part salt to 3 parts ice) and pack it in tightly. (The salt first melts some of the ice, resulting in chips of ice suspended in a saline solution. This prevents the ice settling into a solid igloo round the churn. Then, paradoxically, this saline solution is cooled by the remaining ice to *below* water-freezing point, brine having a lower freezing point than water. Now the ice-chips, surrounded by the below $-0^{\circ}C$ solution, cannot readily melt and the mixture, thus stabilized, rapidly freezes the ice cream.)
3. Pour in the ice cream mixture taking care not to fill the container more than three-quarters full.
4. Insert the paddles and cover the metal churn with a piece of greaseproof paper. Fix the lid on over the paper. Assemble the rest of the machine.

5. Churn steadily, refilling the bucket with ice as it melts.
6. When the handle becomes difficult to turn the ice cream is set.
7. Remove the lid, scrape the paddles clean and replace the lid.
8. If the ice cream is for the day it is made, it should be kept in the refrigerator for one hour before serving.
9. If the ice cream is for a later date, pile it into a suitable container and keep it in the deep freeze until 1 hour before serving, when it should be put into the refrigerator to 'ripen'.

ELECTRIC ICE CREAM BUCKET

Pack the machine as for a hand churn and then set it in operation. When the hum of the motor becomes a high-pitched whine the ice cream is set.

ELECTRIC TRAY FREEZER (or sorbetière)

This is a rectangular aluminium box with plastic paddles. It fits into the freezer compartment of a refrigerator. Set the freezer at its lowest temperature, i.e. the highest setting. Pour the mixture into the sorbetière, place on the lid and put into the freezer. Turn on the machine; when the hum of the motor becomes a high-pitched whine the ice cream is set. Turn off the machine, scrape down and remove the paddles, cover the ice cream and leave to 'ripen' in the refrigerator for 1 hour.

REFRIGERATOR-FREEZER

This method does not rely on an ice cream machine of any sort but on everyday kitchen equipment.

Make sure that the fork, rotary beater, spoon, bowl and ice tray to be used are well chilled and that the freezer is set to the highest setting (lowest temperature). Pour the mixture into a chilled tray, and put into the freezer. Whisk with a fork every 20 minutes until the mixture is half frozen, then tip into a chilled bowl and whisk with a rotary beater. Return to the freezer in the bowl and whisk again at 20-minute intervals until the ice cream has become completely frozen. If the ice cream is to be eaten at a later date, allow 40–60 minutes in the refrigerator before serving, to soften slightly.

Exceptions

If the ice cream mixture already contains a high proportion of trapped air (for example, if it is made with a meringue base) the occasional whisk during the freezing process is not necessary. In addition, if a good processor such as a Magimix is available the ice cream can be completely frozen without whisking, then broken up and whisked in the machine to a creamy airy consistency. It must then be returned to the freezer.

WATER ICES

Water ices are better made in an ice cream machine, because the absence of any fat means that large ice crystals form very easily. The addition of whipped egg whites or gelatine helps to prevent this. A *granita* is a water ice made without egg whites or gelatine, having a rather icy and grainy, not creamy, texture.

BOMBES

Bombes are iced desserts frozen in a special bombe mould or in a pudding basin and turned out before serving. They generally consist of an outside layer of ice cream or sorbet and a filling of a contrasting ice cream, sorbet or a cream mousse or meringue mixture. When cut into segments the slices have a pretty stripey appearance. The traditional bombe mould was completely round, but modern ones are often shaped like jelly moulds. A pudding basin works perfectly well.

Making bombes

1. To line a bombe mould with ice cream:
    (i) Chill the mould in the freezer.
    (ii) Soften the ice cream so that it can be spread.
    (iii) Line the bottom and sides of the mould with ice cream.
    (iv) Freeze until firm.

2. For the filling:
   (i) Chill the filling well.
   (ii) Pour or spoon into the mould.
3. Cover and freeze until firm, preferably overnight.
4. Place in the ordinary refrigerator one hour before serving.
5. To unmould:
   (i) Remove lid. Prick the mixture to release any vacuum.
   (ii) Invert a plate over the mould and turn mould and plate over together.
   (iii) Cover with a cloth wrung out in hot water and hold it there. When the cloth becomes cold, wring it out again in hot water and replace it over the bombe.
   (iv) Remove the cloth. The bombe case should now lift off easily.
   (v) If the ice cream has melted slightly, return the bombe to the freezer until firm.
6. Decorate with fruit, nuts or whipped cream, as appropriate.

Easy bombe filling

Flavour whipped cream as you like (e.g. with a liqueur or with finely chopped fruit or with ginger). Mix it with an equal quantity of broken meringues.

CATERING QUANTITIES

Few people accurately weigh or measure quantities as a control-conscious chef must do. But when catering for large numbers it is useful to know the minimum quantities required to provide well without great waste.

As a general rule, the more people you are catering for the less food *per head* you need to provide, e.g. 250g/½lb of stewing beef per head is essential for 4 people, but 180g/6oz per head would feed 60 people.

POULTRY

Chicken and turkey: 450g/1lb weight per person, weighed when plucked and drawn

Duck: 3 kilos/6½lb bird for 3–4 people; 2 kilos/4½lb bird for 2 people

Goose: 3·4 kilos/8lb for 4 people; 6·9 kilos/15lb for 7 people

GAME

Pheasant: 1 bird for 2 people (roast); 1 bird for 3 people (casseroled)

Pigeon: 1 bird per person

Grouse: 1 young grouse per person (roast); 2 birds for 3 people (casseroled)

Quail: 2 small birds per person, *or* 1 large boned stuffed bird (served on a crouton)

Partridge: 1 bird per person

Venison: 170g/6oz lean meat per person (casseroled); 2 kilos/4½lb cut of haunch weighed on the bone, for 8–9 people (braised or roast); weighed off the bone, 170g/6oz per person (braised or roast)

Steaks: 170g/6oz per person

MEAT

Lamb or mutton

Casseroled: 275g/½lb per person (boneless, with fat trimmed away)
Roast leg: 1·35 kilos/3lb for 3–4 people; 2 kilos/4½lb for 4–5 people; 3 kilos/6½lb for 7–8 people

Roast shoulder: 2 kilos/4½lb shoulder for 5–6 people; 3 kilos/6½lb shoulder for 7–9 people
Roast breast: 450g/1lb breast for 2 people

(British lamb joints are frequently larger than New Zealand joints.)

Grilled best end cutlets: 3–4 per person
Grilled loin chops: 2 per person

Beef

Stewed: 225/½lb boneless trimmed meat per person
Roast (off the bone): if serving men only, 225g/½lb per person; if serving men and women, 200g/7oz per person
Roast (on the bone): 340g/¾lb per person
Roast whole fillet: 2 kilos/4½lb piece for 10 people
Grilled steaks: 200–225g/7–8oz per person depending on appetite

Pork

Casseroled: 170g/6oz per person
Roast leg *or* loin (off the bone): 200g/7oz per person
Roast leg *or* loin (on the bone): 340g/¾lb per person
(2 average fillets will feed 3–4 people)
Grilled: one 170g/6oz chop or cutlet per person

Veal

Stews or pies: 225g/½lb pie veal per person
Fried: one 170g/6oz escalope per person

Minced meat

170g/6oz per person for shepherd's pie, hamburgers etc.
110g/¼lb per person for steak tartare
85g/3oz per person for lasagne, canneloni etc.
110g/¼lb per person for moussaka
55g/2oz per person for spaghetti

FISH

Whole large fish (e.g. sea bass, salmon, whole haddock), weighed uncleaned, with head on: 340–450g/¾lb per person

Cutlets and steaks: 170g/6oz per person
Fillets (e.g. sole, lemon sole, plaice): 3 small fillets per person (total weight about 170g/6oz)
Whole small fish (e.g. trout, slip soles, small plaice, small mackerel, herring): 225–340g/½–¾lb weighed with heads for main course; 170g/6oz for starter
Fish off the bone (in fish pie, with sauce etc.): 170g/6oz per person

Shellfish

Prawns: 55–85g/2–3oz per person as a starter; 140g/5oz per person as a main course
Mixed shellfish: 55–85g/2–3oz per person as a starter; 140g/5oz per person as a main course

VEGETABLES

Weighed before preparation and cooking, and assuming three vegetables, including potatoes, served with a main course: 110g/4oz per person, except (per person):

French beans: 85g/3oz

Peas: 85g/3oz

Spinach: 340g/¾lb

Potatoes: 3 small (roast); 170g/½lb (mashed); 10–15 (Parisienne); 5 (chateau); 1 large or 2 small (baked), 110g/¼lb (new)

Rice

Plain, boiled or fried: 55g/2oz (weighed before cooking) *or* 1 breakfast cup (measured after cooking)
In risotto or pilaf: 1oz per person (weighed before cooking) for starter; 55g/2oz per person for main course

Note: As a general rule men eat more potatoes and less 'greens' than women!

MISCELLANEOUS

Brown bread and butter: 1–1½ slices (3 triangular pieces) per person

French bread: 1 large loaf for 15 people; 1 small loaf for 10 people

Cheese

After a meal if serving one blue-veined, one hard and one cream cheese: 225g/½lb piece of each for 8 people if serving one variety of cheese only: 85g/3oz per person up to 8 people; 55g/2oz per person for up to 20 people; 30g/1oz per person for over 20 people.

At a wine and cheese party: 110g/¼lb per person for up to 8 people; 85g/3oz per person for up to 20 people; 55g/2oz per person for over 20 people.

Inevitably, if catering for small numbers, there will be cheese left over but this is unavoidable if the host is not to look mean.

Biscuits

3 each for up to 10 people
2 each for up to 30 people
1 each for over 30 people

Butter

30g/1oz per person if bread is served with the meal
45g/1½oz per person if cheese is served as well

Cream

20ml/¾oz per person for coffee
50ml/1½oz per person for pudding or dessert

Milk

¼ litre/1 pint for 18–20 cups of tea

SALADS

Obviously, the more salads served, the less guests will eat of any one salad. Allow 1½ large portions of salad, in total, per head – e.g. if *only* one salad is served make sure there is enough for 1½ helpings each. Conversely if 100 guests are to choose from five different salads, allow a total of 150 portions – i.e. 30 portions of each salad.

Tomato salad

450g/1lb tomatoes, sliced, serves 5 people

Cole slaw

1 small cabbage, finely shredded, serves 10–12 people

Grated carrot salad

450g/1lb carrots, grated, serves 6 people

Potato salad

450g/1lb potatoes (weighed before cooking) serves 5 people

Green salad

Allow a loose handful of leaves for each person (i.e. a large Cos lettuce will serve 8, a large Webb's will serve 10, a Dutch hothouse 'butterhead' will serve 4)

COCKTAIL PARTIES

Allow 10 cocktail mouthfuls per head if served at a 'cocktail party'
14 cocktail mouthfuls per head if served at lunchtime when guests are unlikely to go on to a meal
4–5 cocktail mouthfuls with pre-lunch or pre-dinner drinks
8 cocktail mouthfuls, plus 4 miniature sweet cakes or pastries, per head for a wedding reception

Sliced bread

A large loaf, thinly sliced, generally has 18–20 slices

Butter

30g/1oz soft butter will cover 8 large bread slices

Sausages

450g/1lb = 32 cocktail sausages

2
First Courses

SOUPS

Iced Creamy Borscht

450g/1lb raw beetroot
570ml/1 pint water
Salt and freshly ground black
  pepper
30g/1oz butter
1 large onion, sliced
225g/$\frac{1}{2}$lb raw potatoes, peeled
  and sliced
425ml/$\frac{3}{4}$ pint milk

1 chicken stock cube
1 teaspoon cumin seeds *or* $\frac{1}{2}$
  teaspoon ground cumin
Juice of $\frac{1}{2}$ lemon
190ml/$\frac{1}{3}$ pint cream
290ml/$\frac{1}{2}$ pint soured cream
1 tablespoon chopped fresh
  chives

1. Wash the beetroot but do not peel them. Boil them in the
    water with a good pinch of salt for 3 hours or until very tender.
    Do not throw away the water, but peel the beets, discarding
    the skins.
2. Melt the butter in a heavy saucepan and in it slowly fry the
    onion until just turning colour. Add the sliced potatoes and
    cook over gentle heat for a further 5 minutes.
3. Add the milk, cumin and chicken stock cube. Simmer slowly
    until the potato is cooked.
4. Put the beetroot and cooking liquid through a liquidizer,
    vegetable mill or sieve. Then liquidize or sieve the contents
    of the saucepan. Mix with the beetroot.
5. Add the lemon juice and plenty of pepper. Taste for seasoning,
    adding salt if needed. Stir in the cream.

6. Chill well. Serve the soup in individual soup plates or cups, with a good dollop of soured cream in each serving, and the top sprinkled with the chives.

Serves 6

Beef Consommé

1¾ litres/3 pints very well
flavoured beef bouillon
(pages 233–4)
Whites of 3 eggs plus shells

5 tablespoons sherry *or*
Madeira

1. Place the bouillon and sherry in a large clean metal saucepan. Place over a gentle heat.
2. Place the crushed shells in a bowl, add the egg whites, and whisk until frothy. Pour into the bouillon. Whisk with a balloon whisk until the mixture boils and rises. Stop whisking immediately and take the pan off the heat. Allow the mixture to subside. Take care not to break the crust formed by the egg white.
3. Bring the consommé up to the boil again and then again allow to subside. Repeat this once more. (The egg white will trap the sediment in the stock and clear the soup.) Allow to cool for 10 minutes.
4. Fix a double layer of fine muslin over a clean basin and carefully strain the soup through it, taking care to hold the egg white crust back. When all the liquid is through (or almost all of it) allow the egg white to slip into the muslin. Then strain the soup again – this time through both egg-white crust and cloth. Do not try to hurry the process by squeezing the cloth as this will produce murky soup: it must be allowed to drip through at its own pace. The consommé is now ready for serving.

Note: To serve the consommé *en gelée* (jellied) pour the liquid into a shallow pan or tray to cool and refrigerate until set. Chop roughly with a knife and spoon into ice-cold soup cups. Serve with a wedge of lemon and toast.

Serves 6

Garnishes for Consommé

Aux pointes d'asperges

Cooked asparagus tips. Place at the bottom of a hot tureen and pour the soup over.

A la Julienne

Mixed carrot, turnip, leek and celery cut into Julienne strips. Add to the consommé and cook until tender. Chopped chervil or parsley is sometimes added at the last minute.

Lady Curzon

Chill the consommé in ovenproof cups. Flavour 2 tablespoons double cream with curry powder, salt and pepper and pour over each consommé. Place under a hot grill to brown the top. Put into a warm oven to heat the soup.

Aux profiteroles

Choux pastry seasoned with Parmesan, mustard and cayenne, piped in pea-size pieces and baked until crisp. Place in the bottom of a hot tureen, pour the soup over and serve immediately before the profiteroles can become soggy.

Aux quenelles

Small chicken quenelles, poached in stock. Float these in the consommé and sprinkle with chopped chervil or parsley.

Aux vermicelli

Vermicelli cooked in stock until tender. Rinse well, place in a hot tureen and pour the soup over. (Other small-size pastas are also used.)

Consommé Royale

Consommé (page 97)
1 egg white

4 tablespoons cream
Salt and pepper

1. Mix the egg white with a fork and beat in the cream and seasoning.
2. Place in an ovenproof dish and stand in a pan of gently simmering water until set.
3. Cool, cut into neat strips and add to the comsommé just before serving.

Serves 6

Soupe au Pistou

Mediterranean peasant dish which calls for fresh basil and very fresh garlic.

2 tablespoons oil (preferably olive)
225g/½lb potatoes, peeled and diced
2 leeks, finely sliced
2 carrots, finely sliced
450g/1lb dried haricot beans, soaked overnight
110g/¼lb green beans, sliced *or* chopped

2 litres/3½ pints chicken stock
1 heaped teaspoon salt
½ teaspoon coarsely ground black pepper
2 tablespoons vermicelli *or* other small pasta
4 ripe tomatoes, peeled and chopped

For the pistou:
4 garlic cloves, crushed
4 heaped tablespoons fresh chopped basil

3 tablespoons olive oil

To serve:
Grated Gruyère cheese

1. First make the soup: heat the oil and add the potatoes, leeks and carrots. Cover and cook gently until the vegetables are soft.
2. Add the dried beans, green beans, chicken stock, salt and pepper. Simmer until the haricot beans are soft (about 1½ hours). Add the pasta and tomatoes and cook for a further 10 minutes, or until the pasta is tender.
3. Make the pistou: put the garlic and the basil in a mortar or liquidizer and pound to a paste. Add the oil, drop by drop (as when making mayonnaise) mixing all the time, to form an emulsion. Just before serving, stir the pistou into the soup. Hand the cheese separately.

Note: Recipes for this soup vary along the Mediterranean according to local tradition and the season. Courgettes, cabbage and onions sometimes make their appearance. The Italian version of pesto (pages 238–9), from which pistou is derived, is sometimes added to the soup, which is itself a version of the Italian minestrone.

Serves 6

PÂTÉS AND TERRINES

Chicken Liver Pâté

285g/10oz butter
1 large onion, very finely
   chopped
1 large garlic clove, crushed
450g/1lb chicken livers *or*
   225g/½lb duck livers and
   225g/½lb chicken livers

Salt and freshly ground black
   pepper
85g/3oz clarified butter (if the
   pâté is to be stored)
   (page 236)

1. Melt half the butter in a large thick frying pan and gently fry the onion in it until soft and transparent.
2. Add the crushed garlic and continue cooking for 1 further minute.
3. Discard all the discoloured bits from the livers as they are very bitter.
4. Add the livers to the pan, and cook, turning them to brown on all sides, for 8 minutes or so, when they should be firm and cooked inside.
5. Add salt and plenty of pepper.
6. Mince the mixture or liquidize it in an electric blender with the rest of the butter. Put it into an earthenware dish or pot.
7. If the pâté is to be kept more than 3 days cover the top with a layer of clarified butter.

Serves 8

Hare Terrine

Begin preparations for this two days in advance. This recipe is sufficient for one 2 pint terrine.

For the marinade:

4 bay leaves
1 teaspoon salt
6 peppercorns
1 tablespoon redcurrant jelly
3 tablespoons brandy
8 juniper berries, crushed

1 hare
450g/1lb veal, minced

450g/1lb belly pork, minced
170g/6oz fresh white
  breadcrumbs
1 beaten egg
Salt and freshly ground black
  pepper
1 level tablespoon finely
  chopped fresh thyme or
  savory
340g/¾lb streaky bacon rashers

1. Mix together the ingredients for the marinade. Take about 1½lb from the saddle and hind legs of the hare. Cut into slices and leave in the marinade overnight.
2. The next day mince together any meat left on the hare with its cleaned liver, heart and kidney. Mix it together with the veal, belly of pork, crumbs and egg. Season very well and mix in the chopped herbs.
3. Cut the rind off the bacon and stretch the rashers on a board with the back of a knife. Line a 1 litre/2 pint terrine with slightly overlapping slices of bacon, allowing the ends to hang over the sides.
4. Put half the pork and veal mixture into the terrine. Arrange the slices of hare on top and pour over the marinade. Cover with the remaining pork and veal. Press down firmly and fold the bacon ends over the top. Cover with greaseproof paper and foil.
5. Set the oven to 190°C/375°F, gas mark 5. Place the terrine in a roasting tin half-filled with hot water and bake for 1–1½ hours. It is cooked when it feels firm to the touch.
6. Remove from the oven and leave to cool for about 20 minutes. Cover with a clean piece of greaseproof paper and weigh it

down with a 1 kilo/2lb weight. Leave overnight. Turn out and serve in slices.

Serves 8–10

Smooth Duck Pâté with Aspic

This recipe must be started at least one day in advance.

1 large duck	170g/6oz butter
1 onion	3 tablespoons port
1 carrot	Ground mace
1 Stick of celery	15g/½oz gelatine
6 peppercorns	1 egg white
2 bay leaves	2 egg shells
Salt and freshly ground black pepper	1 orange for garnish
1¼ litres/2 pints water	

To serve:
Hot toast

1. Take all the duck flesh off the bones. Put the bones, the onion, carrot, celery, peppercorns and bay leaves in a large saucepan. Season with salt. Add the water, bring to the boil and leave to simmer for at least 3 hours, without allowing the water to reduce to less than 290ml/½ pint.
2. Cut the duck flesh into 5cm/2in pieces. Melt 2 tablespoons of the butter and in it fry the duck, a few pieces at a time, until completely cooked (about 10 minutes). Add more butter and duck pieces as and when necessary.
3. Cut away and discard any discoloured parts from the liver. Melt more butter and fry the liver for 3 minutes.
4. Liquidize or pound together the cooked duck, liver and any remaining butter. Beat in the port and season with salt, pepper and ground mace. Spread flat in a dish, leave to cool and then put in the refrigerator overnight.

5. Strain the duck stock and refrigerate it overnight too.
6. Lift or skim any fat from the stock. Put the 290ml/$\frac{1}{2}$ pint stock into a large saucepan (making up the amount with water if necessary) and sprinkle on the gelatine. Put over a gentle heat.
7. Add the egg white to the crushed shells in a bowl and whisk until frothy. Pour into the warming stock and keep whisking steadily with a balloon whisk until the mixture boils and rises. Stop whisking immediately and draw the pan off the heat. Allow the mixture to subside. Take care not to break the crust formed by the egg white.
8. Bring the aspic, without whisking, to the boil again, and again allow to subside. Repeat this once more (the egg white will trap the sediment in the stock and clear the aspic). Allow to cool for 10 minutes.
9. Fix a double layer of fine muslin over a clean basin and carefully strain the aspic through it, taking care to hold the egg white crust back. When all the liquid is through (or almost all of it) allow the egg white to slip into the muslin. Then strain the aspic again – this time through both the crust and cloth. Do not try to hurry the process by squeezing the cloth or murky aspic will result. Leave to cool until nearly set.
10. Slice the whole orange thinly. Pour a little aspic on top of the duck pâté. Put into the refrigerator until nearly set. Arrange the slices of orange on top of this and return it to the refrigerator until set. Pour on more aspic just to cover the orange slices and return to the refrigerator. When this aspic is set pour over another layer and return to the refrigerator until set again.
11. Serve with plenty of hot toast.

Serves 4–6

OTHER FIRST COURSES AND PASTA

Italian Seafood Salad

450g/1lb fresh squid
Few slices onion
Few parsley stalks
1 bay leaf
Salt
1 medium leek
1 medium carrot
55g/2oz white button
  mushrooms
55g/2oz cooked peeled prawns

For the dressing:
1 scant tablespoon olive oil
2 scant tablespoons other
  (milder) salad oil
1 teaspoon wine vinegar
1 teaspoon fresh lemon juice
Salt and freshly ground black
  pepper
1 small garlic clove, crushed
1 tablespoon finely chopped
  fresh parsley

1. Ask the fishmonger to gut and skin the squid. Alternatively tackle it yourself – it is rather messy, but quite easy: remove the entrails and the blood (ink) under cold running water – they will come out easily. Remove the clear plastic-like piece of cartilege that runs the length of the body on the inside. Cut off and throw away the head (it is the round middle bit with two large eyes). Scrape off the pinkish-purple outside skin – a fine membrane – from the body and the tentacles. Don't worry if you cannot get all the tentacles completely clear of it, Wash the body and tentacles to remove all traces of ink: you should now have a perfectly clean, white, empty squid.

2. Cut it into thin strips. Put them in a saucepan and just cover with water. Add the onion, parsley stalks, bay leaf and a pinch

of salt. Simmer gently until the squid is tender. This can take up to 1 hour for strips cut from a large squid. Drain well.

3. Wash the leek and discard the tough outside leaves and the dark green part. Shred the rest finely and plunge it into boiling salted water for 2 minutes until just tender but still bright green. Rinse under running cold water to set the bright colour.

4. Peel the carrot. With a potato peeler shred it into long thin ribbons. Slice the mushrooms finely.

5. Combine the ingredients for the dressing in a screw-top jar and shake well.

6. When the squid is cool drain it (but keep the fish stock for some future soup or sauce – it is delicious) discard the onion, bay leaf and parsley stalks and put the squid into a bowl. Add prawns, mushrooms, carrot strips, cooked leek and dressing. Chill well before serving.

Note: Other seafood can be used too:

Frozen Cockles: less salty than those in brine. Fresh cockles must be left for an hour in salty water and turned often to rid them of sand before cooking as for mussels.

Mussels: scrub well under running water. Pull away the 'beard' and discard any that are broken or which will not close when tapped. Put in a heavy pan with a few spoons white wine, cover, and shake over heat for 5 minutes until the shells have opened. Discard any which remain closed. Remove the mussels from the shells, and discard the 'rubber bands'.

Frozen cooked prawns: thaw slowly, season with lemon juice, salt and black pepper.

Frozen raw 'scampi': cook with the squid, allowing about 8 minutes. Do not boil.

Raw whole prawns: simmer for 8 minutes with the squid or in a separate pan. Shell carefully. If using whole for decoration remove the legs and any roe after cooking.

Serves 6

Gougères

105g/3¾oz flour
Pinch of salt
Pepper and cayenne
85g/3oz butter
225ml/7½ fl.oz water

3 eggs, lightly beaten
55g/2oz strong Cheddar cheese
  cut into 5mm/¼in cubes
425ml/¾ pint filling (below)
2 tablespoons browned crumbs

1. Set oven to 200°C/400°F, gas mark 6.
2. Sift the flour with the seasonings.
3. In a large saucepan heat the butter in the water and when completely melted bring up to a rolling boil. When the mixture is bubbling all over, tip in all the flour, take off the heat and beat well with a wooden spoon until the mixture will leave the sides of the pan. Allow to cool for about 10 minutes.
4. Beat in the eggs gradually until the mixture is smooth and shiny and of 'dropping consistency' – you may not need the last few spoonfuls of egg. Stir in the diced cheese.
5. Spoon the mixture round the edge of a flattish greased ovenproof dish. Pile the filling into the centre, and sprinkle with the crumbs. Bake until the choux is well risen and golden and the filling is hot (about 35–40 minutes).

Makes a gougère for 6

Chicken Filling for Gougère

30g/1oz butter
1 medium onion, finely sliced
½ teaspoon curry powder
85g/3oz large mushrooms,
  sliced
1 tablespoon flour
2 teaspoons fresh chopped
  parsley

290ml/½ pint chicken stock
Salt and freshly ground black
  pepper
85g/3oz ham, chopped
285g/10oz cooked chicken,
  chopped
Dry breadcrumbs
A little melted butter for the top

1. Melt the butter in a saucepan and in it soften the onion until cooked but not brown. Add the curry powder and the mushrooms and cook for 1 minute.
2. Stir in the flour, cook for 1 minute and add the parsley, stock and freshly ground pepper and salt to taste.
3. Bring to the boil, stirring all the time. Simmer for 2 minutes. Add the ham and chicken.
4. Pile into a gougère case (page 107). Sprinkle with crumbs and melted butter and bake for 35–40 minutes.

Note: This is a good filling for pancakes, vol-au-vents or may be simply served on toast.

Makes filling for a 6-portion gougère

Chicken and Beanshoot Salad

One 1·8 kilos/4lb cooked chicken, preferably poached
450g/1lb beanshoots
1 small onion, finely chopped
1 tablespoon fresh chopped mint
French dressing (page 237)
Soy sauce

1. Pull the chicken into 2·5cm/1in strips, discarding the skin and bones. Mix with the washed but raw beanshoots.
2. Add the onion and mint to the French dressing and mix with the chicken and beanshoots.
3. Pile into a serving dish and sprinkle liberally with soy sauce.

Serves 6

Snails à la Bourguignonne

170g/6oz butter
Juice of ½ lemon
2 tablespoons chopped fresh parsley
6 garlic cloves
Salt
24 snails and 24 shells

1. Soften the butter very well and beat in the lemon juice and parsley. Crush the garlic with salt and beat this into the butter. Leave in a cool place.

2. Push a snail, tail first, into each shell with a teaspoon handle. Fill the remaining cavity of the shell with the garlic butter, scraping the top off neatly. Keep in the refrigerator until needed.

3. Set the oven to 200°C/400°F, gas mark 6. Place a snail, butter upwards in each indentation of snail dishes and cook in the oven for 8 minutes or until the butter has completely melted and starts to sizzle, but no longer. Overcooking snails toughens them.

4. Serve immediately with plenty of fresh French bread.

Note I: In the absence of snail dishes an ovenproof plate filled with dry rice or salt, into which you 'plant' the snails, will do.

Note II: Because preparing fresh snails is a specialized and long process, ready-to-use snails are bought in cans, even by the top French restaurants. Shells are bought separately and can be re-used. Small, but good English snails from the Mendip Hills are available.

Serves 4

Frogs' Legs

450g/1lb raw frogs' legs
55g/2oz butter
1 small garlic clove, crushed
1 tablespoon chopped fresh
  parsley
Lemon juice
Salt and freshly ground black
  pepper

For the marinade:
Olive oil
1 onion, sliced
1 parsley stalk
6 peppercorns
1 bay leaf

1. Split the pairs of frogs' legs and marinate them in a small cupful of olive oil with the other marinade ingredients for 2 hours or more. This is not essential but helps to improve the taste and texture of the meat. Drain the legs.
2. Melt the butter in a large sauté pan and when frothy add the frogs' legs and garlic. Sauté briskly for 5–10 minutes (they should fry to a very pale brown).
3. Add the parsley, lemon juice and seasoning. Serve with French bread to mop up the butter.

Note: Frogs' legs are normally sold frozen and are available at large fishmonger's.

Serves 4

Fried Gnocchi

570ml/1 pint milk
1 onion, sliced
1 clove
1 bay leaf
6 parsley stalks
110g/¼lb semolina
200g/7oz strong Cheddar cheese
2 tablespoons very fresh Parmesan cheese, grated

1 tablespoon chopped fresh parsley
Salt and freshly ground black pepper
Pinch of dried mustard
Pinch of cayenne
Beaten egg
Dried white breadcrumbs
Oil for deep frying

1. Infuse the milk with the onion, clove, bay leaf and parsley stalks over a very gentle heat for 7 minutes. Bring up to boiling point, then strain.
2. Sprinkle in the semolina, stirring steadily, and cook, still stirring, until the mixture is thick (about 1 minute). Draw the pan off the heat and add the cheeses, parsley, salt, pepper, mustard and cayenne. Spread this mixture into a neat round on a wet plate and leave to chill for 30 minutes.
3. Cut the gnocchi paste into eight equal wedges. Chill.

4. Heat the oil until a crumb will sizzle vigorously in it. Dip the gnocchi into beaten egg and coat with breadcrumbs.
5. Deep fry in hot oil until golden brown (about 2 minutes). Drain well on absorbent paper. Sprinkle with salt and serve.

Note: A thin tomato sauce (page 238) is good with fried gnocchi.

Serves 6

Cannelloni

Egg pasta (pages 285–6, using half quantities)
290ml/½ pint tomato sauce (page 238)

45g/1½oz strong Cheddar *or* Gruyère cheese, grated, *or* 30g/1oz Parmesan, grated

For the filling:
2 teaspoons oil *or* dripping
340g/¾lb minced beef
1 onion, chopped
Stick of celery, chopped
1 garlic clove, crushed
2 teaspoons tomato purée
2 teaspoons flour

150ml/¼ pint beef stock
1 bay leaf
1 level tablespoon fresh chopped parsley
1 tablespoon port *or* Madeira
Salt and freshly ground black pepper

1. Cut the pasta into 10cm/4in strips about 6cm/2½in wide. Allow to dry for 1 hour.
2. Heat the oil and add the meat. Brown well all over. Add the onion, celery, garlic and tomato purée and cook for 2 minutes.
3. Add the flour and cook for 30 seconds. Draw the pan off the heat, add the stock, bay leaf and parsley, stir well and return to the heat. Bring slowly to the boil, stirring continuously.
4. Season, cover and simmer for 30 minutes. Then add the port or Madeira and continue to simmer for 15 minutes. Remove the bay leaf.
5. Set the oven to 200°C/400°F, gas mark 6. Heat the grill.

111

6. Cook the pasta in boiling salted water until just tender (about 5 minutes if home-made, 12 if bought). Drain well, and pat dry with a tea-towel or cloth.
7. Divide the meat mixture between the strips of pasta and roll them up to form the cannelloni. Place them in a greased ovenproof dish.
8. Pour over the tomato sauce and sprinkle with grated cheese. Bake for 15 minutes, then place under the grill until nicely browned.

Note I: For a blander version, trickle over a little white sauce or double cream before grilling the finished dish.

Note II: Commercially made cannelloni is usually tube-shaped, and the filling is inserted with a teaspoon.

Serves 4

Ravioli

370g/¾lb flour-quantity egg
    pasta (pages 285–6)

For the meat filling:

85g/3oz cooked beef, minced
85g/3oz cooked veal, minced
15g/½oz butter
2 teaspoons white
    breadcrumbs
2 teaspoons chopped parsley
2 teaspoons beef stock

1 teaspoon tomato purée
Salt and freshly ground black
    pepper
Pinch of nutmeg
Pinch of cinnamon
1 small egg, beaten

To serve:

Parmesan cheese, grated
Melted butter *or* oil *or* tomato
    sauce (page 238)

1. Fry the meats in the butter for 5 minutes. Stir in the breadcrumbs, parsley, stock, tomato purée, salt, pepper, nutmeg and cinnamon. Taste and add more seasonings if required.

2. Add enough egg to bind the mixture together. Allow to cool.

3. Roll the pasta into a very thin rectangle. Cut accurately in half. Keep well covered to prevent drying out.

4. Take one sheet of pasta and place half-teaspoons of filling at 3cm/1½in intervals, in even rows, all over it. Cover loosely with the other sheet of pasta and press together firmly all round each mound of filling. Cut between the rows, making sure that all the edges are sealed. (See drawing.) Allow to dry on a wire rack for 30 minutes.

5. Simmer the ravioli in near-boiling salted water for 15–20 minutes or until just tender. Drain well. Serve with tomato sauce, oil, or melted butter, and hand grated Parmesan cheese separately.

Serves 4

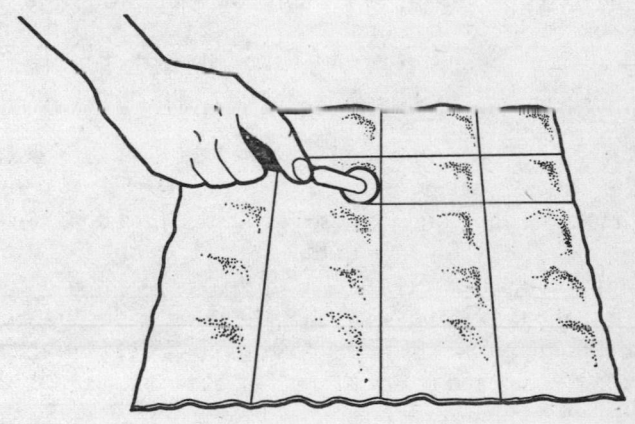

Lasagne Verde Bolognese

Green pasta (page 285, using half quantities)

Parmesan cheese, grated

For the meat sauce:
1 tablespoon dripping *or* oil
340g/¾lb minced beef
1 onion, finely diced
Stick of celery, finely diced
Garlic cloves
30g/1oz flour
290ml/½ pint stock
1 glass white wine
Salt and freshly ground
  black pepper
1 scant tablespoon chopped
  fresh parsley

1 teaspoon chopped fresh
  marjoram
Pinch of cinnamon
1 tablespoon tomato purée

For the cream sauce:
45g/1½oz butter
1 bay leaf
45g/1½oz flour
570ml/1 pint creamy milk
Salt and freshly ground black
  pepper and nutmeg

1. Cut the pasta into strips 15cm/6in long and 3cm/1½in wide. Allow to dry for 1 hour.
2. Heat the fat and in it brown the mince well. Add the finely diced vegetables and the garlic and fry, stirring continuously, for 2 minutes.
3. Stir in the flour. Cook for 30 seconds. Pour in the stock and the wine, and add the salt, pepper, parsley, marjoram, cinnamon and tomato purée. Bring to the boil, stirring. Simmer slowly for 45 minutes, then boil rapidly, stirring, until the sauce is very thick and syrupy.
4. To make the cream sauce melt the butter, add the bay leaf and flour and cook, stirring, for 1 minute. Draw off the heat.
5. Add the milk and return to the heat. Bring slowly to the boil, stirring continuously until you have a thick, creamy sauce. Season to taste and remove the bay leaf.

6. To cook the lasagne drop the pasta a few pieces at a time into a large pan of fast-boiling salted water. They will take about 5 minutes if home-made, 12 minutes if out of a packet, to become tender. Rinse under running cold water and pat dry with a tea-towel.

7. Set the oven to 190°C/375°F, gas mark 5. Butter an ovenproof dish and cover the bottom with a layer of pasta, then spoon on a thin layer of meat sauce. Cover with a layer of cream sauce and dust with Parmesan cheese.

8. Arrange a layer of pasta on top of this. Continue the layers in this manner finishing with cream sauce. Sprinkle with cheese.

9. Bake for 20–25 minutes, until bubbling and just brown on top.

Serves 6

Prue's Easy Party Pasta

110g/¼lb pasta (tagliatelli *or* shell shapes are best)
2 tablespoons olive oil
110g/¼lb mushrooms, sliced
1 garlic clove, crushed
110g/¼lb cooked ham, cut in thin strips

2 hardboiled eggs, quartered
1 level tablespoon chopped fresh basil
Salt and freshly ground black pepper
55g/2oz Cheddar cheese, grated
1 level tablespoon chopped fresh parsley

1. Boil the pasta in fast-boiling salted water until tender.
2. Take a large heavy frying pan and into it put the oil, mushrooms and garlic. Fry gently for 2 minutes, then add the strips of ham, the eggs and the basil. Cover with a lid or foil and put on to a warming plate or into a coolish oven to warm through.

3. When the pasta is tender but not mushy, drain it well and rinse off any excess starch under the *hot* tap, or by pouring a kettle of fresh boiling water through it. Drain again. Tip the hot pasta into a warm serving bowl and season well with salt and pepper. Tip the frying pan ingredients in on top of the pasta. Mix carefully with a fork, then sprinkle with the grated cheese and chopped parsley.

Note: The dish, as long as it is not overmixed, can be made in advance for a party, and reheated gently in a wide saucepan or, covered, in the oven. But if this is done, the cheese and parsley should be added only before serving. Skinned, seeded and quartered tomatoes are a good addition, and should be added to the frying pan with the eggs. Neither eggs nor tomatoes need real cooking – only heating up – before being tipped on to the pasta.

Serves 4

Bean and Salami Casserole

225g/½lb brown kidney beans
55g/2oz bacon rind
1 parsley stalk
Stick of celery
6 peppercorns
225g/½lb pork belly, skinned
Lard, dripping *or* oil for frying
2 medium onions, roughly chopped
2 carrots, roughly sliced
1 red pepper, sliced
2 garlic cloves, crushed
285g/10oz canned tomatoes
290ml/½ pint beef stock
Salt and freshly ground black pepper
225g/½lb Italian salami, in the piece
Small handful of celery tops, finely chopped

1. Place the beans in a bowl, cover with cold water and leave for 3–4 hours.
2. Drain them and place in a large saucepan. Cover with cold water. Add the bacon rind, parsley stalk, celery stick and peppercorns. Bring slowly to the boil, cover and simmer for 1 hour. Drain and remove the flavourings.

3. Set the oven to 190°C/375°F, gas mark 5. Cut the pork belly into small chunks. Fry until golden brown (using a little oil or fat if necessary). Transfer to an ovenproof casserole. Brown the onions (adding more fat if needed). Add them to the casserole.

4. Lightly fry the carrots and pepper for 5 minutes, then add the garlic. Fry for 1 minute and tip them into the casserole too.

5. Pour the tomatoes and stock into the frying pan and bring to the boil. Scrape any sediment from the bottom and pour into the casserole. Add the beans and season well. Cover with a lid and cook in the oven for 2 hours, or until the beans are tender.

6. Skin the salami and slice fairly thickly first into rings, then cut into thin strips. Add to the casserole and cook for another 10 minutes.

7. Strain off the liquid into a saucepan. Allow it to settle then skim off the fat. Boil rapidly until reduced to about a large cupful. Pour over the bean casserole. Stir in the celery tops and serve.

Note: A simpler but very good casserole is made by combining the soaked beans with all the other ingredients (without preliminary frying) and cooking in a very slow oven until tender – about 4 hours.

Serves 4

Cannelloni with Spinach and Mushroom Filling

900g/2lb fresh spinach, well washed, with stalks removed
55g/2oz butter
225g/½lb flat black mushrooms, sliced
Salt and pepper
12 cooked cannelloni (the bought ones can be very good, and thin French pancakes are an excellent substitute (pages 314–15)
55g/2oz Cheddar cheese, grated
425ml/¾ pint creamy white sauce (page 239)

1. Put the wet spinach in a large saucepan and put on the lid. Cook gently for 5 minutes, stirring occasionally. Drain well, pressing out the moisture. Turn on to a board and chop roughly.
2. Set the oven to 180°C/350°F, gas mark 4.
3. Melt the butter, add the mushrooms and fry for 3 minutes. Stir in the spinach and 150ml/¼ pint of the sauce and season with salt and pepper.
4. Fill the mixture into the cannelloni, or roll up in the pancakes. Lay them in an ovenproof dish, pour over the remaining sauce and sprinkle the cheese on top.
5. Bake in the oven for 20 minutes or until the top is lightly browned.

Serves 4

FRUIT AND VEGETABLE STARTERS

Pears with Stilton and Poppy Seed Dressing

110g/¼lb Stilton cheese
110g/¼lb cream cheese
4 ripe dessert pears, washed
  but not peeled
Squeeze of lemon juice
1 Small bunch of watercress,
  washed

For the dressing:
3 tablespoons oil
1 tablespoon lemon juice
1 level tablespoon poppy seeds
Salt and freshly ground black
  pepper

1. Put all the dressing ingredients together in a screw-top jar and shake until well emulsified. Taste and add more seasoning if necessary.
2. Beat together the Stilton and cream cheese until soft. Spoon into a forcing bag fitted with a plain large nozzle.

3. With an apple corer remove the centre of the pears. Sprinkle a little lemon juice into each hole and then pipe in the cheese mixture. Place in the refrigerator until ready to serve (at least 2 hours).
4. Slice each pear across into thin round slices. Spoon over the poppy seed dressing and garnish with watercress.

Serves 4

Leeks Mimosa Vinaigrette

8 small leeks
2 hardboiled eggs

1 tablespoon chopped fresh parsley

For the French dressing:
3 tablespoons oil
1 tablespoon vinegar
Salt and freshly ground black
   pepper

Pinch of dry English mustard
Pinch of sugar (optional)

1. Cut off the roots of the leeks and all but 2½cm/1in of the green part. Split them from the green end towards the root end, cutting through to within 8cm/3in of the root end. This is to enable you to ruffle through the leaves as you hold them under the cold tap to wash out the sand.
2. Cook the leeks in boiling salted water until just tender (about 6 minutes). Cool under running water and drain well.
3. Make the French dressing: put all the ingredients together in a screw-top jar and shake until well emulsified. Pour this over the leeks and leave to marinate for 2 hours.
4. Split the eggs in half and remove the yolks. Wash the whites and dry well. Chop them finely, using a stainless steel knife or push them through a nylon or stainless steel sieve. Sieve the egg yolks.
5. Arrange the leeks on a serving dish, pouring over the French dressing. Garnish with rows of chopped parsley, sieved egg yolk and chopped egg white.

Serves 4

Artichokes with Clarified Butter

4 artichokes   110g/4oz butter, clarified
                                (page 236)

1. Wash the artichokes in salted water. Trim the sharp points of
    the leaves square with a pair of scissors or large knife. Cut
    away any of the very tough leaves and trim the stalk so that
    the artichoke will stand upright.
2. Plunge the artichokes into a pan of boiling salted water and
    cook for about 45 minutes or until a leaf can be easily
    pulled away from the whole. Drain well.
3. To serve, pull out the centre leaves and with a teaspoon care-
    fully scrape out the fibrous 'choke' making sure that every
    particle is removed. Serve with hot clarified melted butter,
    handed separately.

Note I: Clarified butter is not strictly necessary. Plain melted
butter will do, but the crystal clear look of clarified butter is very
pleasing.

Note II: It is a good idea to provide each guest with his own pot
of melted butter to dip the artichoke leaves in, and an empty dish
or plate for the debris, and a fingerbowl.

Note III: Artichokes are also delicious served cold with a French
dressing, or with mayonnaise (pages 241–2) to which a stiffly
beaten egg white has been added just before serving.

Serves 4

Jellied Grape and Mint Ring

450g/1lb large green grapes
1 tablespoon gelatine
570ml/1 pint water
Juice of 3 lemons
1 tablespoon finely chopped
  fresh mint

Caster sugar to taste (about
  55g/2oz)
Green colouring

1. Plunge the grapes for a few seconds into boiling water to make skinning them easier. Peel, halve and seed them, and drop them at once into the lemon juice.
2. In a small pan soak the gelatine in 3 tablespoons of the water. After 10 minutes warm the gelatine very slowly until it is dissolved and clear.
3. Put the grapes, water and mint in a bowl. Sweeten to taste. Stir in the gelatine and add a drop of green colouring.
4. Wet a ring mould or savarin tin and fill with the mixture. Leave to set in the refrigerator.
5. To serve, dip the mould briefly in hot water to dislodge the jelly. Turn out on to a plate.

Note: This jelly is a good lunch-time starter, especially if served with brown bread and butter. Or serve with walnut triangles, made by pressing thin slices of well-buttered brown bread face-down on chopped walnuts, then cutting the slices in half diagonally (cover with plastic wrap and chill before serving).

Serves 6

Cucumber with Soured Cream

1 medium cucumber

For the dressing:
3 tablespoons oil
1 tablespoon wine vinegar
Salt and pepper

Pinch of sugar
1 level tablespoon chopped
  mint

For the topping:

55g/2oz soft cream cheese

2 heaped tablespoons soured
cream

Juice of ½ lemon

1 small garlic clove

1. Slice the cucumber finely. Sprinkle the slices lightly with salt
    and leave for 20 minutes.
2. Put the dressing ingredients in a screw-top jar and shake until
    well emulsified.
3. Beat the cream until soft, then gradually stir in the soured
    cream. Add the crushed garlic, and season with salt, pepper
    and lemon juice to taste.
4. Rinse, drain and dry the cucumber thoroughly. Toss the slices
    in the French dressing and put them into a serving dish, or
    on to individual plates. Spoon the cream cheese mixture on
    top.

Note: This makes a good salad, with others, for a party, or can
be served with hot bread and butter as a light starter.

Serves 4

Pineapple Japonais

1 fresh pineapple

Caster sugar

For the dressing:

1 egg

3 tablespoons tarragon vinegar

2 tablespoons caster sugar

Pinch of salt

2 tablespoons lightly whipped
cream

1. Slice the pineapple in half lengthwise, cutting through the fruit
    and the leaves. Using a grapefruit knife cut out the flesh in
    one piece from each pineapple half. Remove the woody core
    and discard it. Slice the flesh and return it upside down to
    the pineapple shell (i.e. rounded side up). Sprinkle with sugar
    and leave it to stand while preparing the dressing.

2. Beat the egg and add the vinegar and sugar with a pinch of salt. Stand the bowl over a pan of simmering water and whisk continuously until thick. Allow to cool.
3. Stir in the cream and spoon the dressing over the pineapple.

Serves 4

Spinach Roulade

450g/1lb fresh spinach *or*
  170/6oz frozen leaf spinach
15g/½oz butter
Salt and freshly ground black
  pepper
4 eggs, separated
Pinch of nutmeg
Parmesan *or* strong Cheddar
  cheese, grated

For the filling:
15g/½oz butter
170g/6oz mushrooms, chopped
15g/½oz flour
190ml/⅓ pint milk
4 tablespoons cream
1 heaped tablespoon chopped
  fresh parsley
Salt and freshly ground black
  pepper

1. To prepare the spinach remove the stalks and wash thoroughly. Put into a pan without water. Add a sprinkling of salt. Cover and cook gently, shaking the pan occasionally for 5–7 minutes. The spinach will reduce in quantity by about two-thirds. Drain thoroughly by squeezing between two plates. Chop finely and push through a sieve. Beat in the butter.
2. Set the oven to 190°C/375°F, gas mark 5. Take a large roasting pan and cut a double layer of greaseproof paper slightly larger than the tin. Lay this in the tin. Don't worry if the ends stick up untidily around the sides. Brush the paper lightly with oil or melted butter.
3. To make the roulade gradually beat the egg yolks into the spinach and season with salt, pepper and nutmeg. Whisk the egg whites until stiff but not dry and fold them into the spinach. Pour this mixture into the prepared roasting tin, spread it flat and sprinkle with grated cheese. Bake for 10–12 minutes or until it feels dry to the touch.

4. Melt the butter and gently cook the mushrooms in it. Remove the pan from the heat, add the flour and mix well. Return the pan to the heat and cook for half a minute. Add the milk and bring to the boil, stirring continually until you have a fairly thick creamy sauce. Add the cream and parsley and season well.

5. Sprinkle grated cheese on to a piece of greaseproof paper and place on a tea-towel. Turn the roulade on to the paper and remove the original piece of paper. Spread the filling on to the roulade and roll it up as you would a Swiss roll, removing the paper as you go. Serve on a warmed dish either whole or in slices.

Serves 4

Spinach Mould

675g/1½lb fresh spinach
30g/1oz butter
100g/3½oz fresh white bread-
    crumbs
2 eggs, beaten

1 egg yolk
Pinch of ground nutmeg
Salt and freshly ground black
    pepper
345ml/12 fl.oz milk

1. Wash the spinach well and remove the tough stalks. Put, still wet, into a saucepan with a lid and holding the pan in one hand and the lid on with the other shake and toss the spinach until it is soft and reduced in quantity.

2. Drain well and remove about 15 of the best and biggest leaves carefully. Drain these on absorbent paper.

3. Squeeze all the water from the remaining spinach, pressing it between two plates. Tip on to a board and chop very finely. Butter a 15cm/6in cake tin or soufflé dish and line it with the whole spinach leaves.

4. In a saucepan melt the butter, add the spinach and stir until very dry looking. Take off the heat and add the breadcrumbs, eggs, egg yolk, nutmeg and seasoning.

5. Heat the milk and stir it into the mixture.

6. Spoon the spinach mixture into the cake tin and cover with buttered foil or greaseproof paper.
7. Heat the oven to 180°C/350°F, gas mark 4. Stand the cake tin in a roasting pan full of boiling water. Transfer both roasting tin and spinach mould to the oven and bake for 45 minutes or until the mixture is firm.
8. Turn out on a hot serving dish.

Serves 4–6

EGGS, SAVOURY SOUFFLÉS AND MOUSSES

Egg and Prawn Mousse with Aspic

For the decoration:
150ml/¼ pint aspic (pages 229–30)

For the garnish choose from the following:

2 hardboiled eggs, shelled and cut into neat slices *or* wedges

About 10 slices pickled cucumber

About 10 thin slivers black olive *or* radish

Sprig of watercress

For the mousse:

1 level tablespoon gelatine

2 tablespoons water

5 hardboiled eggs

85g/3oz cooked prawns, chopped if large

6 tablespoons mayonnaise (pages 241–2)

1 level tablespoon anchovy essence

3 tablespoons cream, lightly whipped

Salt, pepper and cayenne

1 egg white

1. Start with the decoration: wet the mould, soufflé dish or bowl and pour in half the liquid aspic. Refrigerate until set.

2. Now arrange your chosen garnish in a pattern on the set aspic, bearing in mind that when the mousse is turned out the decoration will be seen from the other side. Dribble enough of the remaining cooled aspic into the dish or mould just to wet the decoration, taking care not to dislodge it. Put back into the refrigerator till set.

3. Carefully pour enough cooled aspic into the dish to cover the decoration, again taking care not to dislodge it. Do not use more aspic than you need as too thick a layer is unappetising. Refrigerate once again until set.

4. For the mousse: first put the water in a small saucepan, sprinkle in the gelatine and leave to soak.

5. Chop the eggs and mix them with the prawns, mayonnaise and anchovy essence. Season with pepper and cayenne, and salt only if necessary.

6. Dissolve the gelatine over very gentle heat and when runny and clear add it to the mixture, stirring briskly. Allow to cool until thickening round the edges. Fold in the cream.

7. Whisk the egg white until stiff and fold it into the mixture. Pour into the dish on top of the aspic layer. Refrigerate.

8. When it is set loosen the sides of the mousse with the fingers and briefly dip the bottom of the dish or mould into hot water to loosen the aspic layer (like turning out a jelly). Put a flat serving plate over the top of the mould, making sure it is dead-centre, then quickly invert both plate and mould. The aspic-covered mousse should fall out on to the plate. If it sticks obstinately, give it a sharp shake.

Note: Commercially available aspic powder (to which boiling water is added) is perfectly satisfactory for this dish, provided a *thin* layer is used.

Serves 6

Sorrel and Cheese Soufflé

110g/¼lb sorrel
340g/¾lb spinach
55g/2oz butter
Dried white breadcrumbs
55g/2oz flour
290ml/½ pint milk
Salt and pepper

Pinch of cayenne
½ teaspoon mustard
55g/2oz strong Cheddar *or* Gruyère cheese
4 eggs
1 dessertspoon Parmesan cheese

1. To prepare the sorrel and spinach, remove the stalks and wash the leaves very carefully. Place in a pan of boiling salted water for 2 minutes. Drain very well, squeezing water out through a colander or sieve or between two plates. Chop finely.
2. Set the oven to 200°C/400°F, gas mark 6. Lightly butter a 15cm/6in soufflé dish. Coat the sides lightly with breadcrumbs.
3. Melt the butter in a saucepan and stir in the flour. Add the milk and bring to the boil, stirring continuously, for 1 minute. Take the sauce off the heat, stir in the salt and pepper, cayenne, mustard, cheese, spinach and sorrel. Cool slightly.
4. Separate the eggs, adding the yolks to the sauce. Whisk the egg whites until stiff but not dry and mix a spoonful thoroughly into the sorrel mixture. Then gently fold in the rest.
5. Pour into the soufflé dish, which should not be more than two-thirds full. With a knife cut through the mixture several times to ensure that there are no large pockets of air. Sprinkle the top with Parmesan cheese.
6. Bake for 20–25 minutes or until the soufflé is still moist in the middle but crisp around the edges. (It should not wobble alarmingly when given a slight shove, nor be absolutely rigid.)

Serves 4

Haddock Pudding

225g/½lb fresh haddock fillet
290ml/½ pint milk
1 small onion, sliced
1 bay leaf
6 peppercorns
30g/1oz fresh white
    breadcrumbs
20g/¾oz plain flour

15g/½oz butter
½ teaspoon fresh chopped
    fennel (the herb)
1 level tablespoon fresh
    chopped parsley
3 eggs, separated
Salt, pepper and paprika
15g/½oz butter for greasing dish

1. Butter a 15cm/6in soufflé dish. Set the oven to 180°C/350°F, gas mark 4.
2. Lay the haddock fillets skin side up in an ovenproof dish, pour over the milk and put in the onion, bay leaf, and peppercorns. Poach in the oven until cooked (about 30 minutes).
3. Take out, but do not switch off the oven. Strain off the liquid into a bowl or jug. Pour enough of the hot fish liquid on to the breadcrumbs to soak them.
4. Melt the butter, add the flour and stir over gentle heat for 1 minute. Pour on the rest of the milk the fish was cooked in and stir while gently bringing to the boil. You should now have a very thick white sauce.
5. Skin and flake the fish very finely. Add it to the sauce with the fennel and parsley and the soaked breadcrumbs. Beat in the egg yolks. Season with salt, pepper and paprika.
6. Whisk the egg whites till stiff but not dry-looking. Using a large metal spoon fold them into the fish mixture, taking care not to over-stir. Turn into the greased soufflé dish. With a knife, cut through the mixture two or three times to release any over-large air pockets.
7. Put in the middle of the oven to bake; it will take about 30 minutes. (It should not wobble alarmingly if given a slight shove, nor be absolutely rigid.)

Note: If for any reason the pudding cannot be served at once, turn off the oven and leave it in there. It should be all right for 10 minutes or so but may become dry. To counteract any possible dryness a crab or lobster sauce (page 243) or a cheese one (page 240) can be served.

Serves 4

SALADS

New Potatoes Vinaigrette

675g/1½lb small new potatoes
French dressing (page 237)
Small bunch of fresh mint

1 tablespoon chopped chives
1 shallot, finely chopped

1. Wash the potatoes and scrape them, but do not peel. Cook in boiling salted water with a sprig of mint until tender. Chop 8–10 mint leaves finely.
2. Mix the French dressing with the mint, chives and shallot.
3. Drain the potatoes well and toss immediately in the French dressing. Leave to cool and toss again just before serving. Decorate with a fresh mint leaf or two.

Note: There is always controversy about peeling new potatoes. The best, very new, pale ones need little more than washing. Most need scraping, and some – usually large, dark and patently not very new – need peeling *after* cooking.

Serves 4

Watercress Salad with Croutons

Oil for deep frying
4 slices white bread

2 bunches watercress

For the dressing:
3 tablespoons oil
1 tablespoon vinegar
Salt and pepper
½ garlic clove, crushed

½ teaspoon chopped
fresh parsley
Pinch of sugar (optional)

1. First make the croutons: heat the oil until a crumb will sizzle vigorously in it. Cut off the crusts and cut the bread into small cubes.
2. Fry the bread in the oil until golden brown and crisp. Drain well on absorbent paper. Sprinkle lightly with salt, and leave to cool completely.
3. Combine all the dressing ingredients in a screw-top jar and shake well.
4. Prepare the watercress by washing it, shaking it dry and discarding any thick stalks or yellow leaves.
5. Just before serving toss the watercress in the French dressing, tip into a clean salad bowl and sprinkle the croutons on top.

Serves 4–5

Bean and Bean Salad

450g/1lb fresh French beans
450g/1lb cooked haricot beans
   or butter beans (canned are
   fine)
2 tablespoons chopped fresh
   basil *or* spring onion tops

1 tablespoon lemon juice
3 tablespoons salad oil
Salt and freshly ground pepper
1 small garlic clove, crushed

1. Top and tail the French beans and boil them in salted water until just tender. Drain and swish under the cold tap water to prevent further cooking and preserve their colour.

2. Drain the haricot or butter beans if they are canned and rinse away any starchy water. When they are dry mix them with the cooked French beans and put into a dish.
3. Place the basil or spring onions in a jar, add the lemon juice, seasoning, garlic and oil and shake vigorously. Pour over the salad.

Note: All types of beans are good – fresh broad beans (especially if the inner skins are removed after cooking), dried lima, canned flageolets etc.

Serves 4

3
Vegetables and Rice

Creamed Brussels Sprouts

290ml/½ pint very fresh double
   cream
900g/2lb Brussels sprouts,
   washed and trimmed

Salt and freshly ground black
   pepper
Grated nutmeg

1. Boil the cream in a small heavy saucepan until reduced in quantity by about half. It will thicken. Stir frequently during boiling to prevent burning. Keep warm.
2. Boil the sprouts in salted water until tender (about 8 minutes). Drain well. Then finely chop or liquidize them.
3. Mix the cream with the sprouts, and add salt, pepper and nutmeg to taste.

Note: This dish may be prepared the day before serving. Allow sprouts and cream to cool before mixing. Reheat by tossing in a heavy frying pan over gentle heat, or in a shallow buttered dish in a hot oven or, best of all, rapidly in a microwave oven.

Serves 6

Lima Beans with Dill and Tomatoes

450g/1lb dried lima beans,
   soaked for 2–3 hours
30g/1oz butter
1 garlic clove, crushed
1 onion, finely chopped

Juice of 1 lemon
1 tablespoon chopped fresh dill
Pinch of sugar
Salt and freshly ground black
   pepper

2 tomatoes, peeled, seeded and
  chopped
1 tablespoon tomato purée

2 tablespoons soured cream
2 tablespoons chopped fresh
  parsley

1. Cook the beans in the water in which they were soaked until tender (1½–2 hours). Drain well.
2. Melt the butter and add the garlic and onion. Fry slowly until the onion is soft but not coloured.
3. Add the tomatoes, beans, tomato purée and lemon juice. Mix thoroughly.
4. Add the dill, sugar, salt and pepper. Taste and correct seasoning if necessary.
5. Stir in the soured cream and serve with the parsley sprinkled on top.

Serves 8

Broad Beans and Bacon

3 rashers rindless streaky
  bacon
450g/1lb shelled broad
  beans

Butter
Salt and freshly ground black
  pepper
1 tablespoon chopped fresh
  savory *or* thyme

1. Dice the bacon and fry the pieces in their own fat until crisp and brown but not brittle.
2. Shell the beans and boil in salted water for 8 minutes.
3. Drain well and toss in melted butter. Season with salt and pepper, and stir in the diced bacon, any bacon fat, and the chopped savory or thyme.

Note: Tough large broad beans are delicious if the inner skins are removed after boiling. Boil the beans as usual, then run under cold water until cold enough to handle. Slip off the skins and put the bright green beans into a frying pan with the butter, bacon and savory or thyme. Toss carefully to reheat. They are inclined to break up.

Serves 4

Whole Broad Beans in Watercress Sauce

30g/1oz butter
30g/1oz flour
425ml/¾ pint milk
Salt and freshly ground black
  pepper

Bunch of watercress
675g/1½lb *very young* small
  broad beans

1. Melt the butter and stir in the flour. Cook, stirring, for 1 minute.
2. Pour in the milk and continue stirring until the sauce boils. Simmer for 2 minutes. Season to taste.
3. Wash the watercress and remove the stalks. Cook the leaves for about 30 seconds in boiling water.
4. Drain and rinse them under the cold tap to stop further cooking and to 'set' the green colour. Press out all the moisture.
5. Liquidize the sauce with the watercress leaves. Failing an electric blender, chop the watercress finely, pound it in a mortar or sieve it, then add to the sauce.
6. Wash the beans but do not shell. Cut them into 3cm/1½in lengths. Cook quickly in boiling salted water until just tender (about 8 minutes).
7. Drain well and tip into a serving dish. Reheat the sauce and pour over the beans.

Serves 4

Spring Cabbage with Cream and Nutmeg

675g/1½lb spring cabbage
Salt and freshly ground black
  pepper
¼ teaspoon grated nutmeg

15g/½oz butter
2 heaped tablespoons soured
  cream

1. Shred the cabbage finely and rinse it. Place in salted boiling water and return to the boil. Boil rapidly until slightly soft but crunchy (3–5 minutes).
2. Drain the cabbage well, then return it to the heat to evaporate excess moisture, shaking the pan and tossing the cabbage so it dries but does not burn.
3. Sprinkle with black pepper and nutmeg. Toss in the butter. Take off the heat, and stir in the soured cream.

Serves 4

Hot Cucumber à la Crème

For the béchamel sauce:

290ml/½ pint milk
Slice of onion
1 bay leaf
Stalk of parsley
20g/¾oz butter
20g/¾oz flour

1 large *or* 2 small cucumbers
2 tablespoons cream
1 level tablespoon fresh
 chopped dill
Salt and freshly ground black
 pepper

1. Infuse the milk with the onion, bay leaf and parsley stalk over a gentle heat for 7 minutes. Strain and allow to cool slightly.
2. Melt the butter, add the flour and cook, stirring, for 30 seconds. Draw the pan off the heat, add the milk and stir well. Return the pan to the heat and bring the sauce to the boil, stirring continuously. Simmer for 2 minutes.
3. Peel the cucumber and cut it into short even-sized sticks. Cook them in boiling salted water until tender (about 3–4 minutes). Drain well.
4. Add the cucumber to the béchamel sauce and stir in the cream, dill, salt and pepper.

Serves 4

Game Chip Baskets Filled with Chestnuts

See the notes on deep frying on pages 30–3.

675g/1½lb potatoes
Oil for deep frying
1 large can whole unsweetened
chestnuts
Handful of raisins

Small bunch of white grapes,
halved and pips removed
30g/1oz pinenuts
45g/1½oz butter

1. Peel the potatoes. Slice finely using a mandolin or a patterned cutter so that the finished basket will look like woven straw.
2. Dip a small wire strainer or sieve into the fat to get it well greased. Heat the fat until a crumb will sizzle vigorously in it.
3. Line the strainer with potato slices overlapping each other. Using a small ladle or a similar round-shaped object to prevent the chips floating away from the strainer as you cook them, deep fry the 'basket' until golden and crisp.
4. Drain well on absorbent paper.
5. Melt the butter and add the drained chestnuts, raisins, grapes and pinenuts. Fry until hot and beginning to brown.
6. Fill the baskets with this mixture just before serving.

Note: A gadget for making the baskets is available in shops selling to the catering trade, but the sieve-and-ladle method works perfectly well.

Serves 4

Marrow with Garlic and Tomato

900g/2lbs marrow
30g/1oz butter
1 onion, finely chopped
1 garlic clove, crushed
2 tablespoons tomato purée

1 tablespoon white wine
1 teaspoon chopped fresh basil
Salt and freshly ground black
pepper

1. Peel the marrow, cut it in half and remove the seeds. Cut the flesh into even-sized chunks (about 2·5cm/1in).
2. Put into a sieve over a pan of boiling water, or into a proper steamer, cover and steam for 30 minutes or until the marrow is completely tender.
3. Melt the butter, add the onion and garlic and cook gently until the onion is soft but not coloured. Add the steamed marrow, tomato purée, wine, basil, and season with salt and pepper.
4. Cover and cook (shaking the pan frequently to prevent sticking and burning) over a moderate heat for about 10 minutes.
5. Taste and season again if necessary. Serve hot or cold.

Note: Marrow is generally steamed because it holds a lot of water and when boiled is apt to be soggy.

Serves 6

Pommes Parisienne

4 large potatoes	Knob of butter
2 tablespoons oil	Salt

1. Peel the potatoes and scoop into small balls with a melon baller. As you prepare the balls drop them into a bowl of cold water (this prevents discolouring). Float a plate on top to keep them submerged.
2. Heat the oil in a sauté pan and add the butter. Dry the potato balls well and toss them in the pan until completely coated with fat. Fry very slowly until they are browned and tender, shaking the pan frequently to prevent them sticking.
3. Drain well, sprinkle with salt and serve immediately.

Note: Allow 15 Parisienne potatoes per head. The larger the potatoes, the easier it is to scoop them into balls.

Serves 4

Brown Rice Pilaff with Sesame Seeds

1 small onion, finely chopped
30g/1oz butter
225g/½lb brown rice
720ml/1¼ pints chicken *or* vegetable stock
3 tablespoons sesame seeds

1 tablespoon chopped mixed fresh herbs
Salt and freshly ground black pepper
Paprika

1. Cook the onion in the butter until it is soft but not coloured.
2. Add the rice and fry, stirring, until it is slightly opaque (about 3 minutes).
3. Add the stock, seeds, herbs, salt and pepper. Bring up to the boil, cover and cook very slowly for 45 minutes, by which time the liquid should be completely absorbed and the rice tender.
4. Serve sprinkled with a little paprika.

Serves 4–6

Sweetcorn Fritters

2 eggs
Salt and freshly ground black pepper
220g/½lb cooked sweetcorn

1 teaspoon baking powder
15g/½oz fresh breadcrumbs
Oil for shallow frying

1. Separate the eggs. Mix the yolks with the seasoning and the sweetcorn.
2. Whisk the whites quite stiff but not dry and fold them into the mixture.
3. Stir in the baking powder and add the breadcrumbs. Taste and add salt and pepper if necessary.
4. Melt the fat in a frying pan and when hot add the batter in spoonfuls. Fry to a golden brown on both sides. Drain well.

Serves 4

Fried Parsley

Fresh parsley   Oil

1. Pick sprigs of fresh but dry parsley and place in a frying basket. Heat the oil until a crumb will sizzle in it, then lower the basket into the fat. It will hiss furiously.
2. Cook for about 30 seconds. It should be bright green and brittle, with a very good concentrated flavour.

Note: If the parsley sprigs are lowered into the fat by a piece of string tied round the stalks, the sprigs will retain their shape well.

4
Fish

Ceviche

225g/½lb fillet of monkfish *or* halibut, skinned and cut into thin slices *or* small strips *or* dice
1 onion, chopped
Juice of 2 lemons *or* 4 limes
1 tablespoon olive oil
Pinch cayenne pepper
2 fresh chillies, seeded and cut in strips (optional)
Salt and freshly ground black pepper
1 peeled tomato, chopped
½ small green pepper, seeded and chopped
Few slices avocado pear, cut small

1. Put the fish, onion, lemon juice, oil, cayenne pepper and chillies together and leave in a cool place for 6 hours, giving an occasional stir. (If the fish is really finely sliced, as little as 30 minutes will do; it is ready as soon as it looks 'cooked' – opaque white rather than glassy.)
2. Season with salt and freshly ground black pepper. Add the chopped tomato, green pepper and avocado and mix well.

Note: Do not add salt until about to serve the Ceviche. It draws the juices from the fish, making the dish too wet.

Serves 2

Grilled Sardines

16 small *or* 8 large sardines,
  fresh *or* frozen, not canned
Oil for grilling

Pepper
Lemon juice
Parsley to garnish

1. To clean the sardines: slit along the belly and remove the innards. Rinse the fish under running cold water and with a little salt gently rub away any black matter in the cavity. Cut off the gills.
2. Heat the grill. Score the fish with three or four diagonal cuts on each side, brush with oil, season with pepper and sprinkle with lemon juice.
3. Grill for about 4 minutes on each side, brushing with the hot oil and juices that run from the fish.
4. Lay the sardines on a warmed platter. Pour over the juices from the grill pan and serve at once.

Serves 4

Crayfish Flan

170g/6oz flour-quantity shortcrust pastry (pages 286–7)
450g/1lb raw crayfish tails
290ml/½ pint milk
1 small onion, sliced
1 small carrot, sliced
1 stick celery, sliced

1 bay leaf
About 6 peppercorns
110g/¼lb mushrooms
55g/2oz butter
30g/1oz flour
1 tablespoon chopped fresh
  parsley

1. Line a 20cm/8in flan ring with the pastry and bake blind until crisp and completely cooked. Keep warm.
2. Remove the flesh from the crayfish shells. Crush the shells roughly.
3. Place the milk, crayfish shells, onion, carrot, celery, bay leaf

and peppercorns in a saucepan, bring gently to the boil and simmer for 10 minutes.

4. Strain the milk, return it to the saucepan and add the crayfish. Poach for 3–4 minutes; do not boil. Strain and reserve the liquor.

5. Chop the mushrooms finely.

6. Heat half the butter in a pan and cook the mushrooms in it for 1 minute. Stir in the flour and cook for 30 seconds. Pour in the flavoured milk and stir while bringing to the boil. Add the remaining butter. Taste for seasoning.

7. Cut the crayfish into chunks and add to the sauce. Reheat and pour into the flan. Serve at once.

Note: The flan case and the filling can be made the day before they are needed, but they should not be put together until just before heating for serving. If both pastry and filling are stone cold the flan can be filled and then heated. But do not pour hot filling into a cold pastry case because it will make the pastry soggy, and the flan will not be in the oven long enough to get crisp again.

Baking blind: To bake a pie-crust or flan case before filling: Line the raw pastry case with a piece of foil or a double sheet of grease-proof paper and fill it with dried lentils, beans, rice or even pebbles or pennies. This is to prevent the pastry bubbling up during cooking. When the pastry is half cooked (about 15 minutes) the beans can be removed and the empty pastry case further dried out in the oven. The beans can be re-used indefinitely.

Serves 4–6

Deep-fried Seafood Envelopes

110g/¼lb cooked prawns	Parsley stalk
Salt and freshly ground black pepper	20g/¾oz butter
	20g/¾oz flour

Lemon juice
110g/¼lb raw scallops
110g/¼lb raw scampi, fresh *or*
  frozen
Slice of onion
6 peppercorns
1 bay leaf

115ml/4 fl.oz milk
½ teaspoon tomato purée
225g/½lb flour-quantity puff
  pastry (pages 293–4)
Beaten egg
Oil for deep frying
Tomato sauce (page 238)

1. If frozen, defrost the prawns slowly, and sprinkle with black pepper and lemon juice.
2. Place the scallops and scampi in a small pan, just cover with cold water and add the onion, peppercorns, bay leaf, parsley stalk and salt. Place over a gentle heat and simmer slowly for 4 minutes. Drain, and boil the stock to reduce to 110ml/4 fl.oz.
3. Cut the prawns and scampi in half. Remove the muscles from the scallops (found on the opposite side to the roe) and cut each scallop into two or three pieces.
4. Melt the butter in a saucepan, add the flour and cook for 30 seconds. Take off the heat. Add the reduced fish stock and mix well. Pour in the milk and return the pan to the heat. Bring to the boil slowly, stirring continuously. Season and add the tomato purée. Simmer for 1 minute by which time the sauce should be well thickened but still sloppy. Stir in the scampi, prawns and scallops.
5. Heat until the oil is hot enough to sizzle when a crumb is dropped into it.
6. Roll the pastry into very thin 8cm/3in squares. Place a spoonful of the fish mixture on each square and fold over on the diagonal. Stick the edges well together with a little beaten egg and brush both sides of the pastry with more beaten egg.
7. Deep fry a few at a time until golden brown; drain well on crumpled kitchen paper. Serve quickly.
8. Hand tomato sauce separately.

Makes about 20

Pain de Poisson

560g/1¼lb sole (filleted weight)
3 egg whites
Salt, freshly ground black pepper and cayenne
425ml/¾ pint double cream
3 eggs
170g/6oz fresh white breadcrumbs
4 level tablespoons chopped fresh parsley
2 level tablespoons chopped fresh tarragon and chives, mixed
Sprig of fresh tarragon
10 thin long rashers mild streaky rindless bacon

To serve:
Hollandaise sauce (pages 242–3)

1. Set the oven to 150°C/300°F, gas mark 2. Set aside four neat fillets of sole. Mince the remaining fillets twice or pound in a blender or mortar. When absolutely smooth beat in two egg whites.
2. Season with salt, pepper and cayenne. Gradually beat in two-thirds of the cream. Cover and set aside.
3. Meanwhile whisk the three whole eggs lightly and add the remaining cream to them. Stir this into the breadcrumbs with the chopped herbs. Season and mix well.
4. Whisk the remaining egg white until frothy. Season the reserved fillets with salt and pepper.
5. Lightly butter a loaf tin or terrine and put the tarragon sprigs on the bottom. Line the terrine with the rashers of bacon leaving the ends to be folded over the top of the terrine. Spread two-thirds of the fish mixture around the base and sides. Brush with a little of the frothy egg white and lay in two fillets of sole.
6. Brush with egg white and cover with half the herb and breadcrumb mixture. Brush with egg white, lay in the remaining two fillets of sole. Cover with remaining one-third of the fish mixture. Brush with egg white and cover with the remaining herb and breadcrumb mixture. Fold the bacon strips over the top of the terrine so that all the fish is covered.
7. Cover with damp greaseproof paper and foil and stand the

terrine in a roasting tin of hot water. Bake for 1½–2 hours. To see if it is ready press a skewer into the centre of the pain de poisson, hold there for about 2 seconds and test its heat against the inside of your wrist – it should be hot. The top of the pain de poisson should feel firm to the touch.

8. To serve invert a dish over the terrine and turn the whole thing over. Give a gentle shake and remove the tin. Serve warm with Hollandaise sauce.

Note: Thin strips of barding fat may be used instead of the streaky bacon. Strong-tasting bacon should be soaked in cold water, then blanched in fresh water and cooled before use. Alternatively the bacon can be omitted, and the dish decorated with a few tarragon sprigs, after unmoulding.

Serves 6

Inkfish Stew

Preparation must begin one day in advance

675/1½lb fresh squid (about 3–4 medium-sized squid)	55g/1½oz butter
	2 garlic cloves
425ml/¾ pint red wine	1 medium onion, sliced

1. Prepare the squid: pull the intestinal bag gently but firmly from inside the body and discard it and the rib-like piece of transparent cartilege called the pen. Scrape off the purplish-red skin from the body and wash the body well inside and out. Cut into rings – there are two edible fins which should be included. Cut the tentacles from the head and chop them into 2cm/¾in pieces. Add them to the squid rings. In the soft part still attached to the head there will be a long ink sac (in a white skin): remove this and break it into a bowl. Discard the head.
2. Marinate the squid in the ink and red wine overnight.
3. Melt the butter, add the garlic and onions and cook slowly until soft but not coloured.

4. Drain the marinated squid (reserving the liquid) and add it to the frying pan. Sauté for 4 minutes. Add the wine and ink and simmer for about 1½ hours or until the squid is tender.

Serves 4

Lobster Thermidor

4 small live lobsters
3 tablespoons oil
30g/1oz butter
1 teaspoon Dijon mustard

1 level tablespoon grated
 Parmesan cheese
Browned crumbs

For the mornay sauce:
20g/¾oz butter
20g/¾oz flour
290ml/½ pint milk

Salt, pepper and cayenne
2 tablespoons grated very fresh
 Parmesan cheese

For the Bercy reduction:
1 tablespoon chopped shallot
110g/¼lb clarified butter
 (page 236)

1 glass white wine

1. First make the mornay sauce: melt the butter, add the flour and cook for 1 minute. Draw the pan off the heat and stir in the milk. Return to the heat and bring slowly to the boil, stirring continuously until you have a creamy white sauce.
2. Season with salt, pepper and cayenne and simmer for 2–3 minutes. Remove from the heat, add the Parmesan and taste for seasoning.
3. Next, the lobsters: set the oven to 180°C/350°F, gas mark 4. Kill each lobster by pushing a sharp knife through its nerve centre (marked by a well-defined cross on the back of the head). When you pierce the middle of the cross the lobster will die instantly, although it will still move alarmingly.
4. Lay the lobster flat out and split it in half lengthwise. Remove the little stomach sac from near the head and the dark thread-like intestine.

5. Heat up the oil and butter and sauté the lobsters, flesh side down, for 5 minutes. Then put the whole pan in the oven for 15 minutes.
6. Make the bercy reduction: soften the shallot in the clarified butter over gentle heat until soft and transparent. Add the wine and boil fast until reduced to 3 tablespoons. Mix this bercy reduction, and the liquid from the lobster pan, with the mornay sauce. Heat up and add the mustard.
7. Remove all the meat from the lobster shells. Chop up the meat from the claws and the creamy greenish flesh from the head. Cut the tail meat into scallops. Mix the chopped meat with some of the sauce and place this in the bottom of the shell. Place the scalloped meat, rounded side up, on top of this. Coat with the remaining sauce and sprinkle with cheese and crumbs.
8. Place in the oven for 5–10 minutes to reheat and then brown under the grill. Serve 2 half-lobsters to each person.

Serves 4

Prawn Pilaff

790/1¾lb unshelled raw prawns
570ml/1 pint water
115ml/1 small glass white wine
Salt and freshly ground black pepper
1 lemon

3–4 parsley stalks
110g/¼lb butter
1 medium onion, finely chopped
225g/½lb long-grain rice
2 hardboiled eggs, chopped
1 tablespoon chopped fresh parsley

1. Put the whole prawns in a saucepan with the water, wine and a little salt. Bring slowly to the boil and simmer for 2 minutes. Lift out the prawns, leaving the liquid. Shell all but three of the prawns, putting the shells back into the saucepan. Add a slice of lemon and the parsley stalks. Simmer for 15 minutes. Strain and keep the liquid to cook the rice in.

2. Melt 85g/3oz of the butter and in it gently cook the onion until soft. Add the rice and fry slowly until the rice looks opaque. Add the liquid. Bring to the boil, stirring with a fork. Cover and simmer gently until the rice is tender and the water absorbed (about 20–30 minutes).
3. Meanwhile melt the remaining butter, add the prawns and eggs and heat through. Season with salt, pepper and lemon juice. Fork the shelled prawns and eggs into the pilaff rice. Pile into a serving dish, and sprinkle with plenty of chopped parsley. Put the three unshelled prawns on top, and serve.

Note I: If raw whole prawns are unavailable cooked ones will do. But it is important that they should be unshelled – the flavour given to the liquid by the shells is very good.

Note II: If the pilaff is to be kept warm, do not garnish with the parsley and whole prawns until serving. The parsley dries out and the prawns go chalky white.

Serves 6

Salmon Mayonnaise

1 whole salmon, cleaned

For the court bouillon:
2¼ litres/4 pints water
150ml/¼ pint vinegar
3 bay leaves
1 onion, sliced

Large bunch of parsley
1 carrot, sliced
12 peppercorns

For the garnish:
290ml/½ pint thick mayonnaise
   (pages 241–2)
Lemon wedges

Cucumber
Bunch of watercress

1. To make the court bouillon put the water, vinegar, bay leaves, onion, parsley, carrot and peppercorns in a large pan. Bring to the boil, cover and simmer for 20 minutes. Strain and cool.

2. Prepare the salmon: mitre the tail by cutting a V with a pair of scissors. Place the fish in a fish kettle or large saucepan, curving it into a C or S shape if it will not fit stretched full length.

3. Cover and poach very gently over a low heat for 4 minutes to the 450g/1lb, calculated from the time the liquid reaches poaching temperature (just below simmering).

4. Lift out the fish, cover with a damp cloth or loosely with foil and allow to get completely cold. Then carefully remove the skin but leave head and tail intact.

5. Now garnish the salmon in any way you like. The following suggestion produces a pretty but easily achieved, result.

6. Pile the mayonnaise into a piping bag fitted with a 1cm/½in fluted nozzle. Pipe 'shells' along the backbone. Thin down the remaining mayonnaise with a little cream, milk or hot water and put in a sauce boat to hand separately.

7. Cut a small piece of cucumber in half horizontally and then slice it finely. Arrange the slices, standing up, between the mayonnaise shells.

8. Arrange the lemon wedges, with more cucumber slices, along one side of the dish and garnish the ends with bunches of watercresss.

Note I: Salmon can be cooked without recourse to careful timing: lay the salmon in a pan into which it just fits nicely and just cover it with cold court bouillon. Bring it to simmering point as slowly as possible. Then remove from the heat. By the time the court bouillon is cold the salmon will be cooked, the theory being that a large salmon, needing a great quantity of liquid, will have longer at cooking temperatures than a small one, with perhaps only 1 litre/2 pints of court bouillon in a small fish kettle.

Note II: A 1·35 kilo/3lb fish will serve 4 people; a 2·4 kilo/8lb fish will serve 10–12 people.

Flat Salmon Pie

450g/1lb flour-quantity pâte
à paté (page 291)
55g/2oz Gruyère or
Cheddar cheese, grated
30g/1oz grated Parmesan
85g/3oz melted butter
50g/2oz fresh white
breadcrumbs

225g/½lb smoked salmon
2 tablespoons chopped fresh
dill
1 large garlic clove, crushed
150ml/5 fl.oz soured cream
Freshly ground black pepper
Juice of ½ lemon
Beaten egg

1. Make up the pâte à paté and roll out into two rectangles, one to fit a Swiss roll tin, the other slightly larger.
2. Set the oven to 200°C/400°F, gas mark 6.
3. Lightly grease and flour the back of a Swiss roll tin or baking sheet. Put the smaller rectangle of pastry on it and prick all over with a fork. Bake for 15 minutes and leave to cool.
4. Mix together the Gruyère or Cheddar cheese, the Parmesan, the melted butter and the breadcrumbs. Scatter half of this mixture all over the half-cooked pastry, leaving a good half-inch clear round the edge.
5. Chop the smoked salmon into small pieces and scatter it on top of the cheese mixture. Then scatter over the chopped dill.
6. Mix the crushed garlic with the soured cream and spread all over the salmon. Season well with pepper but no salt.
7. Sprinkle evenly with the lemon juice and top with the rest of the cheese mixture. Wet the edge of the bottom piece of pastry lightly with beaten egg and put the top sheet of pastry in place, pressing the edges to seal it well.
8. Use any pastry trimmings to decorate the pie and brush all over with beaten egg.
9. Bake until the pastry is crisp and pale brown. Serve hot or cold.

Note: Off-cuts and trimmings of smoked salmon can be bought more cheaply than slices, and do well for this dish.

Serves 6

Salmon en Croûte

One 2·3 kilos/5lb salmon

450g/1lb flour-quantity puff
   pastry (pages 293–4)
Few tablespoons fine semolina
Butter
Lemon juice
Tarragon leaves
White pepper and salt
Beaten egg

For the stock:
2 slices onion
1 bay leaf
Small bunch of parsley
6 peppercorns
Salt
Bones, skin and head from the
   salmon
570ml/1 pint water

For the sauce:
55g/2oz butter
20g/$\frac{3}{4}$oz flour
290ml/$\frac{1}{2}$ pint fish stock
50ml/$\frac{1}{2}$ glass white wine

1 teaspoon chopped fresh
   tarragon *or* parsley
2 tablespoons double cream

1. Fillet the fish keeping the four fillets as intact as possible. Skin the fillets.
2. Use the bones and other trimmings for the stock; put all the ingredients into a saucepan and simmer for 30 minutes. Strain into a measuring jug. Make up to 290ml/$\frac{1}{2}$ pint with water if necessary.
3. Heat the oven to 230°C/450°F, gas mark 8.
4. Roll out a third of the pastry into a long thin piece, about the thickness of a penny. Cut it to roughly the size and shape of the original salmon, i.e. fish-shaped.
5. Place on a wet baking sheet, and prick all over. Leave in a cool place for 15 minutes. Bake it in the hot oven until brown and crisp. If, when you turn it over, it is soggy underneath, put it back in the oven, soggy side up, for a few minutes. Cool.
6. Sprinkle the cooked pastry evenly with semolina (this will prevent the fish juices making the pastry soggy).

7. Lay the fillets of fish on the cooked pastry, dotting them with plenty of butter and sprinkling with lemon juice, tarragon, salt and pepper as you go, and assembling them more or less as they were when on the bone.

8. Roll out the rest of the pastry into a large sheet (slightly thinner this time) and lay it over the fish. Cut round the fish, leaving a good border (about 2·5cm/1in) beyond the edge of the bottom layer of the pastry. Carefully tuck the top 'sheet' under the cooked pastry, shaping the tail and pointed head of the fish carefully.

9. Brush with beaten egg. Using the back of a knife, mark the pastry in a criss-cross pattern to represent fish scales (or, if you have the time, mark the scales with the rounded end of a teaspoon). Cut some pastry trimmings into fine strips and use them to emphasize the tail fins and gills and use a circle of pastry for the eye. Brush again with egg.

10. Bake for 15 minutes in the hot oven to brown and puff up the pastry, then turn down the oven to 150°C/300°F, gas mark 3 for a further 30 minutes to cook the fish. Cover the crust with wet greaseproof paper if the pastry looks in danger of over-browning. To test if the fish is cooked push a skewer through the pastry and fish from the side: it should glide in easily.

11. Melt half the butter in a saucepan, add the flour and cook, stirring, for 1 minute or until the butter and flour are pale biscuit-coloured and foaming. Draw off the heat then add the 300ml/½ pint stock and the wine. Return to the heat and stir until boiling and smooth. Boil rapidly until you have a sauce of coating consistency.

12. Add the chopped tarragon and the cream. Season with salt and pepper as necessary. Beat in the remaining butter, bit by bit. Pour into a warmed sauceboat.

13. Slide the *salmon en croûte* on to a board or salmon dish, and make sure your guests admire it before you cut into it.

14. Hand the sauce separately, or slit the salmon down the middle, lift one side of the pastry case, and pour the sauce inside.

Serves 8

Sea Trout en Papillote

340g/¾lb fillet of sea trout, skinned
55g/2oz butter
1 tablespoon very finely shredded white of leek
1 tablespoon very finely shredded carrot
55g/2oz mushrooms, thinly sliced

1 teaspoon freshly chopped tarragon *or* fennel leaves
Lemon juice
2 tablespoons white wine
Salt and freshly ground black pepper
Oil for brushing baking sheet and paper

1. Heat the oven to 250°C/500°F, gas mark 9.
2. Fold a large sheet of greaseproof paper in half and cut a semi-circle (20cm/8in radius) from it so that when the double sheet is opened out the cut-out will be a 40cm/16in round. Cut out a second 'papillote'.
3. Melt half the butter and add the leek and carrot to it. Cook slowly without browning for 5 minutes, then add the mushrooms. Cook 1 more minute, then add the tarragon or fennel, and season with salt and pepper.
4. Cut the sea trout fillet into four or six diagonal slices about 1cm/½in thick.
5. Brush the inside of the paper rounds with a little oil taking care to leave a margin without oil. Divide the vegetable mixture between the two papillotes, spooning it on to one side only of the paper round. Lay the fish slices on top of the vegetables, two or three on each. Squeeze a few drops of lemon on each and sprinkle each with a tablespoon of wine. Dot with the remaining butter and add salt and pepper.
6. Fold the free half of the papillote paper over to make a parcel rather like an apple turnover. Fold the edges of the two layers of paper over twice together, twisting and pressing hard to make an air-tight seal. (See diagram.)
7. Lightly brush a baking sheet with oil and put it into the oven for five minutes to heat. Then carefully put the papillotes on

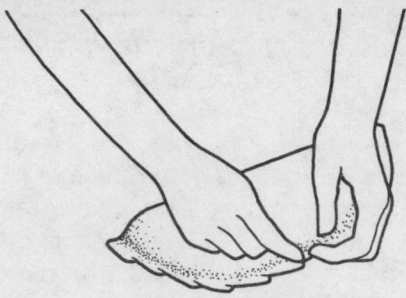

    the baking sheet, taking care that they do not touch each other. Bake for 5 minutes.

8.   Serve immediately on hot flat plates. Each diner unwraps his own puffed-up parcel.

Note I: Halibut, haddock, salmon, indeed almost any fish, can be cooked in this way. Whole trout weighing 340g/¾lb will take 15 minutes to cook. Breast of chicken, boned and skinned, is good too (20 minutes in the piece, 15 if in slices).

Note II: For a richer dish serve with beurre blanc (page 236).

Note III: Papillotes are generally made from circular papers, as in the above recipe, but are better made from heart-shaped pieces if whole small fish or long fillets of fish are to be enwrapped. See below.

Serves 2

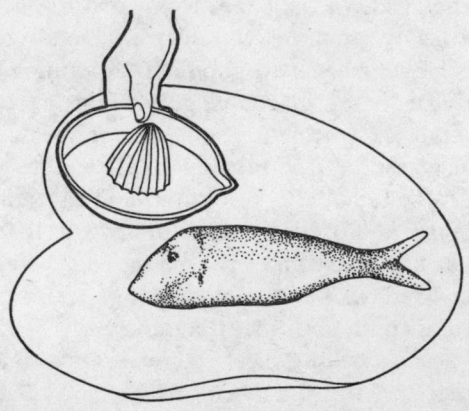

Lemon Sole with Burnt Hollandaise

12 fillets lemon sole, skinned

For the court bouillon:

Skin, bones and trimmings
from the fish
1 onion, sliced
1 carrot, sliced
425ml/¾ pint water

2 tablespoons wine vinegar
6 peppercorns
1 bay leaf
Pinch of salt
1 parsley stalk

150ml/¼ pint Hollandaise sauce   3 tablespoons double cream
(pages 242–3)

1. Place all the ingredients for the court bouillon together in
    a pan. Bring to the boil and simmer for 25–30 minutes.
    Strain and allow to cool.
2. Set the oven to 180°C/350°F, gas mark 4.
3. Roll the fillets up (skinned side inside) or fold into neat
    parcels, tucking the ends under. Lay them in an ovenproof
    dish or roasting pan and pour over the court bouillon. Cover
    and poach in the oven for 15 20 minutes. Alternatively poach
    carefully on top of the cooker.
4. While the fish cooks heat up the grill and make the Hollan-
    daise sauce.
5. Drain the fish well and arrange on a heat-resistant serving
    dish. Mix the sauce with the cream and coat each fillet with
    a spoonful. Brown quickly under the grill and serve im-
    mediately.

Serves 4

Sole Véronique

3 sole, about 450g/1lb each,
skinned and filleted but
bones and skin reserved
150ml/¼ pint white wine

1 bay leaf
6 peppercorns
1 onion, sliced
Salt

For the sauce:
20g/¾oz unsalted butter
20g/¾oz flour

290ml/½ pint milk
2 tablespoons single cream

For the garnish:
110g/¼lb white grapes

1. Set the oven to 180°C/350°F, gas mark 4.
2. Trim the fillets and fold them up with the skinned side in. Lay them in an ovenproof dish. Pour on the wine and add the bay leaf, peppercorns and onion. Add enough water to cover half the fish. Arrange the skin and fish bones on top and bake for 15–20 minutes.
3. Dip the grapes into boiling water for 5 seconds, then skin them. Cut in half then discard the pips. Put into a covered dish and heat through in the oven.
4. When the fish is cooked remove the fillets and keep them warm. Strain the cooking liquor and reduce it by boiling rapidly to 3 tablespoons.
5. Melt the butter, add the flour and cook for 1 minute. Gradually add the milk, stirring continually as you bring it to the boil. Stir in the reduced fish stock (or *fumet*) and simmer for 1 minute. Taste and adjust the seasoning if necessary. Add the cream and half the hot grapes.
6. Arrange the fillets of sole on a warmed serving dish. Coat with the Véronique sauce and arrange the remaining grapes at each end of the dish. Serve immediately.

Note I: The perfectionist cook may like to leave the grapes whole: use the rounded end of a hair grip to extract the pips through the stalk end.

Note II: Canned white grapes are less trouble than fresh ones, and have an excellent flavour and texture for the dish. Do not add the juice, and do not peel them.

Serves 4

Sole Colbert

Four 340g/¾lb Dover soles
Seasoned flour
Beaten egg
Dry white breadcrumbs

Fat for deep frying
Maître d'hôtel butter (page 235)
Lemon wedges

1. Skin and trim the soles, leaving on the heads. With a small sharp knife make a cut *one side only* down the centre of the backbone, through the flesh to the bone. Raise the side fillets (loosening them with a knife) so that you can snip the bone just below the head and above the tail. Later you will remove the whole backbone so work the fillets away from the bones, but leaving them still attached at each end and along the edge of the fish – you are working only from the centre out. See drawing. Rinse and dry the fish.

2. Dip in seasoned flour, shaking away any excess. Brush with beaten egg and press on the dry white breadcrumbs. Be sure to egg and crumb the underside of the raised fillets.

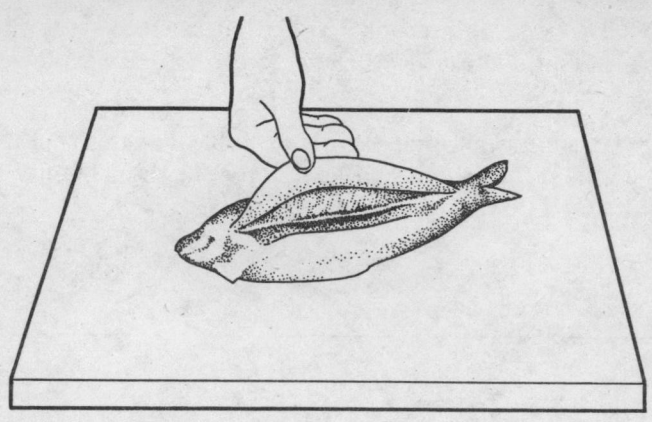

3. Heat up the oil so that a crumb will sizzle in it. Fry the whole fish until a good golden brown, holding the fish down with a fish slice to prevent it curling up. Drain well on absorbent paper.

4. Leave for 1–2 minutes. Then carefully pull out the backbone, cutting round the breadcrumb coating to prevent too much of it being pulled off.

5. Fill the space with slices of maitre d'hotel butter. Dish and serve immediately with wedges of lemon.

Note: For a light lunch dish or a starter 'slip' soles are suitable. They weigh 170–225g/6–8oz.

Serves 4

Chaudfroid of Sole

Four 560g/1¼lb soles, skinned
  and filleted

For the stock and aspic jelly:

1 onion	6 peppercorns
1 carrot	1 glass white wine

Stick of celery
Bones, head and skins of the
  soles
1 bay leaf

55g/2oz gelatine
2 egg whites and 2 egg shells,
  crushed

For the farce:
170g/6oz uncooked salmon,
  minced
1 egg white

2 tablespoons cream
Salt and freshly ground black
  pepper

For the chaudfroid sauce:
290ml/½ pint milk
6 peppercorns
Blade of mace
Slice of onion
20g/¾oz butter

20g/¾oz flour
7g/¼oz gelatine
190ml/⅓ pint aspic jelly
1 tablespoon cream
Salt and white pepper

For the garnish:
Paper-thin slices of truffle *or*
  mushroom

1. To make the stock cut the onion, carrot and celery into small chunks, put into a pan with the fish heads, bones and skins, and add the bay leaf, peppercorns and wine. Pour over ¾ litre/1½ pints cold water. Bring to the boil, skim and simmer for 30 minutes. Strain and leave to cool.

2. Set the oven to 170°C/325°F, gas mark 3.

3. Next tackle the farce. Put the salmon in a bowl. Whisk the egg white until frothy and beat it slowly into the salmon with the cream. Taste and season with salt and pepper.

4. Wash and dry the sole fillets. Divide the farce equally between them. Spread it on the skinned sides and roll or fold up into neat parcels.

5. Put them into a buttered ovenproof dish with a cup of the fish stock. Cover with buttered foil or greaseproof paper. Bake for 12 minutes or until cooked. Strain off and reserve the liquid; leave the fish to cool, covered.

6. To make the sauce first heat the milk with the peppercorns, blade of mace and slice of onion. Strain and mix with the liquid saved from cooking the fish.

7. Melt the butter and add the flour. Cook, stirring, for 1

159

minute. Remove from the heat and add the milky liquid. Leave to cool but stir occasionally to prevent a skin forming.

8. To make the aspic put the stock into a large saucepan, sprinkle on 55g/2oz gelatine and put the saucepan over a gentle heat.

9. Place the crushed shells in a bowl, add the egg white and whisk until frothy. Pour into the warming stock and keep whisking steadily (preferably with a balloon whisk) until the mixture boils and rises. Stop whisking immediately and draw the pan off the heat. Allow the mixture to subside. Take care not to break the crust formed by the egg white.

10. Bring the aspic up to the boil again and again allow to subside. Repeat this once more (the egg white will trap the sediment in the stock and clear the aspic). Allow to cool for 10 minutes.

11. Fix a double layer of fine muslin over a clean basin and carefully strain the aspic through it, taking care to hold the egg white crust back. When all the liquid is through (or almost all of it) allow the egg white to slip into the muslin. Then strain the aspic again – this time through both egg white crust and cloth. Do not try to hurry the process by squeezing the cloth, or murky aspic will result.

12. In a small pan soak the gelatine for the sauce in about 4 tablespoons of the cleared cool aspic for 5 minutes. Melt over a low heat. Beat into the sauce with the cream. Taste for seasoning, adding salt or white pepper if necessary.

13. Lay the fish 'parcels' on a cake rack with a tray underneath. As the sauce thickens, spoon some over each fillet, covering the top and sides. Refrigerate the coated fillets until the sauce is set.

14. Garnish the fish 'parcels' with truffle or mushroom. When the aspic is cool and on the point of setting, carefully coat each fillet with aspic. Refrigerate to set. Repeat the coating if necessary, the aspic layer should be thin, but very shiny.

15. Set the rest of the aspic in a shallow tray.

16. Arrange the fillets on a serving dish. When the aspic in the tray is set cut it into tiny squares with a sharp knife. Garnish the fish with the chopped aspic. Keep cool.

Note: If the aspic is less than crystal-clear it is wise not to chop it – which seems to emphasize its murkiness.

Serves 4–6

Trout with Hazelnuts

55g/2oz hazelnuts
4 medium-sized rainbow trout
Seasoned flour
85g/3oz clarified butter (page 236)

Lemon juice
Salt and pepper
Lemon wedges
Chopped fresh parsley

1. Set the oven to 170°C/325°F, gas mark 3. Brown the hazelnuts in the oven. Rub them in a clean cloth to remove the skins. Chop them roughly.
2. Clean the trout very well. Dip them in the flour and shake off any excess.
3. Fry briefly on both sides in all but a tablespoon of the butter. Transfer to an ovenproof dish, pouring over the butter from the pan. Bake for 15 minutes (or until firm to the touch).
4. Fry the chopped hazelnuts in the remaining butter.
5. Arrange the trout on a warm serving dish, pour over the fried hazelnuts and any butter, then sprinkle with lemon juice, and salt and pepper. Garnish with lemon wedges and sprinkle with parsley.

Note I: If trout is not properly cleaned it tastes bitter.

Note II: This is similar to the classic *truites aux amandes.* For this split or flaked almonds instead of hazelnuts should be used. They are simply fried in butter and sprinkled over the fish.

Note III: The fish may be cooked entirely in the frying pan, but they must be fried slowly, for about 7 minutes a side.

Serves 4

Baked Turbot with Cheese and Shrimp Sauce

4 turbot steaks
Salt and freshly ground black
  pepper
150ml/¼ pint white wine
150ml/¼ pint water
1 bay leaf
Slice of onion
1 parsley stalk
2 peppercorns
30g/1oz butter

30g/1oz flour
150ml/¼ pint milk
110g/¼lb cooked, peeled pink
  shrimps or prawns
55g/2oz Cheddar cheese, grated
Pinch of cayenne
1 tablespoon Parmesan
1 tablespoon fresh white breadcrumbs
30g/1oz butter

1. Set the oven to 190°C/375°F, gas mark 5. If the shrimps are frozen defrost them slowly sprinkled with lemon juice and pepper.
2. Lay the turbot steaks in an ovenproof dish and season with salt. Cover with the wine and water and add the bay leaf, onion, parsley stalk and peppercorns. Cover and poach in the oven for 20–25 minutes or until the fish is firm and cooked.
3. Lift the steaks from the liquor. Carefully remove skins and bones, and place the steaks in a serving dish. Keep them warm. Boil cooking liquor rapidly to reduce by half.
4. Melt the butter in a saucepan. Stir in the flour and cook, stirring, for 1 minute. Remove from the heat and gradually stir in the poaching liquor. Return to the heat, and stir while the sauce comes to the boil and thickens. Add the milk and reheat.
5. Reduce the heat, add the shrimps and poach gently for 1 minute. Take off the heat and stir in the grated cheese. Season to taste with salt, pepper and cayenne. Pour over the fish.
6. Sprinkle the dish with the Parmesan cheese and breadcrumbs. Dot with butter (or sprinkle with melted butter) and brown under the grill.

Serves 4

Deep-Fried Whitebait

450g/1lb whitebait   Oil *or* fat for deep frying
Flour   Lemon wedges
Salt, pepper and cayenne   Deep-fried parsley (page 139)

1. Sort through the whitebait discarding any broken fish. Season the flour very well with salt and pepper.
2. Heat the deep fat until a crumb will sizzle vigorously in it.
3. Once the fat is ready, not before, put the whitebait in a sieve and spoon over the flour. Shake and toss carefully until every fish is coated. (Do this in small quantities if you haven't a very large sieve.)
4. Place a small handful of whitebait (too many stick together) into the fat and cook for no more than 2 minutes. Repeat until all the fish are fried. They should be crisp and pale brown.
5. Drain on absorbent paper. Serve at once with lemon wedges and deep fried parsley.

Note: If for any reason the fried whitebait can not be served at once, they should be spread out in a thin layer on a baking sheet and kept, uncovered, in a just-warm oven until wanted. They will become soggy if piled up or covered. Best of all, serve at once.

Serves 4

Turbot and Scallop Moulds

One 900g/2lb live lobster
16 flat thin slices (about the size of the palm of your hand) turbot *or* brill
4 fillets sole, with skins, bones and heads
Few slices onion
1 bay leaf
Salt, pepper and cayenne
85g/3oz finely chopped shallots
85g/3oz butter
¼ teaspoon crushed garlic

About 30g/1oz flour
85ml/3 fl.oz good white wine
Armagnac
2 teaspoons tomato purée
30g/1oz fresh chopped tarragon *or* chervil
8 fresh scallops in their shells
1 egg white
290ml/½ pint double cream
3 tablespoons dry Vermouth
450g/1lb fresh spinach

1. With a sharp knife kill the lobster by inserting a knife where the head joins the thorax, and splitting the head. Split the lobster in half lengthwise and remove the stomach sac and intestine. Pull out the flesh from the tail shell, and keep it raw for the mousse.

2. Put the head, claws, leg and shell into a small saucepan and set aside in a cool place while you make the fish stock.

3. Put the sole bones, skin and head, any turbot or brill trimmings or bones, and a sliced onion, a bay leaf, salt and pepper into a saucepan and add a pint of water. Simmer for 15 minutes, then strain and allow to cool.

4. When quite cold, pour over the lobster head, claws etc. and poach gently until the lobster is cooked (about 10 minutes).

5. Take the flesh from the claws and head (including the greenish creamy part), and from the legs, and chop it up. Return the shells (crushed and broken up) to the stock pan and simmer for a further 10 minutes.

6. In a small heavy pan sweat 30g/1oz of the chopped shallot in 30g/1oz of the butter until soft and transparent. Add the crushed garlic. Allow to cook for 1 minute, then add 1 heaped teaspoon of flour, stir well, then add 1 tablespoon of white wine, a dash of Armagnac and the tomato purée.

Stir over heat, adding enough fish stock to give a sauce of creamy consistency (about 150ml/¼ pint). Add the cooked lobster meat, the chopped fresh tarragon, and salt and pepper to taste. Set the mixture aside.

7. Lift the scallops from their shells (keeping the shells) and remove the orange/pink corals, which you must set aside for the final sauce.

8. Pound or mince the scallop flesh with the raw lobster and the fillets of sole. Then beat in the egg white, 150ml/¼ pint double cream and season with salt, pepper and a dash of Armagnac.

9. Then make the sauce: gently cook the remaining 55g/2oz chopped shallot in 30g/1oz of the butter until soft. Stir in a heaped tablespoon flour, then add the rest of the white wine and the Vermouth. Add 150ml/¼ pint of the fish stock and bring to the boil, stirring. Simmer for 5 minutes, then strain into a clean saucepan. Stir in the remaining double cream, season with cayenne pepper. Set the sauce aside while you prepare the scallop corals.

10. Strain the remaining fish stock from the lobster shells and boil it rapidly until you are left with a tablespoon or so of thick, clearish liquid. This is concentrated 'glaçe de poisson'. Add the scallop corals to it, simmer for 1 minute, then pound stock and corals together to make a smooth pink creamy paste. Set aside (you will add it to the sauce at the last minute).

11. Now, having prepared the lobster and tarragon mixture, the lobster and scallop mousse and sauce, you are ready to start on the main construction. Wash the spinach leaves, remove any tough stalks and plunge into boiling salted water for a few seconds only. Drain very well and immediately dunk into cold water to set the bright green colour.

12. Set the oven to 180°C/350°F, gas mark 4.

13. Take the 8 deeper scallop shells, wash them, and butter them well. Line each shell with a fillet of turbot or brill. Follow this with a layer of the spinach, and then a layer of the mousse. Into the centre of this put a spoonful of the lobster and tarragon mixture. Then another layer of lobster mousse,

another of spinach and cover with the remaining fish fillets.

14. Brush the top with melted butter. Put the eight filled scallop dishes into a roasting pan and pour in enough water, round the shells, to cover the pan to the depth of 0·75cm/¼in. Cover the whole dish with foil and bake for 20 minutes.

15. While the fish parcels are baking, reheat the sauce, and add the scallop coral paste.

16. To serve: slide each parcel out of its scallop shell, turn it over on to a warmed serving dish, and coat with the sauce.

Serves 8

Easy Fish Quenelles

450g/1lb fish fillet (turbot *or* salmon *or* haddock *or* any lean fish)
225g/½lb whiting fillet
4 slices white bread, crusts off
Milk
2 egg whites
Salt, pepper and cayenne
290ml/½ pint double cream
1 can lobster bisque *or* mussel soup
1 tablespoon sherry

For the poaching liquid:
1·14 litres/2 pints water
3 tablespoons vinegar
Bunch of parsley
1 bay leaf
Slice of onion
Fish heads, skins, bones etc.

1. Simmer the poaching liquid ingredients together for 30 minutes, then strain into a shallow saucepan or large frying pan.

2. Mince the fish flesh twice. Soak the bread in milk, squeeze dryish and beat into the fish. Season with pepper only. Slowly, in a machine or a bowl, work in the egg whites: first beat them with a fork until just frothy, and add bit by bit, mixing well between each addition. When the whites are in, leave the mixture, refrigerated, for at least 1 hour.

3. Heat the poaching liquid. Gradually beat three-quarters of the cream into the fish mixture, and add salt and cayenne

to taste. The mixture should be of 'dropping consistency'.
4. Using two wet dessertspoons mould the mixture into egg-shapes and drop them into the hot fish stock. Poach for 8 minutes, or until the quenelles feel firm to the touch. Take care not to overcook.
5. To make the sauce heat the soup, add the rest of the cream and the sherry, and enough of the cooking stock to get it to the right consistency.
6. With a perforated spoon lift the quenelles on to a serving dish and pour over the sauce.

Note: The recipe calls for tasting the raw fish mixture for seasoning. It is important to do this, and anyway it tastes perfectly good. Being squeamish about tasting raw mixtures leads to disappointing flavourless food – a pity after all the trouble of beating and mixing.

Serves 4–6

Fritto Misto

About 450g/1lb mixture of raw prawns, crayfish tails, crab meat, sole, whiting and whitebait (prepared weight)

Lemon juice
Salt and pepper
Oil *or* fat for deep frying

For the batter:
5g/¼oz fresh yeast
150ml/¼ pint tepid water
110g/¼lb plain flour

Pinch of salt
1 scant tablespoon olive oil
1 egg white

For the garnish:
Deep-fried parsley (page 139)

1. Mix the yeast with the water.
2. Sift the flour and salt into a bowl. Make a well in the centre and pour in the liquid and oil.

3. With a wooden spoon, beat this centre mixture, gradually drawing in the surrounding flour by degrees. Leave in a warm place to rise for 30 minutes.
4. Prepare the fish, shelling them or cutting into strips as appropriate. Sprinkle with lemon juice and pepper and leave for 30 minutes or so.
5. Beat the egg white until stiff and fold it into the batter.
6. Drain the fish. Dip into the batter, coating each piece completely.
7. Heat the fat until a drop of batter will frizzle slowly. Deep fry the pieces, a few at a time, in the hot fat until the batter is golden brown. Drain an absorbent paper, sprinkle with salt and pile on to a serving dish. Garnish with deep-fried parsley.

Serves 4

Eel Pie

340g/¾lb flour-quantity puff pastry (pages 293–4)
900g/2lb smoked eel
900g/2lb fresh spinach, well washed
Grated nutmeg and freshly ground black pepper

For the sauce:
15g/½oz flour
150ml/¼ pint milk
55g/2oz unsalted butter
2 egg yolks

Beaten egg

1. Set the oven to 200°C/400°F, gas mark 6. Wet a baking sheet.
2. Take one-third of the pastry and roll it out to a rectangle, 15cm × 20cm/6in × 8in. Place on a wet baking tray and prick with a fork. Bake to a good brown (about 20 minutes). Do not turn the oven off. Leave the pastry on a wire rack to cool.
3. Meanwhile prepare the fillings. Skin the eel and take it off the bone as neatly as possible.

4. Cook the spinach in a large covered pan with a cupful of water (do not add salt if the eel is very salty). Drain thoroughly, chop roughly, and season with nutmeg and a little freshly ground black pepper.

5. To make the sauce: melt 15g/½oz of the butter, add the flour and cook for 30 seconds. Draw off the heat and stir in the milk. Return to the heat and stir until boiling.

6. Cool slightly, then beat in the rest of the butter and egg yolks. Season with a little freshly ground black pepper.

8. Arrange half the spinach on the cooked pastry base and cover with the eel. Spread the béchamel sauce over the eel and cover with remaining spinach.

9. Roll the remaining 225g/8oz puff pastry on a floured board into a 'blanket' large enough to cover the whole pie. Lay it gently over the spinach. With a sharp knife cut off the corners of the 'blanket', but do not throw away these trimmings.

10. Lift one length of the raw pastry and brush the underside with a little beaten egg. Tuck the 'blanket' neatly underneath the cooked base. Repeat with the other three sides.

11. Shape the trimmings into leaves. Brush the whole pie with beaten egg. Lay on the pastry leaves and brush again.

12. Bake for 40–45 minutes.

Serve hot or cold.

Note: To counteract the saltiness of the smoked eel, salt is not added to the sauce or to the spinach. But if the smoked eel is mild in flavour, salt may of course be added to spinach and sauce.

Serves 6

5
Meat

BEEF

Spiced Beef

This recipe takes 8 days to complete.

1 large garlic clove
One 1·4 kilos/3lb boneless
   sirloin of beef
55g/2oz brown sugar

30g/1oz ground allspice
2–3 bay leaves, chopped
110g/¼lb salt
About 450g/1lb plain flour

1. Peel the garlic and cut it into thin slivers. Stick these into the beef flesh. Rub the surface of the joint with the sugar.
2. Leave in a cool place for 12 hours. Mix together the allspice, chopped bay leaf and salt.
3. Take a little of the salt mixture and rub it well into the meat.
4. Keep for a week, turning and rubbing with more salt and spice each day.
5. Set the oven to 190°C/375°F, gas mark 5.
6. Make enough of a fairly thick doughy paste (by mixing flour and water together) to completely envelop the beef.
7. Wrap the meat in the paste.
8. Put it, paste and all, into a roasting tin and pour in a small cup of water. Bake for 2 hours.
9. Remove and allow to cool. Snip off the crust and discard it before serving the beef.

Note: Especially good eaten cold with Cumberland sauce (page 237) or a sweet pickle.

Serves 8

Boeuf Philippe

560g/1¼lb fillet of beef (ends will do)
Worcestershire sauce
Freshly ground black pepper
1 tablespoon beef dripping
½ cauliflower
170g/6oz French beans

3 tomatoes
½ teaspoon horseradish sauce
1 garlic clove, crushed
3 tablespoons French dressing (page 237)
8 black olives, stoned
Bunch of watercress

1. Set the oven to 200°C/400°F, gas mark 6.
2. Season the meat with Worcestershire sauce and black pepper. Heat the beef dripping in a roasting tin over the cooker ring and add the beef. Brown evenly on all sides. If the beef is in one thick piece put it into the oven for 15 minutes, less if it is thin or in smaller pieces. It should be just pink inside. Allow to cool.
3. Wash the cauliflower and cut into florets. Plunge these into a pan of boiling water for 4–5 minutes. Drain. Rinse under cold water to prevent further cooking. Drain again.
4. Wash and top and tail the beans. Cook in boiling salted water for 5 minutes, then rinse under cold water and drain.
5. Plunge the tomatoes into boiling water for 5 seconds and peel. Cut into quarters.
6. Add the horseradish sauce and crushed garlic to the French dressing. The salad is now ready for assembly but this should not be done until just before serving. The beef will lose its colour if dressed too soon, and the salad will look tired if left to stand for any length of time.
7. Cut the beef into thin slices and then into thin strips, cutting *across* the grain of the meat. Place in a basin with the other ingredients, reserving 1 tomato and 4 olives for decoration.
8. Using your hands, mix in three-quarters of the French dressing and pile into a serving dish. Place the reserved tomatoes and olives on top of the dish and brush with a little French dressing. Garnish with a bunch of watercress dipped into the remaining dressing.

Serves 6

Filet de Boeuf à la Stroganoff

340g/¾lb fillet of beef	1 tablespoon oil
1 medium onion	2 tablespoons brandy
225g/½lb mushrooms	2 tablespoons cream
55g/2oz butter	Salt and freshly ground black
100ml/1 small glass white wine	pepper
150ml/¼ pint good beef stock	2 tablespoons soured cream

1. Cut the beef into 5cm/2in strips the thickness of a pencil. Slice the onion finely. Slice the mushrooms.
2. Melt half the butter in a frying pan and in it gently cook the onion until soft and transparent. Add the mushrooms and toss over the heat for 30 seconds. Add the wine and the stock. Boil rapidly to reduce the liquid to about 2 tablespoons. Stir well and tip the lot out into a bowl, scraping the pan carefully.
3. Now heat the oil and the remaining butter in the pan. Get it as hot as you dare. Drop in the beef strips. Shake and toss over fast heat to brown and seal the edges without overcooking the middle. Then turn the heat down.
4. Pour the brandy into the hot pan. Set it alight. As soon as the flames have died down, pour in the mushroom and stock mixture. Return the meat to the pan and stir in the cream. Taste the sauce. Add salt and pepper as necessary. (If the sauce is too thin remove the meat and boil the sauce rapidly to reduce it to a syrupy consistency.)
5. Reheat, then tip into a warm serving dish and fork the soured cream in roughly.

Note: The essence of a perfect beef Stroganoff is the speed at which the fine beef strips are cooked. If using tougher meat, there is nothing for it but gently to stew the beef (after adding the mushrooms and stock) until tender. However, that is not a true Stroganoff, though it can be very good.

Serves 4

Green Peppercorn Steaks

2 teaspoons green pepper-
corns (frozen *or* canned)
Oil
Four 2½cm/1in thick fillet
steaks

2 tablespoons brandy
2 tablespoons double cream
Salt

1. Rinse the peppercorns if they are canned.
2. Brush a frying pan with oil. Heat until smoking. Fry the steaks as fast as you dare on both sides. Get them to the degree you like them (generally, they need about 1½ minutes per side for blue, 2 minutes for rare, 2½ minutes for medium-rare, 3 minutes for medium and 4½ minutes for well done).
3. Pour in the brandy and set it alight.
4. When the flames die down remove the steaks to a warm serving dish.
5. Add the peppercorns, the cream and a pinch or two of salt to the frying pan. Mix well, scraping up any sediment. Boil up and pour over the steaks.

Serves 4

Steak Wellington

Four 170g/6oz fillet steaks *or*
tournedos
Salt and freshly ground black
pepper
Worcestershire sauce
30g/1oz beef dripping
55g/2oz flat mushrooms,
chopped
85g/3oz chicken liver pâté
(page 101)

225g/½lb flour-quantity rough
puff pastry (pages 292–3)
Beaten egg
⅓ small onion, finely chopped
½ glass red wine
1 scant tablespoon flour
290ml/½ pint beef stock
Watercress

1. Set the oven to 220°C/425°F, gas mark 7. Trim any fat or membrane from the steaks. Season with pepper and a few drops of Worcestershire sauce.

2. Heat the dripping in a pan and brown the steaks quickly on both sides to seal in the juices. The outside should be a good brown, the middle absolutely raw. Reserve the frying pan unwashed. Leave the meat to cool on a wire rack (this is to allow the fat to drip off the steaks rather than cooling and congealing on them).

3. Beat half the mushrooms into the pâté. Taste and add seasoning if necessary. Spread one side of each tournedo with this mixture. Roll out the pastry until it is about the thickness of a large coin. Cut into four equal-sized squares about 18cm/7in square.

4. Place each tournedo, pâté side down, on a piece of pastry. Brush the edges with water and draw them together over the tournedo, making a neat and well-sealed parcel. Place them on a wet baking sheet, pâté side up, and brush with beaten egg. Make a small slit in the top of each parcel so that the steam can escape. Decorate with leaves made from the pastry trimmings. Brush these with egg too. Place in the refrigerator for 10 minutes so that the pastry can relax.

5. Meanwhile make the sauce: fry the onion until soft in the beef dripping left in the frying pan. Add the remaining mushrooms and cook for 30 seconds. Add the wine, and boil rapidly until the liquid is reduced to a tablespoon. Stir in the flour, and then the stock. Stir until boiling. Simmer 1–2 minutes. Season with salt and pepper.

6. Now brush the steak parcels with a little more beaten egg and place in the oven for 15 minutes, by which time the pastry should be golden brown and the meat pink. Dish on a warmed plate. Garnish with watercress and hand the sauce separately.

Serves 4

Fillet of Beef en Croûte

One 1·8 kilos/4lb piece of fillet from the thick end
Freshly ground black pepper
Worcestershire sauce (optional)
30g/1oz beef dripping
340g/¾lb flour-quantity puff pastry (pages 293–4)

110g/¼lb flat mushrooms
30g/1oz butter
110g/¼lb chicken liver pâté (page 101)
Beaten egg

1. Set oven to 200°C/400°F, gas mark 6. Wet a baking sheet.
2. Skin and trim the fillet, season well with pepper and Worcestershire sauce (if used). Melt the dripping in a roasting pan and when hot add the meat and brown on all sides. Roast it in the oven for 20 minutes.
3. Take one-third of the pastry and roll it on a floured board until it is a little more than the length and breadth of the fillet. Place it on a wet baking sheet, prick with a fork and bake in the oven until a golden brown (about 20 minutes). Do not turn the oven off. Leave the pastry on a wire rack to cool.
4. Remove the fillet from the roasting pan and allow to cool.
5. Chop the mushrooms very finely and quickly fry in the butter. Mix this with the pâté. Spread the pâté to cover the cooked pastry base. Place the cold fillet on top of this and with a sharp knife cut away any pastry which is not covered by the fillet.
6. Roll the remaining pastry on a floured board into a 'blanket' large enough to cover the fillet easily. Lift up the new pastry and lay it gently over the fillet. With a sharp knife cut off the corners of the 'blanket'. (Do not throw away these trimmings.)
7. Lift one length of the raw pastry and brush the underside with egg wash. With a palette knife lift the base and tuck the 'blanket' neatly underneath it. Repeat with the other three sides. Shape the extra pastry into leaves. Brush the pastry-

covered fillet with beaten egg. Lay on the pastry leaves and brush again.

8. Place the fillet in the oven for 20 minutes or until the pastry is very dark brown and shiny. (This recipe assumes that rare beef is desired, but longer cooking in the first instance – without the pastry – will ensure a more well-done fillet. For medium beef give it a further 10 minutes and for well-done beef a further 15 minutes.) Serve hot or cold. If served hot it should be carved at the table or the juice will be lost and the meat may have a grey unappetizing look.

Note: The dish may be prepared in advance up to the final baking. It should be left ready for the oven on the baking sheet, loosely covered with plastic film or foil to stop the egg glaze drying. If prepared in advance it is important that the mushrooms and pâté be stone cold before mixing together, and that the meat be cold before covering with the pastry.

Serves 8–10

Boeuf à la Mode

140g/5oz larding fat (usually back pork fat)
1·8 kilos/4lb braising beef (boned)
1 veal knuckle
1 calf's foot, chopped
1·14 litres/2 pints good beef stock
2 tablespoons dripping

For the garnish:
450g/1lb button onions
675g/1½lb carrots
45g/1½oz butter
Sugar

For the marinade:
425ml/¾ pint red wine
1 large onion
1 large carrot
3 bay leaves
Sprig of thyme
Parsley stalks
Salt and freshly ground black pepper
3 tablespoons olive oil
2 garlic cloves, crushed
Stick of celery, chopped

1. First prepare the marinade: place the wine in a bowl large enough to hold the piece of beef. Peel and slice the onion and carrot finely and add to the wine with all the other marinade ingredients.

2. Cut the larding fat into very thin strips, like strings. Using a larding needle, thread them into the beef flesh at regular intervals. Tie the meat neatly but not too firmly with thin string. Lay in the marinade and leave for about 12 hours, turning the meat over after about 6 hours.

3. Put the veal knuckle and calf's foot into a saucepan and cover with the beef stock. Bring to the boil quickly, take off the heat and skim off the scum. Bring back to the boil, remove from heat and skim again.

4. Set the oven to 100°C/200°F, gas mark ½. Take up the meat and wipe dry with absorbent paper or a dry cloth.

5. Melt the dripping in a very heavy casserole and quickly fry all sides of the meat until they are deep brown in colour. Drain off the excess fat. Pour the marinade and the stock over the beef, and add the calf's foot and veal knuckle.

6. Bring to the boil, cover, and then place on the bottom shelf in the oven. Cook for about 4 hours or until the meat is tender, basting and turning frequently.

7. To prepare the garnish: put the onions, still unpeeled, into boiling water and boil for 3 minutes. Take out, tip into cold water, and peel them. Peel the carrots and trim them into baby carrot shapes or thin even strips.

8. Melt half the butter in a sauté pan, add the carrots and put on a lid. Cook over the lowest of heats, shaking the pan occasionally until the carrots are just tender. Take care they do not catch on the pan bottom and burn. Towards the end of the cooking time sprinkle in a little salt, pepper and ¼ teaspoon sugar. Keep warm.

9. Without rinsing the sauté pan, melt the rest of the butter and add half a teaspoon sugar. Put in all the peeled onions and cook as you did the carrots, but this time allowing the onions to colour to an even pale brown all over. Mix with the carrots.

10. When the meat is meltingly tender, lift it out, untie and place on a serving dish. Boil the cooking stock rapidly until you have a thin syrupy sauce. Taste and season as necessary. Place the onions and carrots round the meat and strain over the sauce.

Serves 8–10

Boeuf à la Mode en Gelée

Boeuf à la mode (pages 176–8)   *For the garnish:*
2 egg whites   Mustard and cress
2 crushed egg shells
75ml/2½ fl.oz sherry

1. Allow the meat to cool in the cooking liquid. To speed this up, stand the covered casserole in a large basin of cold water into which the cold tap trickles steadily, so constantly cooling it. When the meat is lukewarm, lift it out on to a wire rack set over a tray. Wipe off all the fat.
2. To make the jellied aspic strain 570ml/1 pint of the cooking stock. Allow to cool and set to a jelly. Then remove any vestige of fat from the surface.
3. Put the stock and sherry into a large clean saucepan over gentle heat.
4. Place the crushed shells in a bowl, add the egg whites and whisk until frothy. Pour into the warming stock and keep whisking steadily with a balloon whisk until the mixture boils and rises. Stop whisking immediately and draw the pan off the heat. Allow the mixture to subside. Take care not to break the crust formed by the egg white.
5. Bring the aspic up to the boil again and again allow to subside. Repeat this once more (the egg white will trap the sediment in the stock and clear the aspic). Allow to cool for 10 minutes.
6. Fix a double layer of fine muslin over a clean basin and carefully strain the aspic through it, taking care to hold the

egg white crust back. When all the liquid is through (or almost all of it) allow the egg white to slip into the muslin. Then strain the aspic again – this time through both egg white crust and cloth. Do not try to hurry the process by squeezing the cloth, or murky aspic will result. Leave to cool.

7. When the jelly is on the point of setting carefully coat the meat with it. Allow to set, then repeat the process until a thin clear layer of aspic is obtained.

8. Set a thin layer of aspic in the bottom of a large serving dish. Set another ½cm/¼in layer in a clean tray or roasting tin. When set carefully cut this last aspic into tiny even dice. Put the meat on the aspic-covered serving dish and decorate with two or three small piles of diced aspic, and the cress.

Note: If the aspic is less than crystal clear it is wise not to chop it – which seems to emphasize its murkiness.

Serves 10

LAMB

Lamb Steak à la Catalane

4 lamb steaks, about 1cm/½in thick, cut across the upper leg, bones removed

Bunch of watercress

For the marinade:

290ml/½ pint olive oil

6 garlic cloves, crushed

1 tablespoon dried *or* a good handful of fresh, thyme

1 large onion, finely sliced

24 peppercorns, slightly crushed

Salt

1. Lay the lamb steaks in a roasting pan or shallow dish. Pour over the oil and add all the other marinade ingredients. Leave

the steaks to marinate for at least 8 hours, preferably 24, turning them over two or three times – unless they are left in the refrigerator, where the oil solidifies and can simply be spread with the slices of onion etc., over the top of the steaks.

2. Get a thick frying pan or griddle really hot. Alternatively preheat the grill for at least 10 minutes.

3. Remove most of the oil from the steaks and immediately put them in the hot pan, or under the grill. Grill or fry, turning once, until both sides are a good brown. Like beef steaks they can be eaten in any state from blue to well done, but if overcooked they become very tough. They are best pink in the middle. Serve immediately with a sprig or two of watercress.

Serves 4

Lamb Daube

900g/2lb lean lamb (preferably from the leg)
150ml/¼ pint stock
110g/¼lb streaky bacon
1 onion
1 tablespoon oil
55g/2oz flour

For the bouquet garni:
1 bay leaf
Sprig of thyme
Sprig of rosemary
Sprig of parsley
1 strip of orange rind

For the marinade:
290ml/½ pint red wine
1 medium onion, cut in rough slices
Stick of celery, roughly chopped
1 garlic clove
Sprig of parsley
1 bay leaf
Sprig of rosemary
4 whole allspice berries

1. Trim the lamb and cut into large pieces.
2. Prepare the marinade by mixing all the ingredients together. Lay the pieces of meat in it and leave overnight.

3. Set the oven to 150°C/300°F, gas mark 2.
4. Drain the meat from the marinade and pat dry with a cloth.
5. Dice the bacon. Chop the onion. Heat the oil in a heavy pan and in it brown the bacon and the onion. Lift out with a perforated spoon and place in a casserole.
6. Brown the meat (in the same pan) a few pieces at a time. Lay them on top of the bacon and onions.
7. Strain the marinade into the empty pan. Add the stock. Bring to the boil, scraping the bottom of the pan to loosen any sediment. Pour over the meat.
8. Tie the bouquet garni herbs and orange rind together with a piece of string and sink them in the liquid in the casserole.
9. Make a stiff dough by adding water to the flour. Put the lid on the casserole and press a band of dough around the join of lid and dish to seal them completely.
10. Cook in the oven for 3 hours. Remove the lid.
11. Lift the meat out and put it on a serving dish. Keep it warm.
12. Boil the sauce to reduce it to a syrupy consistency and pour over the meat.

Serves 4

Lamb Curry

30g/1oz clarified butter (page 236) *or* ghee

1 small onion, grated *or* chopped

675g/1½lb boneless lamb, preferably shoulder, cut into 4cm/1½in cubes

2 teaspoons turmeric

½ teaspoon ground ginger

1 garlic clove, crushed

1½ tablespoons ground coriander

¼ teaspoon salt

¼ teaspoon cayenne

425ml/¾ pint stock (preferably, but not necessarily, meat stock)

1 tablespoon fresh chopped parsley

½ tablespoon chopped fresh mint

1. Melt the butter in a large saucepan and brown the onions in it. Remove onto a plate.
2. Put the meat into the pan and brown all over. Add the turmeric, ginger, crushed garlic and half the coriander seeds. Return the onions and stir and cook for 1 minute over a low heat.
3. Season with salt and cayenne and add enough stock to come 1cm/½in below the top of the meat. This level should be kept constant. Bring to the boil, cover and simmer gently until the meat is tender (about 1½ hours), adding stock as necessary.
4. Add the remaining coriander, chopped parsley and mint. Stir, cover and simmer for 15 minutes, allowing the liquid to reduce. If at the end of cooking there appears to be too much liquid, remove the meat and reduce the liquid by boiling rapidly. The meat should be moist but not swimming in liquid.

Note I: More (or fewer) spices may be added according to taste.
Note II: Ghee is clarified fat bought in tins in Indian stores.
Serves 4

Lamb Cutlets Soubise

8 French-trimmed cutlets (pages 74–5)
Seasoned flour
Beaten egg
Dried breadcrumbs

55ml/2fl.oz oil and 15g/½oz butter
Watercress
290ml/½ pint soubise sauce (page 241)

1. Dip each cutlet into seasoned flour, shake off the excess, and brush with beaten egg. Press on the dried breadcrumbs.
2. Heat the oil in a frying pan. When hot, add the butter. Fry the cutlets for 3–4 minutes on each side, until golden brown on the outside but not hard to the touch. Drain briefly on absorbent paper to remove any grease. Serve garnished with washed watercress. Hand the soubise sauce separately.

Note: An alternative method is briefly to brown the cutlets to seal them without cooking the meat through; to cool them and then to dip them into a very thick cold soubise sauce, then into beaten egg and finally into breadcrumbs. They are then sprinkled well with melted butter and baked in a moderate oven until done (about 8 minutes for pink meat, 12 for well done).

Serves 4

Noisettes of Lamb with Onion and Mint Purée

2 best ends lamb each with
  5–7 cutlet bones
Salt and freshly ground black
  pepper
1 scant tablespoon fresh
  chopped mint

Dripping
4 tablespoons thick onion and
  mint sauce, warmed
  (page 238)
Small bunch of watercress

1. First prepare the noisettes of lamb, seasoning the meat with chopped mint, pepper and salt before rolling up. See page 75.
2. Set the oven to 180°C/350°F, gas mark 4.
3. Heat 1 tablespoon of dripping in a heavy roasting pan and over brisk heat brown the noisettes quickly on both sides. Transfer to the oven. Baste once or twice until the meat is cooked but still slightly pink inside (about 15 minutes). Alternatively the noisettes can be fried in the dripping, fast at first to seal them, then more gently for about 3 minutes on each side; or they may be plainly grilled (about 4 minutes per side).
4. Arrange on a warmed serving dish.
5. Spoon a little of the hot onion and mint sauce on top of each noisette and garnish with washed watercress.

Note: Cutlets (trimmed and shortened, but not boned into noisettes) can be used instead of the more elaborate noisettes.

Serves 4

Lamb Cutlets in Pastry

4 double best end lamb cutlets
Dripping *or* oil for frying
2 tablespoons ham, chopped
1 tablespoon tomato purée
55g/2oz mushrooms, chopped
1 tablespoon chopped fresh
  parsley

Salt and freshly ground black
  pepper
225g/½lb flour-quantity puff
  pastry (pages 293–4)
1 egg beaten with salt (egg
  wash)
Tomato sauce (page 238)

1. Set the oven to 200°C/400°F, gas mark 6.
2. Trim off the excess fat from the cutlets and fry briskly in a little dripping or oil to seal the meat. The cutlets must be brown on both sides but raw in the middle. Leave to cool on a wire rack (this prevents the fat from solidifying on the cutlet). Wipe any congealed fat off the cutlets.
3. Mix the ham, tomato purée, mushrooms and parsley together. Season with salt and pepper.
4. Roll out the pastry into a square 23 × 23cm/9 × 9in. Cut it diagonally into four triangles.
5. Put a quarter of the filling on to the centre of each triangle and put a cutlet on top of this, so that the meaty part is exactly in the middle of the piece of pastry.
6. Fold over the flaps of pastry on to the top of the cutlet, leaving the bone sticking out. Make sure the pastry 'seams' slightly overlap. Trim away any extra pastry, but keep the trimmings.
7. Turn the cutlets over and place them on a wet baking sheet. Brush the tops with egg wash. Cut 4 leaves out of the pastry trimmings and put one on each cutlet. Brush again with egg.
8. Bake in the oven for 20 minutes or until the pastry is a good brown. The meat inside will be faintly pink. For well-done cutlets cover the pastry with foil to prevent burning, and continue baking for a further 5 minutes.
9. Hand tomato sauce separately.

Note: Double cutlets are thick ones achieved by cutting through the best end so that each piece of meat has two bones to it. One bone is then carefully removed. It is vital that all fat is removed.

Serves 4

Lamb with Dill Sauce

900g/2lb lean leg of lamb, cut
　into large chunks
1 onion, sliced
1 carrot, sliced
1 tablespoon crushed dill seeds
　or 3–4 sprigs fresh dill
1 bay leaf
12 peppercorns

¼ teaspoon salt
About ¾ litre/1¼ pint chicken
　stock
1 tablespoon flour
30g/1oz butter
1 egg yolk
3 tablespoons cream
2 teaspoons lemon juice

1. Put the meat, onion, carrot, stalks (or seeds) of dill (but not the fresh leaves), bay leaf, peppercorns and salt into a saucepan.
2. Cover with the stock and bring slowly to the boil. Turn down the heat and cook as slowly as possible for 30 minutes, or until the meat is tender.
3. Lift out the cubes of meat, discarding the bay leaf and dill stalks, and put them into a casserole or serving dish. Cover to prevent drying out, and keep warm.
4. Strain the stock, and skim off all the fat. Measure the remaining liquid and make up to 500ml/¾ pint with water if necessary. Return to the saucepan.
5. Mix the butter and flour together to a smooth paste. Whisk this gradually into the hot stock, and whisk steadily until the sauce is smooth. Bring to the boil and simmer for 2 minutes.
6. Mix the egg yolk and cream in a bowl. Mix a little of the hot sauce into the cream mixture, and then stir this back into the sauce. Be careful not to boil the sauce now or the yolk will scramble. Flavour the sauce with the lemon juice and add salt and freshly ground black pepper to taste. Chop the

dill leaves if you have them, and stir in. Pour over the meat and serve at once.

Serves 4

PORK AND HAM

Jambon Persillé

One 900g/2lb piece mild
   gammon *or* unsmoked lean
   bacon
Slice of onion
1 bay leaf
½ carrot
2 parsley stalks
6 peppercorns
1·14 litres/2 pints veal stock plus
  15g/½oz gelatine if the stock
  is not jellied

2 egg shells
150ml/¼ pint dry white wine
1 scant tablespoon tarragon
  vinegar
2 egg whites
2 tablespoons finely chopped
  fresh parsley

1. Soak the bacon in cold water overnight.
2. Simmer it in fresh water (to cover) with the onion, bay leaf, carrot, parsley stalks and peppercorns until tender (about 1½ hours). Leave to cool in the liquid.
3. Put the veal stock into a large clean saucepan. If it is not set to a solid jelly sprinkle in the gelatine. Add the wine and vinegar. Put over gentle heat.
4. Place the crushed shells in a bowl, add the egg white and whisk until frothy. Pour into the warming stock and keep whisking steadily with a balloon whisk until the mixture boils and rises. Stop whisking immediately and draw the pan off the heat. Allow the mixture to subside. Take care not to break the crust formed by the egg white.

5. Bring the aspic up to the boil again and again allow to subside. Repeat this once more (the egg white will trap the sediment in the stock and clear the aspic). Allow to cool for 10 minutes.

6. Fix a double layer of fine muslin over a clean basin and carefully strain the aspic through it, taking care to hold the egg white crust back. When all the liquid is through (or almost all of it) allow the egg white to slip into the muslin. Then strain the aspic again – this time through both egg white crust and cloth. Do not try to hurry the process by squeezing the cloth, or murky aspic will result. Allow to cool.

7. Cut the ham into thick slices and then into neat strips. Arrange a neat layer in the bottom of a mould or soufflé dish which has been rinsed out with cold water.

8. Pour in enough almost-cold jelly to hold the ham in place when the jelly sets. Leave in the refrigerator to set.

9. Mix the chopped parsley into half the just-liquid jelly and pour 1cm/½in into the soufflé mould. Allow to set. Arrange a second layer of ham on top and set it in place with clear jelly.

10. Continue the layers in this way finishing with clear jelly. Chill well.

11. To turn out: dip the mould into hot water to loosen the jelly. Invert a plate over the mould and turn plate and mould over together. Give a slight shake to dislodge the jelly and remove the mould.

Note: A good but less elegant jambon persillé is made with uncleared veal jelly, chopped parsley and cubes of cooked ham simply combined in a dish and allowed to set.

Serves 6

Spiced Cherry Pork with Tarragon Dressing

This recipe was devised by Caroline Waldegrave for the party to launch Leith's School of Food and Wine.

1·35 kilos/3lb loin of pork with belly flap attached, skinned and boned
1 small can spiced stoned cherries *or* 1 small can stoned black cherries, juice of ½ lemon, pinch of ginger, stick of cinnamon, 4 cloves
1 shallot, finely chopped

15g/½oz butter
1 tablespoon vinegar
6 tablespoons fresh white breadcrumbs
1 tablespoon finely chopped fresh tarragon
Salt and freshly ground black pepper

For the tarragon cream dressing:
1 large egg
3 tablespoons tarragon vinegar
2 tablespoons caster sugar
Pinch of salt
3 tablespoons lightly whipped cream

For the garnish:
6 large tomatoes
Chopped fresh parsley

1. Remove the excess fat from the pork loin, leaving only a thin layer. Set the oven to 150°C/300°F, gas mark 2. If the cherries are not spiced, drain them and infuse them over a very gentle heat with the lemon juice, ginger, cinnamon and cloves for 20 minutes.
2. Cook the shallot gently in the butter until soft but not coloured. Mix together the cherries (with no juice), vinegar, breadcrumbs and tarragon. Season well with salt and freshly ground black pepper.
3. Lay the pork loin skinned side down on the table. Pile the stuffing on to the loin. Roll up from the thick side towards the thin flap and tie neatly, at intervals, with string.
4. Put into a roasting pan. Season with salt and pepper. Roast for 3–3½ hours or until a skewer will glide into the thickest

part of the meat easily, and clear, not pink, juices run out. Lift the pork out of the fat and allow to cool.

5. While the pork is cooling, make the tarragon cream dressing. Beat the egg in a small bowl with a wooden spoon. Add the vinegar and sugar with a pinch of salt. Set the bowl over a pan of simmering water, or place the mixture in a double boiler, over gentle heat. Beat continuously until the mixture thickens slightly. Then whisk until almost doubled in bulk. Then allow to cool. When the mixture is stone-cold, stir in the whipped cream and adjust the seasoning.

6. Slice the pork neatly. Arrange the slices on a large platter and coat with the tarragon dressing.

7. Dip the tomatoes into boiling water for 5 seconds. Peel and quarter them. Remove the seeds. If the tomatoes were very big split each piece in half lengthwise. Dip the tip of each segment into the chopped parsley and arrange down the sides of the dish. Carefully sprinkle a little salt over this garnish.

Note: If using stoned fresh cherries you will need about 225g/1½lb of them plus 2 tablespoons of sugar, and the spicing ingredients.

Serves 6

Jambalaya

450g/1lb pork fillet
2–3 tablespoons oil
1 onion, finely chopped
2 sticks celery, finely chopped
2 Frankfurters, sliced
55g/2oz garlic sausage, diced
110g/¼lb rice
290ml/½ pint chicken stock

110g/¼lb shelled prawns, preferably raw
Lemon juice
Salt and freshly ground black pepper
2 teaspoons ground ginger
½ teaspoon turmeric
½ teaspoon paprika

1. Trim the fillet and cut it into 1cm/½in cubes. Heat half the oil in a heavy saucepan and quickly fry the pork until well-browned. Lift the pieces out and put them aside. Add the

onion and celery to the saucepan, reduce the heat and fry gently until soft and evenly coloured. Lift them out.

2. Now fry the Frankfurters and garlic sausage, adding more oil if necessary and turning them until evenly browned. Lift them out. Heat the remaining oil, stir in the rice and fry, stirring constantly, until pale brown (about 10 minutes).

3. Add the chicken stock and prawns and put all the fried food back. Bring to the boil, season with a dash of lemon juice, salt, pepper, ginger, turmeric and paprika. Reduce the heat, cover and simmer until all the stock has been absorbed and the rice is cooked (about 20 minutes).

Serves 4–6

Sweet and Sour Pork

675g/1½lb lean pork
½ teaspoon salt
1 level tablespoon cornflour

Oil for deep frying
1 green pepper

For the sweet and sour sauce:

1 teaspoon cornflour
4 tablespoons water
2 tablespoons sugar
2 tablespoons vinegar
2 tablespoons tomato purée

2 tablespoons orange juice
2 tablespoons soy sauce
2 tablespoons finely chopped pineapple
½ teaspoon oil

1. Start with the sauce: blend the cornflour with the water and mix it with the sugar, vinegar, tomato purée, orange juice and soy sauce.

2. Fry the chopped pineapple in the oil for 1 minute. Add this to the sauce.

3. Cut the pork into 2cm/¾in cubes. Sprinkle with salt and toss in the cornflour.

4. Heat the oil in the fryer until a crumb will sizzle vigorously in it. Deep fry the pork for 7–8 minutes. Drain on absorbent paper.

5. Heat 1 tablespoon oil in a wide pan. Slice the green pepper and fry it quickly for 30 seconds. Lower the temperature, add the sauce and cook for 1 minute, until it thickens. Add the pork and cook together for 1 further minute.
minute.

Serves 4

VEAL

Hungarian Veal Goulash

675g/1½lb veal shoulder *or* leg
450g/1lb onions, sliced
20g/¾oz butter
290ml/½ pint veal stock
Squeeze of lemon juice
1 glass white wine
2 teaspoons tomato purée

1 tablespoon paprika
Salt and freshly ground black
   pepper
1 teaspoon flour
150ml/5 fl.oz carton soured
   cream
Fresh parsley for garnish

1. Cut the veal into 5cm/2in cubes.
2. In a large saucepan cook the onions in the butter until soft.
3. Add the veal, stock, lemon juice, wine, tomato purée, salt, pepper and paprika, bring to the boil and simmer until the meat is tender (45–60 minutes).
4. Strain the stock into a jug and place the meat in an oven-proof dish. Return the stock to the pan, mix the flour with a little of the soured cream and add some of the hot veal stock to it. Mix thoroughly and return the paste to the veal stock. Bring slowly to the boil, stirring continuously; cook for 2 minutes.
5. Check the seasoning and pour the sauce over the veal. Streak in the remaining soured cream and scatter chopped parsley on top.

Serves 4

Veal Escalopes with Rosemary

Four 170g/6oz veal escalopes, preferably from the noix (the best part of the leg) *or* from the loin *or* neck
30g/1oz butter
2 teaspoons chopped fresh rosemary

Freshly ground black pepper
1 tablespoon dry white wine *or* sherry
2 tablespoons single cream
Salt

1. If the escalopes are not very thin place them between grease-proof paper and beat out with a mallet or rolling pin.
2. Melt the butter in a frying pan and add the rosemary. Put over a moderate heat until foaming hot.
3. Season the veal with black pepper and lay in the frying pan. Cook for 2–3 minutes on each side until a very delicate brown. Take up the veal with a perforated spoon or fish slice and keep warm in a very low oven.
4. Pour the wine into the pan and heat gently, scraping the surface of the pan with a wooden spoon to incorporate the sediment. Boil up well and add the cream and salt. Pour over the veal and serve immediately.

Serves 4

Veal Marsala

Four 170g/6oz veal escalopes
30g/1oz butter
Salt and freshly ground white pepper

2 tablespoons Marsala
4 tablespoons single cream
Lemon juice

1. Put the veal escalopes between two sheets of greaseproof paper and beat out with a mallet or rolling pin.
2. Melt the butter in a frying pan and when it is foaming fry

the escalopes briskly to brown them lightly on both sides (2–3 minutes per side). Dish them on a warm plate.

3. Add the Marsala to the pan, swill it about and bring to the boil. Add the cream, season well with salt, pepper and a few drops of lemon juice.

4. Return the veal to the pan to heat through gently.

Serves 4

Veal Cordon Bleu

Four 170g/6oz veal escalopes
4 thin slices ham
4 slices Edam *or* Gruyère cheese
Seasoned flour

1 egg, beaten
Dried white breadcrumbs
Oil and butter for frying

1. With a sharp knife slice horizontally through each escalope without cutting right through. Open the meat out flat.

2. Put the slices between two sheets of polythene or greaseproof paper and with a mallet or rolling pin beat out to tenderize and flatten well.

3. Put a slice of ham and one of cheese on one side of each escalope and fold over the other to make a 'sandwich'.

4. Dip each sandwich in seasoned flour and shake off any excess. Brush with beaten egg. Be sure to brush the edges to hold it together. Press on the dried breadcrumbs.

5. Heat up ½cm/¼in oil in a frying pan and when hot add a knob of butter. When the butter bubbles lay in the veal escalopes and fry gently for 4 minutes on each side until the crumbs are brown. Drain well on absorbent paper.

Serves 4

Veal Escalopes with Ragout Fin

110g/¼lb lambs' or calves'
sweetbreads
20g/¾oz butter
1 small onion, finely chopped
30g/1oz diced bacon
55g/2oz button mushrooms,
sliced but not peeled
1 level tablespoon chopped
fresh parsley

7g/¼oz flour
150ml/¼ pint well-flavoured
chicken stock
Salt and freshly ground black
pepper
Four 170g/6oz veal escalopes
Extra butter for frying
Squeeze of lemon juice

For the garnish:
Sprig of watercress
Lemon wedges

1. Soak the sweetbreads in cold water for 4 hours, changing the water every time it becomes pink; probably four times. There should be no blood at all when the sweetbreads are ready for cooking.
2. Place them in a pan of cold water and bring up to boiling point, but do not allow to boil. Simmer for 2 minutes. Rinse under running cold water and dry well.
3. Pick over the sweetbreads, removing all the skin and membrane. Chop them coarsely.
4. Melt the butter and add the onion. Cook slowly until soft but not coloured. Add the bacon and sweetbreads and cook for 3 minutes. Stir in the mushrooms and parsley and leave over a gentle heat for 1 minute.
5. Mix in the flour and cook for 30 seconds. Remove from the heat and stir in the stock. Return to the heat and bring slowly to the boil, stirring continuously. Season with salt and pepper. Simmer for 30 seconds and set aside to cool and solidify.
6. Place the veal escalopes between two pieces of greaseproof paper or polythene and with a rolling pin or mallet beat them out until thin.
7. Divide the sweetbread mixture between the escalopes and

wrap each one up so that they look like flat parcels. Tie them up with fine cotton.

8. Melt some butter in a large frying pan and when foaming add the escalopes. Brown lightly on both sides. Reduce the temperature and cook slowly for 4–5 minutes. Lift out the escalopes on to a warmed serving plate.
9. Increase the heat under the frying pan and brown the butter, adding a squeeze of lemon juice. Pour over the escalopes and serve garnished with watercress and lemon wedges.

Serves 4

Vitello Tonnato

900/2lb boned loin of veal
1 tablespoon oil
1 glass vermouth
Bouquet garni (1 parsley stalk, 1 bay leaf, sprig of thyme)
Salt and freshly ground black pepper

For the decoration:
570ml/1 pint aspic jelly (pages 229–30)
4 large ripe tomatoes
290ml/½ pint French dressing (page 237)

For the tuna mousse:
1 small can tuna fish
30g/1oz butter
150ml/¼ pint béchamel sauce (page 240)
1 teaspoon tomato purée
3 tablespoons double cream, lightly whipped
Squeeze of lemon juice

1. Set the oven to 190°C/375°F, gas mark 5.
2. Season the veal and tie it up into a neat roll. In a heavy pan or roasting tin brown it evenly on all sides in the oil over a high heat.
3. Add the vermouth and bouquet garni. Cover and bake in the oven until tender (about 1–1½ hours).
4. Meanwhile prepare the tuna mousse: pound the tuna (without its oil) well with the butter. Beat in the béchamel and stir

in the tomato purée and lightly whipped cream. Add a squeeze of lemon juice. Taste and add more salt and pepper if necessary.

5. Remove the veal when cooked and allow it to cool. When cold slice evenly and sandwich the slices together with the tuna mousse in a loaf-like shape, taking care that the tuna mixture is not squeezed out of the top. Leave in the refrigerator until quite firm.

6. Melt the aspic jelly, then allow to cool to the point of setting. Brush or spoon a layer carefully over the vitello. Chill very well and brush again with aspic jelly so that the veal looks very shiny. Carefully lift on to a serving dish.

7. If there is any aspic left over set it in a shallow tray, then cut it into tiny dice. Use to surround the veal.

8. Dip the tomatoes into boiling water for 5 seconds. Peel and slice them. Arrange them around the veal, and spoon the French dressing over.

Note: If the aspic is less than crystal clear it is wise not to chop it – which seems to emphasize its murkiness.

Serves 6

OFFAL

Brawn

1 pig's head, split in two
55g/2oz saltpetre
Coarse pure salt
8 lambs' tongues
2 pigs' trotters
2 bay leaves
2 onions, peeled and sliced
2 carrots, peeled and sliced
2 parsley stalks

6 peppercorns
Juice of 1 lemon
2 small turnips, peeled and
  sliced
12 whole allspice
2 whole cloves
Blade of mace
Pinch of paprika, salt and
  pepper

1. Prepare the head: cut off the ears, remove the brains and eyes and wash the head thoroughly in plenty of water. Reserve the ears and brains.
2. Rub plenty of salt over the head and leave it to drain for 24 hours.
3. Mix together the saltpetre with 55g/2oz of salt and rub it all over the head. Leave to stand for 3 days.
4. Place in a pan of cold water and leave in a refrigerator or larder to soak for 2 days.
5. Place the head with the ears and brains, lambs' tongues and pigs' trotters in a large saucepan and cover with cold water. Bring slowly to the boil, skimming off froth or fat carefully. Simmer for 2 hours or until the meat will easily leave the bone.
6. Lift out the head, tongues and trotters. Strip off all the flesh from the head.
7. Return the bones to the cooking liquid in the pan with the bay leaves, onions, carrots, parsley stalks, peppercorns, lemon juice, turnips, allspice, cloves and mace. Boil, skimming as necessary, until the stock has reduced to 1·14 litres/2 pints (about 45 minutes). Strain and allow to become completely cold.

8. Skin the ear, remove the membranes from the brain and chop both roughly. Skin the tongues and dice them finely. Put all the meat in a large bowl and mix it together thoroughly by hand, discarding any pieces of gristle.
9. Remove the fat from the stock. Warm the stock until just melted and strain through a J-cloth or muslin. Bring to the boil and stir in the prepared meat.
10. Wet a 1·14 litres/2 pint tin mould and pour in the brawn. Cover with a wooden board, or heavy flat object. (This is to prevent the meat floating above the surface of the liquid.)
11. Allow to cool, then refrigerate until set.
12. To serve, dip the mould briefly in hot water, and turn out on to a serving plate.

Serves 10

Veal Kidneys Robert

150ml/¼ pint dry white wine
450g/1lb veal kidneys
55g/2oz butter
2 teaspoons flour
1 teaspoon made English
  mustard
1 dessertspoon chopped fresh
  parsley
Squeeze of lemon juice
Salt and freshly ground black
  pepper
2 tablespoons cream

1. Put the wine in a saucepan and boil until reduced by half.
2. Remove the membranes and cores from the kidneys, and slice them fairly finely.
3. Fry a handful of kidney slices at a time in hot butter, shaking the pan until the kidneys are brown but still pink inside.
4. Return all the kidneys to the pan and stir in the flour. Cook for 30 seconds and then add the mustard, wine, parsley, lemon juice and seasoning. Bring to the boil, stirring continuously. Stir in the cream. Taste, adding salt and pepper if necessary.
5. Turn into a warm dish and sprinkle with chopped parsley.

Serves 2–3

Braised Lambs' Hearts

4 lambs' hearts (total weight 675g/1½lb)
1 tablespoon dripping
290ml/½ pint good strong stock
1 bay leaf
1 parsley stalk
Salt and freshly ground black pepper

For the stuffing:
15g/½oz butter
1 onion, finely chopped
110g/¼lb breadcrumbs
125g/4½oz grated carrot
1 teaspoon cumin powder
1½ tablespoons finely chopped fresh mint
1 teaspoon grated root ginger
1 egg

For the mirepoix:
1 tablespoon finely diced celery
1 tablespoon finely diced onion
1 tablespoon finely diced carrot

For the gravy:
2 tablespoons port
½ teaspoon redcurrant jelly

1. Wash the hearts, removing the veins and arteries. Leave the hearts to soak in cold water for 1 hour.
2. Put the hearts into a saucepan, cover with cold water and bring slowly to the boil. Drain and pat dry.
3. Prepare the stuffing: melt the butter and add the onion, cook until soft but not coloured. Combine with all the stuffing ingredients except the egg. Season with salt and pepper and add just enough beaten egg to bind. Too much egg will make the stuffing too solid.
4. Set the oven to 150°C/300°F, gas mark 2.
5. Fill the heart cavities with the stuffing.
6. Heat the dripping in a large heavy pan with a lid and brown the hearts all over.
7. Remove the hearts and put in the mirepoix ingredients. Cook slowly in the fat until soft and lightly coloured. Return the hearts and pour on the stock. Add the bay leaf and parsley stalk and season well with salt and pepper. Bring to the boil, cover with a piece of greased paper and the lid and place in the oven.

8. Bake for 2½–3 hours or until tender, basting occasionally and topping up with extra stock as necessary. The mirepoix must not become at all dry.

9. When they are tender remove the hearts and turn off the oven. Put the hearts on a serving dish. Slice them carefully or leave whole, as preferred. Keep warm, well covered.

10. Now make the gravy: strain the cooking juices into a saucepan. If very thin, reduce by boiling rapidly to a syrupy consistency, or thicken by whisking 1–2 teaspoons of beurre manié (flour and butter mixed in equal proportions to a paste) into the simmering liquid.

11. Add the port and boil up well. Stir in the redcurrant jelly. Taste and season with salt and pepper. Spoon the gravy over the meat.

Serves 4

6
Poultry and Game

CHICKEN AND TURKEY

Chicken à la King

One 1·8 kilos/4lb chicken, not
  trussed
1 small onion, sliced
1 small carrot, sliced
2 bay leaves
Few parsley stalks
Salt
6 peppercorns
45g/1½oz butter
1 onion, finely sliced
1 small green pepper, sliced
1 canned pimento, sliced

110g/¼lb mushrooms, sliced
45g/1½oz flour
1 tablespoon sherry
150ml/¼ pint milk
3 tablespoons single cream
Freshly ground black pepper

To serve:
Boiled rice

1. Clean the chicken. Put a large pan of water on to simmer with the sliced onion, sliced carrot, bay leaves, parsley stalks, salt and peppercorns. Add the whole chicken, breast side up. Cover and simmer until tender (about 1 hour). To test if the chicken is cooked push a skewer into the thickest part of the thigh. It should glide in easily. Also the drumstick should be loose and wobbly.

2. Remove the chicken from the stock and allow both of them to become completely cold (see note below).

3. Skim the fat off the stock. Reduce the stock by rapid boiling until it measures 425ml/¾ pint.

4. Skin the chicken and remove the bones.
5. Melt the butter, add the sliced onion and cook gently for 2 minutes. Add the green pepper and cook for 1 further minute. Add the pimento, mushrooms and flour and cook, stirring, for 1 minute.
6. Remove the pan from the heat and add the reduced stock. Mix well and return the pan to the heat. Bring slowly to the boil, stirring continuously. Add the sherry. Simmer 1 minute.
7. Add the milk and cream and reheat without boiling. Season with salt and pepper.
8. Add the chicken in large pieces and allow to warm through without boiling for 2 minutes.
9. Serve with boiled rice.

Note: Although cooling a chicken in the liquid it was cooked in gives a very juicy bird, it is a dangerous practice as, if the liquid does not cool rapidly the chicken will be kept at a warm temperature that encourages the breeding of salmonella and other dangerous bacteria. But the bird may be safely cooled if the pan is stood in a bowl of cold water and put in the sink, with the cold tap running into the cold water surrounding the hot pan. This will speed up the cooling process. If the chicken is lifted out of the liquid to cool, put it on a dish and loosely cover it with a piece of plastic film, foil, or a cloth (not a lid which would trap the heat and create an incubating temperature).

Serves 6

Tarragon Chicken

One 1·8 kilos/4lb roasting
  chicken
55g/2oz butter
Slice of lemon
4 sprigs fresh tarragon

150ml/¼ pint chicken stock
20g/¾oz flour, sifted
150ml/¼ pint double cream
Salt and pepper

1. Heat the oven to 200°C/400°F, gas mark 6. Wipe inside and

outside of chicken. Place inside the cavity a small nut of the butter, the lemon slice and half the tarragon. Season inside and out with salt and freshly milled pepper.

2. Melt the remaining butter in a casserole the size of the chicken and brown all sides of the bird in it. Place the giblets (except the liver) in the casserole, pour over the stock, cover with a lid and place in the oven. Leave to cook for 1½ hours or until the juice runs out clear, rather than pink, when the thigh is pierced with a skewer.

3. Take the chicken out of the casserole, draining the juices back in. Joint the chicken neatly and put the pieces in a covered dish. Keep warm.

4. Skim all the fat from the stock. Mix 1 tablespoon of this fat with the flour in a teacup. When thoroughly blended pour more of the stock into the cup and mix well. Return this to the casserole and stir over direct heat until boiling.

5. Strain into a clean saucepan and add the remaining leaves of tarragon. Simmer for 1–2 minutes, then stir in the cream. Taste and season if necessary.

6. Pour over the chicken joints and serve.

Serves 4

Chicken Maryland

One 1·4 kilos/3lb chicken
1 tablespoon seasoned flour
1 egg, beaten
1 tablespoon dry white
   breadcrumbs
55g/2oz butter

To garnish:
Sweetcorn fritters (page 138)
8 rashers bacon
4 bananas
30g/1oz butter
Oil for frying
Bunch of watercress

1. Joint the chicken into eight pieces.
2. Dip each piece in seasoned flour, brush with beaten egg and coat with dry white breadcrumbs, pressing them on firmly.
3. Melt 55g/2oz butter in a large sauté pan and when foaming, add the chicken pieces, a few at a time, and fry both sides to

a good brown. Reduce the heat and cook uncovered for a further 20–25 minutes.

4. Meanwhile prepare the garnishes: make the sweetcorn fritters and set aside until ready to fry them.

5. Cut the rind off the bacon rashers, stretch the rashers on a board with the back of a knife (this prevents shrinkage), roll up loosely and thread on two skewers. Set aside until ready to grill.

6. Peel the bananas and split them lengthways. Dip in seasoned flour and set aside until ready to fry.

7. When the chicken pieces are cooked and tender, transfer them to a cool oven to keep warm, but do not cover them.

8. Light the grill. You now have to fry the bananas in the butter in one frying pan, the sweetcorn fritters in oil in a second pan and at the same time grill the bacon until crisp. So watch everything carefully, turning the food over as one side cooks. Drain well when cooked.

9. Arrange the chicken on a large serving platter and garnish with the corn fritters, bacon rolls and fried bananas. Arrange a small bunch of watercress on the dish and serve at once.

Serves 4–6

Chicken St Menehould

1 leek	140g/5oz butter
2 tablespoons white wine	85g/3oz flour
1 onion, sliced	Salt and pepper
1 garlic clove	1 tablespoon fresh chopped
1 bay leaf	parsley
6 peppercorns	Breadcrumbs
Pinch of thyme	Oil for deep frying
570ml/1 pint water	Beaten egg
One 1·8 kilos/4lb chicken	2 parsley stalks
150ml/¼ pint milk	

1. Slice the white part of the leek. Put the leek, white wine,

onion, garlic, bay leaf, peppercorns, thyme and 570ml/1 pint of water with the chicken into a saucepan. Cover and poach until tender (about 1½ hours). Remove the chicken, set aside and allow to cool. Carefully joint the chicken and remove the bones and skin from the joints. Skim the fat from the stock.

2. Boil the stock rapidly until you have about 150ml/¼ pint left. Strain and add the milk.

3. Melt 85g/3oz of the butter, add the flour and cook for 1 minute. Remove from the heat and beat in the milky stock. Return to the heat and bring slowly up to the boil, stirring continually, until you have a very thick white sauce panade. Check the seasoning and beat in the chopped parsely. Allow to cool.

4. Dry the chicken joints on absorbent paper. Spread them all over with the thick white sauce and roll them in the breadcrumbs. Chill in the refrigerator until firm.

5. Heat the fat in the fryer until a crumb will sizzle gently in it. Mix the egg with a little salt and use to coat the chicken joints well. Press on more breadcrumbs.

6. Fry the chicken until golden brown. To test if the chicken is hot right through, press a skewer into the centre, hold it there for 30 seconds and then lay the skewer on the palm of your hand. It should be hot rather than warm.

7. Drain well on absorbent paper and serve at once.

Serves 4

Poussins with Pernod

Four 450g/1lb one-portion
   poussins (baby chickens)
Seasoned flour
30g/1oz butter
2 shallots, finely chopped
5 tablespoons Pernod

For the garnish:
Lemon wedges
Chopped fresh parsley

1. Bone the chickens completely (see page 83).

2. Put the chickens between two pieces of greaseproof paper and flatten them with a wooden mallet or rolling pin.

3. Dip them in seasoned flour. Shake off the excess flour.

4. Melt the butter in a large sauté pan. When foaming brown the poussins for about 4 minutes on each side. Reduce the temperature and add the shallots. Continue to sauté the poussins for about 4 further minutes on each side.

5. Increase the temperature and pour in the Pernod. When hot set the alcohol alight with a match and turn off the heat. When the flames die away, scrape the pan with a spoon to loosen any sediment stuck to the bottom.

6. Take out the poussins; arrange on a warm serving dish. Boil up the pan juices and pour, sizzling, over the poussins. Garnish with lemon wedges and parsley and serve immediately.

Note: Two-portion poussins are called 'double' poussins, one-portion birds 'single'.

Serves 4

Boned Stuffed Poussin

A very small poussin normally serves one, but if it is boned and stuffed it will be enough for two not over-hungry people.

2 poussins
85g/3oz butter
1 large onion, finely chopped
110g/¼lb button mushrooms, sliced
55g/2oz fresh white breadcrumbs
2 tablespoons finely chopped fresh parsley
Grated rind of ½ lemon
Salt and freshly ground black pepper

About 1 tablespoon beaten egg
170g/6oz mixed chopped onion, carrot, turnip and celery (mirepoix)
290ml/½ pint chicken stock (made from bones of the poussin)
1 bay leaf
Bunch of watercress

1. Bone the poussins without removing the legs or wings (see page 83).
2. Make the stuffing: melt 30g/1oz of the butter, add the onion and cook slowly until soft but not coloured. Add the mushrooms and cook for 1 further minute.
3. Mix the onions and mushrooms with the breadcrumbs, parsley and lemon rind. Season with salt and pepper and add enough egg to just bind the mixture together. (Do not add too much egg or the stuffing will be heavy.)
4. Lay the poussins, skin side down, flat on the table top. Divide the stuffing between them and sew them up using cotton or very fine string. Try to shape them to their original form.
5. Melt half the remaining butter in a flameproof casserole. When it is foaming add the poussins and brown lightly all over, then remove them from the pan.
6. Add the remaining butter to the casserole with the mirepoix of diced vegetables. Fry until the vegetables are lightly brown.
7. Set the poussins on top of the vegetables. Add the chicken stock, bay leaf, salt and pepper. Bring to the boil, cover and simmer slowly for 40–50 minutes.
8. When the poussins are cooked – when pierced with a skewer the juices that run out should be clear, not pink – place them on a plate and remove the cotton or string. Keep warm.
9. Liquidize the cooking liquor and vegetables or press through a sieve to make a sauce. Reheat, checking the seasoning. Spoon a little sauce over the poussins and hand the rest separately in a warmed gravy boat. Garnish with watercress.

Note: For a thinner, more elegant sauce simply press the vegetables to extract most of their juices, but discard the vegetables. If necessary boil the sauce to reduce to a syrupy consistency.

Serves 4

Jambonneaux de Poulet

55g/2oz cooked ham, minced
55g/2oz cooked chicken livers, mashed
55g/2oz butter, softened
Salt and freshly ground black pepper
2 legs taken from 1 large chicken
45g/1½oz butter for frying

110g/4oz mixed finely chopped onion, celery and carrot (mirepoix)
75ml/4–5 tablespoons Madeira
225ml/8 fl.oz chicken stock
1 bay leaf
Sprig of watercress

1. Beat together the ham, chicken livers and softened butter. Taste and add pepper or salt if needed.
2. Remove the bone from the chicken legs without splitting the skin, working carefully from the thick end. Stuff the ham mixture into the boned-out chicken legs. With a trussing needle and fine string sew up the chicken joints so that they resemble miniature hams.
3. Melt half the butter in a flameproof casserole. When it is foaming and hot add the chicken legs and brown lightly all over, then remove them from the pan. Add the remaining butter to the casserole with the mirepoix of vegetables. Fry until the vegetables are lightly brown.
4. Place the jambonneaux (chicken legs) on top of the vegetables. Heat the Madeira in a small pan or ladle held over the flame. When hot set it alight with a match and pour it, flaming, into the pan. Add the chicken stock, bay leaf, salt and pepper. Bring to the boil, cover and simmer slowly for 1 hour.
5. When the chicken is cooked – when pierced with a skewer the juices that run out should be clear, not pink – remove to a plate and keep warm.
6. Strain the cooking liquor and press the vegetables to extract most of the juice. Reduce to a syrupy consistency, checking the seasoning. Hand the sauce separately in a warmed gravy boat. Garnish the jambonneaux with a sprig of watercress.

Serves 2

Boned Stuffed Chicken

One 1·8 kilos/4lb chicken
A little oil
1 teaspoon butter
1 bay leaf
425ml/¾ pint chicken stock
(made from the chicken
bones)

For the mirepoix:
1 small onion, finely chopped
1 small carrot, finely chopped
Stick of celery, finely chopped
Bunch of watercress

For the stuffing:
15g/½oz butter
1 small onion, finely chopped
225g/½lb sausage-meat
2 tablespoons fresh white
breadcrumbs
1 small apple, chopped
Pinch of fresh sage
1 egg
Salt and freshly ground black
pepper

1. Bone the chicken completely, including the legs and wings (see page 83).
2. Make the stuffing: melt the butter, add the onion and cook until soft but not coloured. Mix together the sausage-meat, onion, breadcrumbs, apple, sage and egg and season well with salt and pepper.
3. Use this stuffing to fill the boned chicken. Draw up the sides and sew together with cotton or fine string.
4. Set the oven to 190°C/375°F, gas mark 5. Heat the oil in a large casserole dish, add the butter. When foaming add the chicken and brown all over. Remove the bird, reduce the heat and then lightly brown the mirepoix of vegetables.
5. Return the chicken to the casserole, add the bay leaf and stock and season well with salt and pepper. Cover and put into the oven for 1½ hours.
6. When the chicken is cooked remove it on to a warmed serving plate and remove the string or cotton.

7. Meanwhile make the sauce. Skim the fat from the top of the cooking juices and liquidize or sieve the remaining liquid and mirepoix. Return this to a rinsed-out saucepan and boil rapidly until a syrupy consistency is reached. Pour into a warmed gravy boat. Garnish the chicken with a small bunch of watercress.

Note: For a thinner, more elegant sauce, simply press the vegetables to extract most of their juices, but discard the vegetables. If necessary, boil the sauce to reduce to a syrupy consistency.

Serves 6

Chicken Chaudfroid

One 1·8 kilos/4lb chicken,
    not trussed
1 onion, sliced
½ carrot

2 bay leaves
Sprig of parsley
6 peppercorns
½ teaspoon salt

For the aspic jelly:
860ml/1½ pints chicken stock
55g/2oz gelatine
5 tablespoons white wine
5 tablespoons sherry
1 tablespoon wine vinegar
3 egg whites
3 egg shells, crushed

For the garnish:
Fine slices cooked button
    mushroom *or* truffle *or* fresh
    tarragon leaves
1 punnet mustard *or* cress

For the chaudfroid sauce:
1 bay leaf
4 peppercorns
Slice of onion
Blade of mace
Sprig of parsley
425ml/¾ pint milk
30g/1oz butter
30g/1oz flour
Salt
150ml/¼ pint chicken aspic
15g/½oz gelatine
5 tablespoons cream

This is cold chicken coated with a white sauce, glazed with aspic jelly, and garnished with slices of truffle or mushroom. The chicken should be cooked the day before serving because the stock in which it is cooked becomes the aspic jelly.

1. On the first day place the chicken in a saucepan, just cover with cold water, add the vegetables, herbs, peppercorns and salt. Bring to the boil, cover and simmer gently until the chicken is tender (about 1¼ hours). When it is cooked a skewer will glide easily into the thigh, and the drumstick should feel loose.

2. Remove the bird from the pan (but see *Note II*), allow it to cool, (loosely covered with foil) and place it in the refrigerator overnight. Strain the stock and leave it to cool. If possible, refrigerate it (this will set the fat and make it easier to remove the next day).

3. The next day remove all the fat from the chicken stock. Put the stock (which should be about 860ml/1½ pints) and gelatine into a clean pan. Add the wine, sherry and vinegar. Put over a gentle heat.

4. Place the crushed shells in a bowl, add the egg white and whisk until frothy. Pour into the warming stock and keep whisking steadily with balloon whisk until the mixture boils and rises. Stop whisking immediately, and draw the pan off the heat. Allow the mixture to subside. Take care not to break the crust formed by the egg white.

5. Bring the aspic up to the boil again and again allow to subside. Repeat this once more (the egg white will trap the sediment in the stock and clear the aspic). Allow to cool for 10 minutes.

6. Fix a double layer of fine muslin over a clean basin and carefully strain the aspic through it, taking care to hold the egg white crust back. When all the liquid is through (or almost all of it) allow the egg white to slip into the muslin. Then strain the aspic again – this time through both egg white crust and cloth. Do not try to hurry the process by squeezing the cloth, or murky aspic will result.

7. Make the chaudfroid sauce: place the bay leaf, peppercorns,

onion slice, mace and parsley sprig in a saucepan with the milk. Set over a gentle heat and bring slowly to the boil. Leave to cool for 10 minutes.

8. Melt the butter, add the flour and cook for 1 minute. Draw off the heat and slowly, stirring all the time, strain over the milk. Return the pan to the heat and bring slowly up to the boil, stirring continually until you have a slightly thickened shiny sauce. Season well with salt and simmer gently for 2–3 minutes.

9. In a small pan put 150ml/$\frac{1}{4}$ pint of the aspic, and sprinkle on the gelatine. Allow to soak for 10 minutes then heat gently until clear and warm. Stir this into the white sauce with the cream. Taste and add more salt if necessary. The sauce must be very smooth and shiny: it can be strained through a tammy cloth or strainer or whizzed in a liquidizer to give it a good sheen. Stir the sauce as it cools and begins to set. When it is the consistency of thick cream it is ready to use for coating.

10. To prepare the chicken, skin and joint it very neatly into four or eight pieces, removing the wing tips and drumstick knuckle. Place the pieces on a wire rack with a tray underneath.

11. Coat each chicken joint very carefully with the nearly set chaudfroid sauce. Allow to set and if necessary give it a second coating, scraping extra sauce (which will need reheating slightly to return it to coating consistency) from the tray underneath the wire rack.

12. When nearly set arrange the slices of mushroom or truffle or the tarragon leaves in a formal simple pattern on each chicken piece. Allow to set.

13. Coat with some of the cool but still liquid aspic. Allow to set. Give a second and perhaps third coating, allowing each coating to set before attempting the next.

14. Pour the remaining aspic on to a shallow tray. Allow to set, then cut it into neat dice. Use it to cover a large flat serving dish and make a slight dome in the centre. Arrange the chicken chaudfroid around this and surround with small clumps of mustard or cress.

Note I: Chaudfroid is classically decorated with sliced truffles. These are delicious if fresh but disappointing and expensive if bought in tins. Mushrooms make an inexpensive and satisfactory substitute. Fresh tarragon leaves are pretty and give the dish a delicious flavour.

Note II: The chicken is undeniably juicier if it is cooled in the cooking stock, rather than out of it. But the cooling must be rapid (prolonged lukewarm temperatures lead to the growth of bacteria). For this reason the recipe suggests cooling stock and bird separately. To get the best of both worlds, however, the whole suacepan, containing chicken and stock, can be stood in a large bowl of cold water in the sink, with the cold tap keeping the water refreshed and cold. In this way cooling will be very quick.

Note III: If the aspic is less than crystal clear it is wise not to chop it – which seems to emphasize its murkiness.

Serves 4

Vinegar Chicken

One 1·8 kilos/4lb chicken, jointed into 8 pieces
30g/1oz butter
5 large garlic cloves, unpeeled
5 tablespoons wine vinegar
290ml/½ pint dry white wine
2 tablespoons brandy
2 teaspoons pale French mustard
1 heaped teaspoon tomato purée
290ml/½ pint very fresh double cream
2 tomatoes, peeled and seeded

1. Heat the butter and in it brown the chicken pieces, skin side first. Add the unpeeled garlic and cover the pan. Cook gently for 20 minutes or until the chicken is tender. Pour off all but a tablespoon of the fat.
2. Add the vinegar to the pan, stirring well and scraping any sediment from the bottom. Boil rapidly until the liquid is reduced to about two tablespoons. Lift out the chicken and keep warm.

3. Add the wine, brandy, mustard and tomato purée to the remaining vinegar in the pan, mix well and boil to a thick sauce (about 5 minutes at a fast boil).
4. In a small heavy-bottomed saucepan boil the cream until reduced by half, stirring frequently to prevent burning. Take off the heat and fit a small wire sieve over the saucepan. Push the vinegar sauce through this, pressing the garlic cloves well to extract their pulp.
5. Mix the sauce and add salt and pepper as necessary. Cut the tomato into thin strips and stir into the sauce. Arrange the chicken on a hot serving dish, and spoon over the sauce.

Note I: The deliciousness of this dish – and it *is* delicious – depends on the vigorous reduction of the vinegar and wine. If the acids are not properly boiled down the sauce is too sharp.

Note II: Five cloves of garlic seems a lot. But the resulting smooth sauce does not taste particularly strongly of garlic.

Serves 4

Christmas Turkey Stuffed with Ham

One 2·3 kilos/5lb piece of boiled bacon *or* ham, skinned
One 6·7 kilos/15lb turkey, boned (page 83)

For roasting:
55g/2oz butter
1 onion, sliced
3 bay leaves
2 parsley stalks
425ml/¾ pint water

For the gravy:
About 2 tablespoons flour
290ml/½ pint turkey stock
Bunch of watercress

For the stuffing:
30g/1oz butter
1 large onion, finely chopped
900g/2lb belly of pork, minced
450g/1lb unsweetened canned chestnut purée *or* mashed cooked fresh chestnuts
225g/½lb fresh white breadcrumbs
2 eggs lightly beaten
1 teaspoon dried sage
2 tablespoons chopped parsley
Salt and freshly ground black pepper

1. Set the oven to 200°C/400°F, gas mark 6.
2. To make the stuffing, melt the butter, add the onion and cook until soft but not coloured.
3. Once cold mix with all the other stuffing ingredients.
4. Open the turkey out flat on a board, skin side down. Spread the stuffing on the turkey and put the ham or bacon on top.
5. Draw up the sides and sew together with needle and fine string. Turn the bird right side up and try to push it into an even, rounded shape.
6. Smear the butter all over the turkey and put it into a roasting tin. Add the giblets (except the liver) and the neck. Add the onion, bay leaves and parsley stalks. Pour in the water. If the turkey looks too flat, wedge the sides with bread tins to hold it in shape.
7. Roast the bird for 1 hour, lower the temperature to 180°C/350°F, gas mark 4 and roast for a further 3 hours. Baste occasionally as it cooks and cover with foil or grease-proof paper if it is browning too much.
8. When the turkey is cooked (that is when a skewer will glide through the thigh easily) lift it on to a serving dish and keep warm while you make the gravy.
9. Lift the pan with its juices on to the top of the cooker. Pour off as much fat as possible.
10. Stir in (using a wooden spoon or wire whisk) enough flour to absorb the remaining fat. Add 290ml/½ pint stock and stir until the sauce boils. Strain into a warmed gravy boat.
11. Garnish the turkey with the watercress and hand the gravy separately.

Note I: This turkey is delicious served cold with a herby mayonnaise.

Note II: The turkey may be stuffed the day before cooking. If this is done care should be taken that both turkey and stuffing are well chilled before the bird is stuffed. Refrigerate until ready to cook.

Note III: If the turkey is roasted covered in 2 layers of muslin (or J-cloths) completely saturated in melted butter, there is no need for basting during cooking, and when the cloths are removed the bird will be brown and crisp.

Serves 20

DUCK AND GOOSE

Pressed Duck

Pressed duck, requiring an expensive duck press, expensive ingredients, skill, timing and showmanship, is seldom made today. But it is a remarkably fine dish, and is the speciality of the famous Tour d'Argent restaurant in Paris. For true pressed duck Rouen duckling is used – its characteristic red flesh and gamey flavour is due to the method of killing: the bird is smothered rather than bled, so loses none of its blood before cooking. Unfortunately dangerous toxins can develop in ducks killed by this method, so they should be eaten very fresh, preferably on the day of killing.

In England, Aylesbury ducks, which have certain similarities to the Rouen breed, although they are killed by the conventional bleeding method, are used. A little demi-glace sauce may be added to the final sauce to make up for the extra juices produced by the Rouen duck but lacking in the Aylesbury.

Two 2·3 kilos/5lb very fresh ducklings

Salt and freshly ground black pepper

Pinch of ground cloves

150ml/$\frac{1}{4}$ pint good red wine

3 tablespoons brandy

150ml/$\frac{1}{4}$ pint demi-glaçe sauce (page 244) if using Aylesbury duck

1 tablespoon butter

1. Heat the oven to 450°F/230°C, gas mark 8.
2. Clean the ducks, prick all over and sprinkle with salt. Roast for 15 minutes only. Remove from the oven.

3. In classic pressed duck the legs are not used. But if they are to be used proceed as follows: remove the legs (which will still be raw), make a few cuts on the underside, and season with salt, pepper and ground cloves. Brush with a very little melted butter. Heat the grill, then grill the legs on both sides until cooked. Keep warm.

4. Remove each side of the breast from the carcases in one piece. Set them aside and chop the carcasses up roughly, putting them and any juices into a bowl.

5. The rest of the preparation and cooking should be done in the dining room, using board, knife, duck press, sauté pan, small saucepan and flame lamp or hot plate. You also need to have a napkin, the brandy, wine, butter, duck carcasses, metal serving dish, and of course the duck breasts and legs (if used) close at hand. But the whole dish can be made as well, if less dramatically, in the kitchen.

6. Reduce the wine to 2 tablespoons, by rapid boiling.

7. Cut the breasts across into small pieces and lay them on the serving dish.

8. Put the duck carcasses, the reduced wine and salt, pepper and a pinch of cloves into the press. Put the sauté pan under the spout and press well to extract all the juices. Put the sauté pan over direct heat and add the brandy and demi-glaçe sauce if used; heat carefully without boiling. Taste, add more salt and pepper if necessary, and finally beat in the butter bit by bit.

9. Put the legs (if used) at each end of the serving dish and put over direct heat to warm through. Pour over the hot sauce and serve at once.

Serves 4–6

Roast Duck with Cherry or Apple Sauce

One 3 kilos/6½lb duck
Salt and freshly ground black
  pepper
½ onion
½ orange

30g/1oz flour
290ml/½ pint duck *or* strong
  chicken stock
Apple sauce (page 239) *or*
  cherry sauce (page 245)

1. Set the oven to 190°C/375°F, gas mark 5. Wipe the duck clean, inside and out. Season the cavity well with salt and pepper. Place the onion and orange inside the duck. Prick the skin all over and sprinkle with salt.
2. Put the duck upside down, on a rack in a roasting pan and roast for 45 minutes. Then pour off the fat. Turn the duck over and continue roasting until cooked (about 45 minutes). Test by sticking a skewer into the thigh – if the juices come out pink the duck needs further cooking.
3. Tip the juices from the cavity into a bowl and reserve them. Joint the duck into six pieces and arrange the joints on a serving dish; or leave whole for carving at the table. In any event keep it warm, without covering (this would spoil the crisp skin).
4. To make the gravy pour off all the fat in the roasting pan except a tablespoon. Stir the remaining spoon of fat and any juices over a low heat, scraping the bottom of the pan to loosen all the sediment. Whisk in the flour, add the juices from inside the duck and the stock and whisk until smooth. Simmer, stirring, for 1 minute. Taste and season.
5. Pour the gravy into a warmed gravy boat. Fill a second gravy boat with hot or cold apple or cherry sauce.

Serves 4

Cold Boned Goose with Aspic

1 medium-sized goose
1 carrot, chopped
1 onion, chopped
2 leeks, chopped
Stick of celery, chopped
6 peppercorns
Bouquet garni (bay leaf, parsley stalk, mace and thyme)

For the aspic:
150ml/¼ pint dry cider
55g/2oz gelatine
2 egg shells, crushed
2 egg whites

For the garnish:
1 small orange
Bunch of watercress

For the stuffing:
30g/1oz butter
1 onion, fincly chopped
4 dates, finely chopped
170g/6oz sausage-meat
2 tablespoons chopped mint
225g/½lb dessert apples, peeled and chopped
225g/½lb cooking apples, peeled and chopped
85g/3oz breadcrumbs
Salt and freshly ground black pepper
1 egg, beaten

1. Bone the goose completely, including the legs and wings (see page 83).
2. To make the stock for the aspic place the goose bones and giblets (except the liver) in a large pan with the chopped carrots, onion, leeks, celery, peppercorns and bouquet garni. Bring to the boil, cover and simmer for 1 hour.
3. To make the stuffing melt the butter, add the onion and cook slowly until soft but not coloured. Add the apples and cook for 1 further minute. Allow to cool.
4. Stir the apple and onion mixture into the breadcrumbs, dates and sausage-meat. Add the mint and season well. Add enough beaten egg just to bind the mixture together.
5. Lay the goose, skin side down, on a wooden board. Remove any excess fat. Pile on the stuffing and roll up the goose into a neat roll, making sure that all the untidy ends are tucked

in. Sew up very neatly using a needle and fine string. Wrap the goose in a piece of muslin or a clean tea-towel and tie it securely.

6. Strain the stock and taste for seasoning. Put the goose into a heavy saucepan or fish kettle and pour on the stock. Bring to the boil, cover tightly and simmer slowly for 2 hours. Turn the goose over once during the cooking. Drain, reserving the stock for the aspic.

7. As soon as the goose is cool enough to handle tighten the wrappings, and put on a plate. When cold, refrigerate.

8. Pour the stock into a bowl and leave to cool overnight. If the stock can be transferred to the refrigerator once it is cold so much the better – it will set the fat and make removing it easier. Next day lift or skim off any fat from the goose stock. It must be absolutely fat-free.

9. Put 860ml/1½ pints of the goose stock (make up with water if not enough) into a very large saucepan with the cider and gelatine. Put over a gentle heat.

10. Place the crushed shells in a bowl, add the egg white and whisk until frothy. Pour into the warming stock and keep whisking steadily with a balloon whisk until the mixture boils and rises. Stop whisking immediately, and draw the pan off the heat. Allow the mixture to subside. Take care not to break the crust formed by the egg white.

11. Bring the stock up to the boil again and again allow to subside. Repeat this once more (the egg white will trap the sediment in the stock and clear the aspic). Allow to cool for 10 minutes.

12. Fix a double layer of fine muslin over a clean basin and carefully strain the aspic through it, taking care to hold the egg white crust back. When all the liquid is through (or almost all of it) allow the egg white to slip into the muslin. Then strain the aspic again – this time through both egg white crust and cloth. Do not try to hurry the process by squeezing the cloth or you will get murky jelly. Allow to cool until on the point of setting.

13. Unwrap the goose. Wipe away all grease. Place it on a wire rack with a tray underneath.

14. Coat it with the nearly-set aspic. Place in the refrigerator until set.
15. Cut the orange, skin and all, across into very thin even slices. You should end up with seven or eight. Dip the orange slices in a little cool aspic and arrange them in a neat over-lapping row down the centre of the goose. Leave to set. Coat the goose with more aspic. Once this layer has set add further layers until really shiny. Place on a serving dish.
16. Set the remaining aspic in a shallow tray. Cut into neat squares and use to surround the goose. Garnish with water-cress.

Note: If the aspic is less than crystal clear it is wise not to chop it – which seems to emphasize its murkiness.

Serves 10

Confit D'oie
(Preserved goose)

This recipe, still common in France, is for goose flesh preserved in fat. The pieces of goose are lifted from the jar, and wiped clean of fat before being served either cold or reheated, or used in composite dishes. The confit takes 3 days to complete. Use a very fat goose.

One 4·5 kilos/10lb goose	2 bay leaves, pounded
900g/2lb salt	Pinch of thyme
7g/¼oz saltpetre	1·8 kilos/4lb goose fat
4 cloves, crushed	450g/1lb lard

1. Cut the goose into quarters.
2. Mix together the salt, saltpetre, cloves, bay leaves and thyme and rub some of this over the whole surface of the goose.
3. Put the goose into a glazed earthenware pot and add the re-maining spiced salt. Cover and leave for 24 hours.
4. Slowly melt the goose fat in a large saucepan. Remove the goose pieces from the salt, wipe clean and put into the fat. Place over slow heat and cook very gently for 1½ hours.

To test if the goose is cooked prick it with a skewer. The juices that run out should be clear, and the flesh feel tender.

5. Drain the pieces of goose and remove the bones. Strain a thick layer of fat in which the goose was cooked into a large glazed earthenware jar.

6. When this fat has completely solidified arrange the pieces of goose on top, being careful to prevent any of them touching the wall of the jar.

7. Cover the pieces of goose with just-liquid cool goose fat. Put into a cool place.

8. Leave to rest for 2 days. Strain some more liquid goosefat into the jar to seal any holes which may have occurred.

9. When this is set melt the lard and pour a layer about 1 cm/½in thick over the surface. When this is set put a circle of grease-proof paper on top, pressing it down to exclude any air. Cover the top of the jar with a double thickness of paper and tie with string.

10. The confit d'oie will keep for months in a cool place. To use it, wipe off all the fat, then treat as fresh-cooked goose. The fat can be simmered, strained and kept for re-use.

Note: Goosefat is seldom available in Britain, but beef dripping, lard (or a mixture of melted duck fat and lard) will do.

Serves 6

GAME

Partridge Baked with Cabbage

Butter *or* bacon dripping for
frying
3 partridges
2 tablespoons each of brandy
and Madeira
10 large cabbage leaves
4 rashers rindless streaky bacon
225g/½lb belly of pork, minced
Salt and freshly ground black
pepper

Pinch of fresh sage
225g/½lb smoked pork

For the sauce:
1 bay leaf
1–2 slices onion
1 carrot, chopped
Bunch of parsley
15g/½oz flour
15g/½oz butter

1. Melt the fat and fry the partridges fairly fast for 5 minutes
   on each side, so that they are well browned. Pour in the
   brandy and the Madeira and set them alight. Leave the birds
   in the pan(s) to cool so that you can collect any juices that
   run out.
2. Briefly cook the washed cabbage leaves in boiling water for
   2–3 minutes, then lift them out, keeping the water.
3. Butter a large ovenproof pie dish or casserole and lay the
   rashers of bacon in the bottom. Line the dish with some of
   the cabbage leaves.
4. Cut the flesh from the partridges and put the breast meat into
   the dish inside the cabbage lining. Pour on any pan juices.
5. Mince the leg meat and mix it with the minced pork. Flavour
   with salt, pepper and sage. Roll this mixture (with floured
   hands) into tiny sausages. Fry these quickly, to brown them
   only, in butter or bacon fat and add to the partridge meat.
6. Dice the smoked pork and fry it briefly in the pan, then add
   a little of the cabbage water. Cover and allow to simmer for

10 minutes. Then lift out the smoked pork pieces and add them to the other meats with the pan juices.

7. Put the partridge bones, with the bay leaf, onion, carrot and parsley in a saucepan and cover with water (preferably that in which you cooked the cabbage). Simmer for 45 minutes.

8. Set the oven to 170°C 325°F, gas mark 3.

9. Sprinkle some salt and pepper into the pie dish and cover the meat with a layer of cabbage leaves. Stand the dish in a roasting tin of hot water, cover with buttered foil bake for 2½–3 hours, or until a skewer will glide easily through.

10. Meanwhile make the sauce: reduce the partridge stock to 290ml/½ pint by rapid boiling. Strain into a clean saucepan. Taste and add salt and pepper if necessary. Work the butter and flour together to a paste. Whisk by degrees into the stock. Stir until boiling. Simmer for 2 minutes.

11. Turn out the partridge and cabbage, upside down, on a serving dish and hand the sauce separately.

Serves 6

Cold Game Pie

Preparation for this dish must start two or three days in advance.

For the forcemeat:

1 pheasant, boned (page 83) and skinned

450g/1lb belly of pork, skinless

3 shallots, finely chopped

Piece of pig's caul about 30cm/12ins square

110g/¼lb poultry livers

2 sage leaves, finely chopped

1 teaspoon fresh chopped thyme

1 clove garlic, crushed

2 teaspoons salt

1 teaspoon coarsely ground black pepper

1 tablespoon brandy

3 tablespoons dry white wine

For the jelly:
Stick of celery
1 carrot, sliced
Slice of onion
1 bay leaf
Sprig of parsley
Sprig of marjoram
Bones, giblets (except the liver)
  and skin of the pheasant
15g/½oz gelatine

For the pastry crust:
285g/12oz flour quantity pâte
  à paté (page 291)
Beaten egg

1. Trim any discoloured parts, and sinew, from the livers.
2. Reserve one pheasant breast, the pheasant liver and one other poultry liver. Mince the rest of the pheasant meat with the rest of the livers and the pork belly. Add the shallot, sage, thyme, garlic, salt, pepper, brandy and wine. Mix well and put into a deep bowl.
3. Lay the breast meat and livers on top, and cover. Refrigerate for 24 hours.
4. Make up the pâte à paté..
5. Use two-thirds of it to line a raised pie mould or a loose-bottomed cake tin.
6. Line the empty pie shell with the pig's caul, allowing the sides to hang down over the edge.
7. Put half the minced mixture into the mould. Cut the pheasant breast into strips and lay them on top of the forcemeat.
8. Lay the livers on top of the pheasant strips. Cover with the rest of the forcemeat, pressing down well to eliminate any air pockets.
9. Draw the caul up over the forcemeat to envelop it.
10. Set the oven to 190°C/375°F, gas mark 5.
11. Use the remaining pastry to cover and elaborately decorate the top of the pie. Press the edges of the top firmly to the base pastry. Make a hole in the middle of the pastry top to allow steam to escape.
12. Brush with beaten egg.
13. Bake the pie for 15 minutes, then turn the oven down to 150°C/300°F, gas mark 2, for a further 1¾ hours. Allow to cool overnight.

14. Make the stock by simmering the jelly ingredients (except the gelatine) in 1·15 litres/2 pints water for 2 hours. Strain through muslin or a double J-cloth and chill overnight.

15. Remove all traces of fat from the stock. Put it into a saucepan and sprinkle on the gelatine. Leave to soak for 10 minutes, then bring slowly to the boil. Boil until there is approximately 290ml/½ pint of liquid left.

16. Allow to cool until cold but not set. It should be syrupy. Carefully pour, little by little, into the pie, through the hole in the pastry. (A small funnel will make this operation easier.) Continue until the liquid level is visible, and will no longer gradually sink. (If by some mischance the pastry case has a hole in it allowing the liquid to leak out, plug the hole with softened butter.)

17. Chill the pie until the liquid is set (about 2 hours).

Note: If pouring the liquid into the pie proves difficult, carefully make, with the tip of the knife, another hole in the cooked pastry towards the edge, and pour the liquid through this.

Serves 10–12

Galantine of Pheasant

1 large pheasant, cleaned
225g/½lb raw chicken meat, minced
170g/6oz sausage-meat
2 shallots, chopped
2 tablespoons Madeira
1 tablespoon chopped fresh parsley
Salt and freshly ground black pepper
2 slices cooked tongue, cut into strips
1 flat dark mushroom, sliced

For the stock:
1 carrot, sliced
1 onion, sliced
Stick of celery, chopped
6 peppercorns
1 bay leaf
1 parsley stalk
Salt
Pinch of thyme

For the decoration:
Slices button mushrooms *or*
    thin rings of carrot *or* fresh
    tarragon leaves *or* slices
    truffle *or* stuffed olives,
    sliced, *or* pieces tomato *or*
    diamond-shaped pieces of
    cucumber skin

For the aspic:
2 egg shells, crushed
2 egg whites
15g/½oz gelatine

1. Bone the pheasant completely, including the legs and wings (see page 83). Cut off any excess fat from the vent end.
2. Place the bones in a pan of water with the stock ingredients, bring to the boil, cover and simmer gently for about 1 hour.
3. Meanwhile prepare the farce (stuffing). Mix together the raw chicken meat, sausage-meat, chopped shallot, Madeira and parsley. Season with salt and pepper.
4. Open the bird on a board, skin side down. Spread with half the farce and lay on the tongue and the mushroom slices. Season and cover with the remaining farce. Fold over the sides of the bird and stitch them together with a needle and thread. Wrap the bird in a piece of muslin and tie the ends together.
5. Strain the stock. Place the pheasant in a heavy pan and pour over the stock. Bring to the boil, cover tightly with a lid and simmer slowly for 1½ hours, turning the pheasant over once during the cooking.
6. Lift out the bird and keep the stock for the aspic.
7. When cool tighten the muslin cloth round the bird and leave overnight, refrigerated.
8. Pour the stock into a bowl and leave to cool overnight. If the stock can be transferred to the refrigerator once it is cold it will set the fat and make removing it easier. There should be 570ml/1 pint of stock.
9. Lift or skim off any fat from the pheasant stock. If it is well set do not add gelatine. If it is not, put it in a large saucepan and sprinkle on the gelatine. Put over a gentle heat.
10. Place the crushed shells in a bowl, add the egg white and whisk until frothy. Pour into the warming stock and keep

whisking steadily with a balloon whisk until the mixture boils and rises. Stop whisking immediately and draw the pan off the heat. Allow the mixture to subside. Take care not to break the crust formed by the egg white.

11. Bring the aspic up to the boil again and again allow to subside. Repeat this once more (the egg white will trap the sediment in the stock and clear the aspic). Allow to cool for 10 minutes.

12. Fix a double layer of fine muslin over a clean basin and carefully strain the aspic through it, taking care to hold the egg white crust back. When all the liquid is through (or almost all of it) allow the egg white to slip into the muslin. Then strain the aspic again – this time through both egg white crust and cloth. Do not try to hurry the process by squeezing the cloth, or murky aspic will result. Allow to cool until on the point of setting.

13. Unwrap the cold pheasant, wipe off all the grease and place it on a wire rack with a plate underneath. Coat it with the nearly set aspic. Place in the refrigerator until set.

14. Decorate with the garnish you have chosen and coat again with aspic. Allow to set and coat again until the pheasant is shiny.

15. Place on a serving dish. Set the remaining aspic in a shallow tray. Cut into dice and use to surround the pheasant.

Note: If the aspic is less than crystal clear it is wise not to chop it because this seems to emphasise its murkiness.

Serves 6

7
Savoury Stocks, Butters and Sauces

STOCKS

White Stock

Onion	Fresh parsley
Celery	Fresh thyme
Carrot	Bay leaf
Chicken *or* veal bones, skin *or* flesh	Peppercorns

1. Peel the onion. Slice it and the celery and carrot roughly.
2. Put all the ingredients into a saucepan. Cover generously with water and bring slowly to the boil. Skim off any fat and/or scum.
3. Simmer for 2–3 hours, skimming frequently and topping up the water level if necessary. The liquid should reduce to half the original quantity.
4. Strain, cool and lift off all the fat.

Aspic

1·14 litres/2 pints white stock (above)
2 egg shells, crushed
2 egg whites

30g/1oz gelatine (use this if the stock is not firmly set when chilled, *or* half if the stock is half-set)

229

1. Lift or skim any fat from the stock.
2. Put the stock into a large saucepan and sprinkle on the gelatine if you need it. Put over gentle heat.
3. Place the crushed shells in a bowl, add the egg whites and whisk until frothy. Pour into the warming stock and keep whisking steadily with a balloon whisk until the mixture boils and rises. Stop whisking immediately and draw the pan off the heat. Allow the mixture to subside. Take care not to break the crust formed by the egg white.
4. Bring the aspic to the boil again and again allow to subside. Repeat this once more (the egg white will trap the sediment in the stock and clear the aspic). Allow to cool for 10 minutes.
5. Fix a double layer of fine muslin over a clean basin and carefully strain the aspic through it, taking care to hold the egg white crust back. When all the liquid is through (or almost all of it) allow the egg white to slip into the muslin. Then strain the aspic again – this time through both egg white crust and cloth. Do not try to hurry the process by squeezing the cloth, or murky aspic will result.

Brown Stock

Onion

Turnip

Carrot

Celery

Marrow bones *or* beef bones, veal bones, duck carcass, bacon – green *or* smoked – *or* pieces of raw meat, but not mutton, lamb or pork

Dripping

Fresh parsley stalks

Bay leaf

Pinch of fresh thyme

Black peppercorns

1. Peel the onion but keep the skin.
2. Peel the turnip, wash the carrot and the celery.
3. Chop all the vegetables into large dice.

4. Chop the meat or bacon up into small pieces.
5. Heat the fat in a large heavy-bottomed pan and brown the bones, meat and vegetables really well all over, scraping the bottom of the pan frequently.
6. Add the herbs, onion skin and pepper (but not salt).
7. Cover with water and bring very slowly to the boil, skimming off any scum as it rises to the top.
8. When clear of scum, simmer gently for at least 2 hours, preferably all day, skimming off the fat as necessary, and topping up with water if the level gets dangerously low. The longer it simmers, and the more the liquid reduces by evaporation. the stronger the stock will be.
9. Strain, cool and lift off any remaining fat.

Note: Cooked bones are less satisfactory than raw bones as they have lost a good deal of their flavour.

Fish Stock

Onion	Fresh parsley stalks
Carrot	Bay leaf
Celery	Pinch of fresh thyme
Fish bones, skins, fins, heads	Pepper
or tails, crustacean shells	
(e.g. prawn, mussel etc.)	

1. Slice the peeled onion, the carrot and the celery.
2. Put everything together in a pan, with water to cover, and bring to the boil. Turn down to simmer and skim off any scum.
3. Simmer for 20 minutes if the fish bones are small, 30 minutes if large. Strain.

Note: Care should be taken not to overcook fish stock as the flavour is impaired if the bones are cooked too long. Once strained, however, fish stock may be strengthened by further boiling and reducing.

Fond Brun

1·35 kilos/3lb beef and veal
  bones, broken
A little bacon rind
110g/¼lb onion, peeled and
  chopped roughly
110g/¼lb carrot, chopped
  roughly

3 bay leaves
Pinch of fresh thyme
2 fresh parsley stalks
4 fresh peppercorns
1 litre/2 pints water

1. Set the oven to 200°C/400°F, gas mark 6.
2. Place the broken bones in a large, deep-sided roasting-pan.
3. Roast in the oven until all the ingredients are very brown (about 2 hours), turning the bones occasionally. Add the vegetables and bacon rind and continue roasting for a further 45 minutes.
4. Transfer everything to a heavy saucepan. Add the herbs, peppercorns and water. Simmer slowly, covered, for 2–3 hours.
5. Strain and leave to get cold.
6. Skim off all the fat.

Glace de Viande

570ml/1 pint fond brun,
  absolutely free of fat
  (above)

1. In a heavy-bottomed saucepan reduce the stock (fond brun) by boiling over a steady heat until thick, clear and syrupy.
2. Pour into small pots. When cold cover with polythene or jam covers and tie down.
3. Keep in the refrigerator until ready for use.

Note: Glace de viande keeps for several weeks and is very useful for enriching sauces.

Court Bouillon

1·25 litres/2 pints water
150ml/¼ pint vinegar
1 carrot, sliced
1 onion, sliced
Stick of celery

12 peppercorns
2 bay leaves
2 tablespoons salad oil
Salt

1. Bring all the ingredients to the boil and simmer for 20 minutes.
2. Ideally the liquid should now be allowed to cool and the fish, meat or vegetables placed in the cool liquid and then brought slowly to simmering point.

Pork Jelly

1 pig's trotter
450g/1lb pork bones, broken
1·75 litres/3 pints water
1 onion, sliced

Stick of celery
Pinch of thyme
Bunch of parsley
1 bay leaf

1. Put the bones in a saucepan and cover with the water. Bring to the boil and skim.
2. Add the other ingredients and simmer all day, the longer the better, skimming occasionally.
3. When the liquid is reduced to about 570mls/1 pint, strain and allow to cool.

Beef Bouillon (broth)

1 veal bone
55g/2oz fat bacon pieces
3 carrots
2 turnips

1 kilo/2lb shin of beef, cut into
   cubes
3·5 litres/6 pints water
½ teaspoon salt

233

2 leeks	2 bay leaves
Stick of celery	3 cloves
1 small parsnip	Good handful of parsley stalks
3 onions	Pinch of thyme

1. Put the bone and fat bacon into a roasting tin and brown in a moderate oven (200°C/400°F, gas mark 6) for 1 hour. Cut the vegetables up roughly (reserving the onion skin, which will be added later). Put the vegetables and the meat in the pan with the bones. Stir them about to coat them with dripping, then put over direct heat and fry until well browned, stirring occasionally to prevent sticking or burning.
2. Drain off the fat (which is worth keeping as dripping). Put the bones and vegetables with the onion skin, water and salt in a large saucepan. Bring slowly to the boil, skimming off the scum and fat as it rises to the surface. When the water is boiling well, pour in a glass of cold water, and immediately skim off fat and scum again. (This is called to *dépouiller* the liquid. The sudden addition of cold water causes the fat and scum to rise to the surface.) Repeat the process once the liquid is boiling again.
3. Add the flavourings. Turn down the heat and allow the stock to simmer for a good 3 hours. Inspect it occasionally and repeat the skimming process if it is necessary. You should now have about 1·45 litres/2½ pints of stock.
4. Strain and allow to cool, then chill so that any remaining fat sets on the top. Lift off the fat. The bouillon should be jellied, but will of course melt on reheating.

Note: The addition of the veal bone is to ensure a stock that will set to a jelly, but is not always necessary. The addition of poultry giblets (excluding the liver) will give a richer stock, but this will not keep as long as stock made without them.

BUTTERS

Maître d'Hôtel Butter

Butter
Chopped fresh parsley
Chopped fresh tarragon
  (optional)

Salt and pepper
Squeeze of lemon

1. Flavour the butter with the other ingredients, beating to a soft paste.
2. Spoon the mixture on to a piece of foil or greaseproof paper and shape into a block or long sausage.
3. Wrap up and chill, or freeze, until needed.

Mint and Mustard Butter

110g/¼lb butter
1 teaspoon Dijon mustard
1 tablespoon finely chopped
  fresh mint

Salt and freshly ground black
  pepper

1. Cream the butter until very soft and beat in the mustard and mint. Season with salt and pepper.
2. On a piece of damp greaseproof paper or foil shape the butter into a cylinder and wrap up. Refrigerate until hard. Serve cut in ·5cm/¼in slices.

Clarified Butter

Method 1: Put the butter in a pan with a cupful of water and heat until the butter is melted and frothy. Allow to cool and set solid, then lift the butter, now clarified, off the top of the liquid.

Method 2: Heat the butter until foaming without allowing it to burn. Pour it through a fine muslin or a double layer of J-cloth.

Method 3: Melt butter in a heavy pan and skim off the froth with a perforated spoon.

Note: Clarified butter will act as a 'seal' on pâtés or potted meats, and is useful for frying as it will stand great heat before burning.

Beurre Blanc

225g/½lb butter, unsalted
1 tablespoon shallot, chopped
3 tablespoons wine vinegar

3 tablespoons water
Salt, white pepper
Squeeze of lemon

1. Chill the butter then cut it in three lengthwise, then across into thin slices. Keep cold.
2. Put the shallot, vinegar and water into a thick-bottomed sauté-pan or small shallow saucepan. Boil until the liquid remaining is about 2 tablespoons.
3. Lower the heat under the pan. Using a wire whisk and plenty of vigorous continuous whisking, gradually add the butter, piece by piece. The process should take about five minutes and the sauce should become thick, creamy and pale – rather like a thin hollandaise. Add salt, pepper and lemon juice.

SAUCES

French Dressing (*vinaigrette*)

3 tablespoons salad oil
1 tablespoon wine vinegar

Salt and freshly ground black
pepper

Put all the ingredients into a screw-top jar. Before using shake until well emulsified.

Note I: This dressing can be flavoured with crushed garlic, mustard, a pinch of sugar, chopped fresh herbs etc. as desired.

Note II: If kept refrigerated the dressing will more easily form an emulsion when whisked or shaken, and has a slightly thicker consistency.

Cumberland Sauce

2 oranges
1 lemon
225g/½lb redcurrant jelly
1 shallot, chopped

150ml/¼ pint port *or* red wine
½ teaspoon pale mustard
Pinch of cayenne pepper
Pinch of ground ginger

1. Peel one orange and the lemon finely, removing only the outer skin, but no pith. Cut the rind into very fine needleshreds.
2. Squeeze all the fruit juice and strain into a pan, add the remaining ingredients with the needleshreds. Simmer for 10 minutes. Leave to cool.

Makes 290ml/½ *pint*

Tomato Sauce

396g/14oz can tomatoes
1 small onion, chopped
1 carrot, chopped
Stick of celery, chopped
½ garlic clove, crushed
1 bay leaf
Fresh parsley stalks

Salt and freshly ground black
   pepper
Juice of ½ lemon
Dash of Worcestershire sauce
1 teaspoon sugar
1 teaspoon chopped fresh *or*
   pinch dried basil *or* thyme

1. Put all the ingredients together in a thick-bottomed pan and simmer over medium heat for 30 minutes.
2. Sieve the sauce and return it to the rinsed-out pan.
3. If it is too thin reduce by boiling rapidly. Check the seasoning, adding more salt or sugar if necessary.

Thick Onion and Mint Sauce

1 large Spanish onion
55g/2oz butter
3 tablespoons water

2 tablespoons chopped
   fresh mint
Salt and freshly ground black
   pepper

1. Chop the onion very finely. Cook slowly in the butter and water until very soft but not coloured. Push through a sieve, or liquidize in a blender.
2. Mix in the finely chopped mint and season with salt and pepper.

Pesto Sauce for Pasta

2 garlic cloves
2 large cups basil leaves
55g/2oz fresh Parmesan cheese,
   finely grated

150ml/¼ pint olive oil
Salt
55g/2oz pinenuts

1. In a liquidizer or mortar, grind the garlic and basil together to a paste. Add the cheese, oil and plenty of salt. Keep in a covered jar in a cool place.
2. Add the pinenuts just before serving on freshly boiled pasta.

Note: Pesto is sometimes made with walnuts instead of pinenuts, and the nuts may be pounded with the other ingredients to give a smooth paste.

Apple Sauce

450g/1lb cooking apples
Finely grated rind of ¼ lemon
3 tablespoons water

1 teaspoon sugar
15g/½oz butter

1. Peel, quarter, core and slice the apples.
2. Place in a heavy saucepan with the lemon rind, water and sugar. Cover with a lid and cook very slowly until the apples are soft.
3. Beat in the butter. Serve hot or cold.

White Sauce

(coating consistency)

20g/¾oz butter
20g/¾oz flour
Pinch of hot dry mustard

290ml/½ pint creamy milk
Salt and white pepper

1. Melt the butter in a thick saucepan.
2. Add the flour and the mustard and stir over the heat for 1 minute. Draw the pan off the heat, pour in the milk and mix well.
3. Return the pan to the heat and stir continually until boiling.
4. Simmer for 2–3 minutes and season with salt and pepper.

Béchamel Sauce

(coating consistency)

290ml/½ pint creamy milk
Slice of onion
Blade of mace
Few fresh parsley stalks
4 peppercorns

1 bay leaf
20g/¾oz butter
20g/¾oz flour
Salt and white pepper

1. Place the milk with the onion, mace, parsley, peppercorns and bay leaf in a saucepan and slowly bring to simmering point.
2. Lower the temperature and allow the flavour to infuse for about 8–10 minutes.
3. Melt the butter in a thick saucepan, stir in the flour and stir over heat for 1 minute.
4. Remove the pan from the heat. Strain in the infused milk and mix well.
5. Return the sauce to the heat and stir or whisk continuously until boiling.
6. Simmer for 2–3 minutes.
7. Taste and season.

Mornay Sauce (Cheese Sauce)

45g/1½oz butter
45g/1½oz flour
570ml/1 pint milk
85g/3oz grated Gruyère or
  strong Cheddar cheese

30g/1oz grated Parmesan
  cheese
Salt and pepper

1. Melt the butter and stir in the flour. Cook, stirring, for 1 minute. Draw the pan off the heat. Add the milk slowly, beating out the lumps as you go.
2. Return the pan to the heat and stir until boiling. Simmer for 2 minutes.
3. Add all the cheese and mix well, but do not re-boil.
4. Season with salt and pepper as necessary.

Soubise Sauce

For the béchamel sauce:
20g/¾oz butter   20g/¾oz flour
1 bay leaf   290ml/½ pint milk

For the soubise:
30g/1oz butter   3–4 tablespoons cream
4 tablespoons water
225g/½lb onions, very finely
  chopped

1. To make the soubise melt the butter in a heavy pan. Add the water and finely chopped onions and cook very slowly, preferably covered with a lid to create a steamy atmosphere. The onions should become very soft and transparent, but on no account brown. Add the cream.
2. Now prepare the béchamel: melt the butter, add the bay leaf and flour and cook, stirring, for 1 minute. Draw off the heat and stir in the milk. Return to the heat and bring slowly to the boil, stirring continuously. Simmer for 2 minutes. Remove the bay leaf and mix with the soubise.

Note: This sauce can be liquidized in a blender or pushed through a sieve if a smooth texture is desired.

Mayonnaise

2 egg yolks   Squeeze of lemon juice
1 teaspoon pale mustard   1 tablespoon wine vinegar
290ml/½ pint olive oil *or*   Salt and pepper
  150ml/¼ pint each olive and
  salad oil

1. Put the yolks into a bowl with the mustard and beat well with a wooden spoon.
2. Add the oil, literally drop by drop, beating all the time. The

241

mixture should be very thick by the time half the oil is added.

3. Beat in the lemon juice.
4. Resume pouring in the oil, going rather more confidently now, but alternating the dribbles of oil with small quantities of vinegar.
5. Add salt and pepper to taste.

Note: If the mixture curdles another egg yolk should be beaten in a separate bowl and the curdled mixture beaten drop by drop into it.

Tartare Sauce

150ml/¼ pint mayonnaise
1 tablespoon chopped capers
1 tablespoon chopped gherkins

1 tablespoon chopped fresh parsley
1 shallot, finely chopped
Squeeze of lemon juice

Mix everything together. Taste and add salt or pepper as necessary.

Note: Chopped hardboiled egg makes a delicious addition.

Hollandaise Sauce

3 tablespoons wine vinegar
6 peppercorns
1 bay leaf
Blade of mace

2 egg yolks
Salt
110g/¼lb softened butter
Lemon juice

1. Place vinegar, peppercorns, bay leaf and mace in a small heavy saucepan and reduce by boiling to a tablespoon.
2. Cream the egg yolks with a pinch of salt and a nut of butter in a small bowl. Set this in a bain-marie on a gentle heat. With a wooden spoon beat the mixture until slightly thickened, taking care that the water immediately around the bowl does not boil. Mix well.

3. Strain in the reduced vinegar. Mix well. Beat in the softened butter bit by bit, increasing the temperature as the sauce thickens and you add more butter, but take care that the water does not boil.
4. When the sauce has become light and thick, take it off the heat and beat or whisk for 1 minute. Taste for seasoning and add lemon juice, and salt if necessary. Keep warm by standing the bowl in hot water. Serve warm.

Note: Hollandaise sauce will set too firmly if allowed to get cold and it will curdle if over-heated.

Crab or Lobster Sauce

About 450g/1lb fish heads *or* bones *or* skin
860ml/1½ pints water
Few slices onion
Bunch of parsley
150ml/¼ pint milk
1 small can crab *or* lobster meat

30g/1oz butter
2 teaspoons flour
1 teaspoon paprika
1 tablespoon sherry
1 tablespoon thick cream
Salt and pepper

1. Put the fish heads and/or the bones and skin into a saucepan with the water, onion and parsley. Cover and simmer for 30 minutes. Strain and mix the stock with the milk.
2. Break up the crab or lobster meat with a fork, removing any inedible membranes.
3. Melt the butter in a saucepan and stir in the flour. Cook gently for 30 seconds. Add the paprika and cook for a few more seconds. Draw the pan off the heat, blend in the stock and milk and return to the heat. Stir or whisk until the sauce boils.
4. Heat the crab or lobster meat in a separate pan with the sherry and when hot add it to the sauce. Stir in the cream and season with salt and pepper.

Note: If fresh lobster or crab shells are available, add them to the pan when making the stock. They will colour and flavour it excellently.

Demi-Glace (*Sauce Espagnole*)

(short method)

2 tablespoons oil
1 small carrot, finely chopped
½ onion, finely chopped
½ stick of celery, finely chopped
½ tablespoon flour

290ml/½ pint stock
½ teaspoon tomato purée
A few mushroom peelings
Bouquet garni (2 parsley stalks, 2 bay leaves, blade of mace)

1. Heat the oil in a heavy saucepan, add the vegetables and fry until brown.
2. Stir in the flour and continue to cook slowly, stirring occasionally and scraping the bottom of the pan to loosen the sediment. Cook to a good russet brown.
3. Draw aside, add three-quarters of the stock, the tomato purée, mushroom peelings and bouquet garni.
4. Return to the heat, bring to the boil, half-cover and simmer for 30 minutes.
5. *Dépouille* twice to remove scum. Strain.

Dépouille: To *dépouiller*, add a splash of cold stock to the boiling liquid to help bring scum and fat to the surface. Tilting the pan slightly, skim the surface with a large metal spoon. Repeat as necessary.

Makes 150ml/¼ pint strong sauce.

Demi-Glace

(long method)

290ml/½ pint short-method demi-glace

290ml/½ pint fond brun (page 232) or good brown stock

1. Combine the demi-glace with the fond brun.
2. Simmer over gentle heat, skimming repeatedly until reduced by half.

Note: A good demi-glace looks like a rich syrupy gravy when hot, setting to a jelly when cold.

Sauce Bordelaise

1 shallot
6 peppercorns
Pinch of thyme
1 bay leaf

1 glass claret
290ml/½ pint demi-glace
(page 244)

1. Place the shallot, peppercorns, thyme, bay leaf and claret into a small heavy pan and boil rapidly until reduced by half. Strain into the demi-glace sauce and reheat.
2. Bring to the boil, stirring continuously, and simmer for 2 minutes. Pour into a warmed gravy boat.

Note: Sauce Bordelaise, often served with steaks, should not be confused with Steak Bordelaise, which is topped with chopped, cooked shallot and pieces of beef marrow. A steak served with the above sauce should be described as Steak à la Sauce Bordelaise.

Cherry Sauce for Duck

55g/2oz canned pitted black
   cherries
3 tablespoons red wine
Pinch of cinnamon
Pinch of ground ginger

Pinch of ground cloves
55g/2oz sugar
290ml/½ pint demi-glace
   (page 244) *or* good duck
   gravy

1. Soak the cherries overnight in the red wine with the cinnamon, ginger, cloves and sugar.
2. Place over a gentle heat and simmer slowly until tender. Drain the cherries, reserving the liquid.
3. Chop the cherries. Mix into the gravy or demi-glace sauce with the liquid in which they were cooked. Reheat and serve hot.

Sauce Poivrade

1 tablespoon oil
1 small onion, chopped
1 shallot, chopped
1 small carrot, chopped
3 tablespoons red wine
2 tablespoons vinegar
1 bay leaf

2 parsley stalks
15g/½oz butter
15g/½oz flour
290ml/½ pint beef stock (cold)
4 juniper berries, crushed
Salt and freshly ground black
   pepper

1. Heat the oil and soften the onion, shallot and carrots in it.
   Add the wine, vinegar, parsley stalks and bay leaf and boil
   over a moderate heat to reduce by half. Set aside.
2. Melt the butter, stir in the flour and cook until a pale biscuit
   brown. Pour in the stock. Bring to the boil, stirring well. Add
   the wine and vegetables and simmer for 30 minutes.
3. Add the juniper berries and seasoning. Simmer for a further
   10 minutes. Strain through a very fine sieve, tammy strainer or
   piece of muslin into a clean pan. Return to the heat and
   simmer for 20 minutes.

8
Puddings and Desserts

BAKED PUDDINGS AND PANCAKES

Rhubarb Lattice Flan

170g/6oz flour-quantity
 shortcrust pastry (pages
 286–7)
450g/1lb rhubarb
150ml/¼ pint sugar syrup
 (page 320)
15g/½oz caster sugar

For the glaze:
1 teaspoon arrowroot
1 tablespoon smooth apricot
 jam

1. Make the pastry and line a 15cm/6in flan ring, reserving the trimmings. Chill for 20 minutes.
2. Set the oven to 190°C/375°F, gas mark 5.
3. Prepare the rhubarb: cut it into 4cm/1½in lengths and stew very gently in the sugar syrup until tender. Drain the fruit very well and reserve the juice.
4. Bake the pastry case blind for 20–25 minutes.
5. Arrange the rhubarb neatly in the flan case.
6. Mix the arrowroot with enough of the fruit juice to make it smooth. Put the arrowroot mixture and the juice into a saucepan and bring it to the boil, stirring all the time. Add the jam and boil to a thick syrupy consistency. Cool until warm then pour into the flan, all over the fruit.
7. Roll out the pastry trimmings into long strips 1cm/½in wide.

Twist the strips like barley sugar and arrange them in a latticed pattern over the flan, sticking the ends down with a little water. Brush each strip with water and sprinkle with caster sugar.

8. Return the flan to the oven until the pastry becomes a pale golden brown. Leave to cool on a wire rack.

Baking blind: see page 142, *note.*

Serves 4–5

Jalousie

110g/¼lb flour-quantity rough puff pastry (pages 292–3)
225g/½lb fresh apple marmalade (pages 322–3)

2 tablespoons smooth apricot jam
Milk
Caster sugar

1. Set the oven to 230°C/450°F, gas mark 8.
2. Roll the pastry into two thin rectangles, one about 2·5cm/1in bigger all round than the other (the smaller one should measure about 13 × 20cm/5 × 8in, the larger 18 × 25cm/7 × 10in). Leave to relax for 20 minutes.
3. Prick the smaller one all over and bake until crisp and brown. Take it out and turn it over on the baking sheet. Allow to cool.
4. Melt the jam in a small pan, and brush over the top of the cooked pastry.
5. Lay the larger piece of pastry on the board, dust it lightly with flour and fold it, gently so that nothing sticks, in half lengthwise. Using a sharp knife, cut through the folded side of the pastry, at rightangles to the edge, in parallel lines, as though you were cutting between the teeth of a comb. Leave a margin uncut about 1in wide, all round the other edges, so that when you open up the pastry you will have a solid border.
6. Spread the apple all over the cooked piece of pastry, on top of the jam.
7. Now lay the cut pastry on top, and tuck the edges under.

Brush the top layer carefully all over with milk (this is a bit messy as the apple keeps coming up between the pastry cuts, but don't worry). Sprinkle well with sugar.

8. Bake in the oven until well browned (about 20 minutes).

Serves 4

Crêpes Suzette

12 French pancakes
 (pages 314–15)

For the orange butter:
85g/3oz unsalted butter
30g/1oz caster sugar
Grated rind of 1 orange
2 tablespoons orange juice
2 tablespoons orange Curaçao

To flame:
Caster sugar
2 tablespoons orange Curaçao
1 tablespoon brandy

1. Put the butter, sugar, orange rind. juice and Curaçao into a large frying pan and simmer gently for 2 minutes.
2. Put a pancake into the frying pan and using a spoon and fork fold it in half and then in half again. Add a second pancake and repeat the process until the pan has been filled.
3. Sprinkle the pancakes with caster sugar and pour over the orange Curaçao and brandy. Light a match, stand back, and light the alcohol. Spoon it over the pancakes until the flames have died down. Serve immediately.

Serves 4–6

MERINGUES

Meringues

4 egg whites
225g/½lb caster sugar

For the filling:
Whipped cream

1. Set the oven to 110°C/225°F, gas mark ½.
2. Place greaseproof paper on two baking sheets, brush with oil and dust lightly with sugar.
3. Whisk the egg whites until stiff but not dry.
4. Add 2 tablespoons of the sugar and whisk again until very stiff and shiny.
5. Fold in the rest of the sugar.
6. Put the meringue mixture out on the paper-covered baking sheets in spoonfuls set fairly far apart. Use a teaspoon for tiny meringues, a dessertspoon for large ones.
7. Bake in the oven for about 2 hours until the meringues are dry right through and will lift easily off the paper.
8. When cold sandwich the meringues together in pairs with whipped cream.

Makes 50 miniature or 12 large meringues

Meringue Mont Blanc

For the meringue:
3 egg whites
170g/6oz caster sugar
Icing sugar

Chocolate caraque (page 332)
  or coarsely grated chocolate

For the filling:
450g/1lb chestnuts
85g/3oz granulated sugar
150ml/¼ pint water
30g/1oz butter
Vanilla essence
150ml/¼ pint double cream,
  whipped

1. Set the oven to 100°C/200°F, gas mark ½. Cover a baking sheet with foil, brush lightly with oil and dust with flour.
2. Whisk the egg whites until stiff but not dry, add 1 tablespoon of the sugar and whisk again until very stiff and shiny. Fold in the remaining sugar.
3. Fill the meringue into a forcing bag with a 1cm/½in plain nozzle. Pipe the mixture into an 18cm/7in circle on the prepared baking sheet, starting from the centre and spiralling outwards. Pipe a rim 3cm/1½in deep. Dust lightly with icing sugar.
4. Bake in the oven for at least 2 hours until the meringue is dry and crisp. When cooked remove carefully, immediately peel off the foil, and allow the meringue to cool on a wire rack.
5. Cut a slit in the skin of each chestnut, place them in a pan of water and bring slowly to the boil. Draw off the heat, then lift out one by one and peel.
6. Dissolve the granulated sugar in the water, add the chestnuts and simmer slowly until soft. Liquidize or sieve the mixture, then return to the pan.
7. Simmer until you have a thick purée, stirring well to prevent the mixture burning. Allow to cool.
8. Beat in the butter and vanilla essence.
9. To assemble the vacherin pile the chestnut filling into the meringue case, spoon over the whipped cream and arrange chocolate caraque on top.

Note: Canned sweetened purée of chestnuts is as good as freshly cooked, and convenient; however it is very expensive.

Serves 6

Pavlova

4 egg whites
Pinch of salt
225g/½lb caster sugar
1 teaspoon vanilla essence
1 teaspoon white vinegar *or* lemon juice
1 heaped teaspoon cornflour

For the filling:
290ml/½ pint double cream, whipped
1 small fresh pineapple
1 tablespoon roughly chopped walnuts

1. Set the oven to 150°C/300°F, gas mark 2. Prepare a baking sheet with a covering of foil brushed with a thin film of oil.
2. Beat the egg whites with the salt until stiff. Gradually add the sugar, beating until you can stand a spoon in the mixture. Add the vanilla, vinegar or lemon juice and cornflour.
3. Pile the mixture on to the prepared baking sheet, shaping to a flat oval or round 3cm/1½in thick. Bake for about 1 hour. The cake is cooked when the outer shell is pale biscuit coloured and hard to the touch. Remove carefully and gently peel off the foil.
4. When quite cold spoon on the whipped cream and sprinkle on the fruit and nuts.

Note I: It is vital to peel off the backing foil while the meringue is warm. Once cold it will stick like a limpet.

Note II: If the backing foil does not come off cleanly, put the pavlova upside down on the serving dish and fill the hollow with the cream mixture.

Serves 6–10

Floating Islands

For the custard:
425ml/¾ pint milk
280ml/½ pint cream
2 teaspoons caster sugar
Vanilla pod *or* 3 drops vanilla
  essence
2 level teaspoons cornflour
4 egg yolks

For the meringue:
3 egg whites
Salt
110g/¼lb caster sugar

To serve:
Grated chocolate

1. Place half the milk, the cream and the sugar in a saucepan with the vanilla. Bring gently to the boil, remove from heat and leave to infuse for 30 minutes. Remove the vanilla pod.
2. Mix the cornflour with a little water. Stir a few ounces of the hot milk mixture into it and then pour it back into the milk. Place over a gentle heat and bring slowly to the boil, stirring continuously. Simmer for 4 minutes to cook the cornflour.
3. Beat the egg yolks then pour the cream mixture on to the yolks in a thin stream, beating well all the time. The custard will probably thicken at once to the consistency which will coat the back of a wooden spoon. If it does not, return to the saucepan and stir steadily over very gentle heat until it does. Take care not to boil or it will curdle. Pour into a shallow wide serving dish, and cover with plastic film to prevent a skin forming.
4. Meanwhile make the islands: put the remaining milk plus 570ml/1 pint of water into a deep frying pan and set over the heat.
5. Whisk the whites with a pinch of salt until stiff but not dry. Whisk in the caster sugar gradually until you have a smooth shiny meringue mixture.
6. The milk and water mixture should now be simmering. Put a tablespoon of meringue mixture into the frying pan and cook gently for only 30 seconds on each side, by which time they will have almost doubled in size. (Do not add more than three

or four islands at a time and do not overcook.) Lift out with a perforated spoon and leave on a wire rack or tea-towel to drain completely. Lay the islands carefully on the 'lake' of custard.

7. Sprinkle the islands with the chocolate.

Makes 6–8 islands

Floating Islands with Caramel

Floating islands (pages 253–4)   85g/3oz sugar

Place the sugar in a heavy pan and set over a gentle heat until the sugar has dissolved and cooked to a golden brown. Remove from the heat, and immediately trickle over the islands already in the custard.

Floating Islands with Coffee Custard

Floating islands (pages 253–4)   2 teaspoons boiling water
1 teaspoon coffee

Proceed as for floating islands but dissolve the coffee in boiling water and add it to the custard sauce just before removing it from the heat.

Floating Islands with Orange

Floating islands (pages 253–4,   1 orange
  omitting the vanilla)   1 tablespoon Grand Marnier

Proceed as for floating islands but, in addition, pare the rind from the orange, being careful to discard all the pith. Infuse the rind in the cream and milk mixture in place of the vanilla pod. Add the Grand Marnier to the custard before pouring into the serving dish.

FRUIT PUDDINGS AND DESSERTS

Spiced Ginger Roll

For the roll:
110g/¼lb plain flour
1 teaspoon mixed spice
1 teaspoon ground ginger
70g/2½oz butter
2 tablespoons treacle
2 tablespoons syrup
1 egg
150ml/¼ pint water
1 teaspoon bicarbonate of soda
Caster sugar

For the filling:
450g/1lb cooking apples
30g/1oz butter
1 teaspoon cinnamon
55g/2oz sugar

To serve:
Whipped cream

1. First make the filling: peel and core the apples. Slice them roughly.
2. Melt the butter in a saucepan and add the cinnamon, sugar and apples. Cover with a lid and cook very gently, stirring occasionally, until the apples become pulpy. Beat until smooth, adding more sugar if the apples are still tart.
3. Set the oven to 180°C/350°F, gas mark 4. Prepare a Swiss roll tin by greasing the inside, then covering the base with greaseproof paper, and greasing again. Dust with caster sugar.
4. Sift the flour, mixed spice and ginger together. Melt the butter in a pan with the treacle and syrup. Whisk the egg with the water and soda. Draw the syrup mixture off the heat and pour in the egg and water. Mix well.

5. Now pour this into the flour and whisk together for 30 seconds. Pour into the prepared tin and bake for 12–15 minutes or until firm to touch.
6. Turn out on to a sheet of greaseproof paper dusted with caster sugar. Remove the paper now stuck to the back of the cake. Spread the cake with the apple purée, roll up like a Swiss roll and serve, preferably with whipped cream.

Note: The pudding is not pretty, being squashy and dark brown, but the taste is wonderful. A last-minute dusting with icing sugar will help the appearance.

Serves 4

Greek Iced Fruit Salad

A selection of:
    cantaloupe melon
    red apples
    bananas
    black grapes
    oranges
    strawberries
    cherries
    etc.

Lemon juice
Crushed ice

1. Put all the fruit, unprepared, into the refrigerator for a few hours to chill well.
2. Prepare the fruit for eating with the fingers, i.e. peel the oranges and break into segments, picking off any pith. Wash, quarter and core the apples and slice, using a stainless steel knife. Break the grapes into bunches of three or four grapes each. Peel the bananas and cut into largish pieces. Cut the melon into quarters, remove the peel and cut the flesh into fingers. Leave the strawberries whole and unhulled, washing them only if they are sandy. Wash the cherries leaving the stalks on.

3. Arrange the fruit attractively on a very well chilled dish and sprinkle with lemon juice. Sprinkle with the ice just before serving.

Note I: Apples can of course be peeled. Shiny red ones look good unpeeled.

Note II: Fruit liable to discolour such as bananas, pears or apples should be cut up shortly before serving.

Note III: To crush ice cubes, put them in a stout plastic bag or cloth and beat with a rolling pin.

Pêches Cardinales

4 large peaches
570ml/1 pint sugar syrup (page 320), for unripe peaches only

290ml/½ pint Melba sauce (page 321)
About 30g/1oz blanched flaked almonds

1. Place the peaches in a pan of boiling water for 10 seconds and then remove the skins. If the peaches are unripe put them unskinned into the sugar syrup and allow it to boil up over them – this will prevent discolouring – then poach gently until tender (about 20 minutes), and skin.
2. Put the peaches, cooked or raw, on to a serving dish. Coat with Melba sauce and scatter over a few almonds.

Note: When peaches are out of season Japanese or South African canned whole white peaches can be used. They are not as good as fresh ones but very acceptable.

Serves 4

Peaches Stuffed with Praline Cream

55g/2oz granulated sugar
150ml/¼ pint water
4 large peaches
55g/2oz crushed praline
 (page 332)
290ml/½ pint lightly whipped
 cream

For the decoration:
8 unblanched almonds *or* whole
 praline almonds

1. In a small heavy saucepan dissolve the sugar in the water and bring to the boil. Simmer gently for a few minutes then allow to cool.
2. Dunk the peaches in boiling water for 10 seconds. Peel, cut in half and remove the stones.
3. Dip each peach half in the sugar syrup, making sure it is completely coated. Arrange cut side up on a serving dish.
4. Stir the praline into the cream. Spoon a little of this mixture into the spaces left by the peach stones. Decorate with an unblanched almond or a whole praline almond.

Note: If the peaches are unripe put them unskinned into sugar syrup and allow it to boil up over them – this will prevent discolouring – then poach gently until tender (about 20 minutes) and skin.

Serves 4

Summer Pudding

6 slices stale white bread
900g/2lb raspberries,
 redcurrants, blackcurrants
 or blackberries *or* a mixture
 of all

2 tablespoons water
170g/6oz sugar
Double cream

1. Lightly grease a pudding basin with butter and line it with pieces of crustless stale bread.

2. Cook the fruit gently in the water and sugar until soft but still bright in colour. Taste and add more sugar if necessary. While the fruit is still just warm pour it into the bread-lined basin, with the juice. Cover with a round piece of bread dipped on both sides in the juice. Stand the basin on a dish.
3. Press a saucer or plate with a 450g/1lb weight on it on top of the pudding. Leave in a cool place overnight. Remove the saucer and the weight and keep any juices that have been pressed out of the pudding.
4. Invert a serving dish over the bowl and turn both over together. Give a sharp shake and remove the bowl. Spoon over the reserved fruit juice. Serve with whipped cream.

Serves 4

Pineapple Fritters

For the fritter batter:
125g/4½oz plain flour
Pinch of salt
2 eggs
1 tablespoon oil
150ml/¼ pint milk

1 medium-sized fresh pineapple
Oil for deep frying
Caster sugar

1. Separate one of the eggs, reserving the white.
2. To make the batter, sift the flour and salt into a bowl. Make a well in the centre and drop in the whole egg and the egg yolk. Mix this without disturbing the flour. Now add the milk, gradually drawing in the surrounding flour as you do so. Keep mixing until you have a perfectly smooth batter (alternatively the flour, eggs, oil and milk can be blended together in a liquidizer). Cover and leave to rest for 30 minutes.
3. Cut the top and bottom off the pineapple so that you are left with a cylinder of fruit. With a sharp knife cut off the skin.

Slice the pineapple into rings and cut away the core from each slice with a small round pastry cutter. Drain the slices well on absorbent paper.

4. Heat the oil until a crumb will sizzle vigorously in it.
5. Whisk the egg white until stiff and fold it into the batter.
6. Dip each pineapple ring into the batter and lower carefully into the hot oil. Increase the temperature slightly as you add the rings. Fry until golden brown and crisp.
7. Drain the fritters well on absorbent paper and dredge with caster sugar. Serve at once.

Makes 4

Chinese Apple Fritters

450g/1lb sugar
150ml/¼ pint water
3 dessert apples
Lemon juice

85g/3oz cornflour
Oil for frying
2 tablespoons sesame seeds
1 teaspoon wine vinegar

1. Lightly oil a flat serving dish, or have ready a bowl of icy water.
2. Place the sugar and water together in a heavy pan and set over a gentle heat to dissolve without boiling.
3. Peel, core and quarter the apples. Cut into chunks. Sprinkle with lemon juice and roll in cornflour.
4. Put the oil on to heat.
5. Meanwhile toast the sesame seeds in a small heavy dry pan.
6. Deep fry the apples in hot oil for about 8 minutes until golden brown. Drain well on absorbent paper.
7. When the sugar has dissolved boil rapidly until the mixture caramelizes (goes toffee-brown) then add the vinegar, taking care as the mixture will splutter and sizzle.
8. Stir, then add the apples. Mix well and pour in the sesame seeds.
9. Turn on to the oiled serving dish, separating the apple chunks with two spoons – the toffee hardens as it cools and will

stick the pieces together unless separated. An alternative method of serving this – and the usual Chinese method – is to dip each fritter into cold water to rapidly cool the caramel and harden it, and then to drain and serve them immediately.

Note: The fritters are easy enough to make but they require organization and timing. It is wise to assemble everything – oiled dish or bowl of icy water, caramel pan, deep-fryer, draining paper, bowl of cornflour, toasted sesame seeds etc. before starting.

Serves 6

CUSTARDS, CREAMS, MOUSSES AND SOUFFLÉS

Ginger Syllabub

4–5 tablespoons Advocaat
  liqueur
2 heaped tablespoons ginger
  marmalade

290ml/½ pint double cream
1–2 pieces preserved ginger

1. Mix the Advocaat and ginger marmalade together.
2. Whip the cream stiffly and stir in the marmalade mixture.
3. Spoon into small glasses, little china pots or coffee cups.
4. Put 2–3 thin slivers of preserved ginger on top of each syllabub. Chill before serving.

Note I: For a smoother texture the ginger marmalade and the Advocaat can be liquidized or sieved together.

Note II: In the absence of ginger marmalade use orange marmalade well flavoured with finely chopped bottled ginger and its syrup.

Serves 6

Pear Caramel Custard

2 ripe pears
290ml/½ pint sugar syrup
(page 320)
55g/2oz granulated sugar
2 whole eggs

2 egg yolks
2 tablespoons caster sugar
570ml/1 pint milk
Vanilla essence

1. Set the oven to 170°C/350°F, gas mark 4.
2. Peel, core and quarter the pears. Poach them until tender in the sugar syrup. Drain well.
3. Place the granulated sugar in a heavy saucepan with 4 table-spoons water and allow it to melt slowly. When melted boil rapidly until it has turned a rich brown.
4. Pour the caramel into the bottom of a warmed ovenproof dish.
5. Beat the eggs, yolks and caster sugar together. Scald the milk and stir this into the eggs. Add the vanilla essence. Strain.
6. Liquidize the pears with a little of the custard. Add the rest of the custard and pour the mixture on to the set caramel in the dish.
7. Place the dish in a roasting tin three-quarters full of hot water and bake in the oven for 45 minutes or until the custard is set. Leave to cool until lukewarm.
8. Run a knife around the edge of the dish, and carefully turn out on to a shallow-lipped serving dish.

Serves 4–6

Orange Bavarois with Meringues

For the meringues:
1 egg white   55g/2oz caster sugar

For the Bavarois:

3 tablespoons water	425ml/¾ pint milk
2 level teaspoons gelatine	3 egg yolks
5 lumps sugar	1½ tablespoons caster sugar
1 orange	150ml/¼ pint double cream

To serve:
Grated chocolate

1. First prepare the meringues. Whisk the egg white until stiff, add 2 teaspoons of the sugar and continue whisking until stiff again; then fold in the rest. Put this mixture into a forcing bag and pipe into tiny button meringues on baking parchment or greased and floured foil, using a 0·5cm/¼in plain pipe. Dry in a slow oven (130°C/260°F, gas mark ½) for about 40 minutes. Immediately peel off the paper and leave to cool.
2. Put the water into a small saucepan and sprinkle on the gelatine. Leave to soak.
3. Rub the sugar lumps over the orange until the sugar is well coloured by the oils in the rind. Put the lumps into the milk and dissolve over a gentle heat.
4. Cream the egg yolks and caster sugar together until thick and light, then pour the milk on to the mixture. Return to the pan and put over a gentle heat to thicken the custard. Stir constantly and do not allow to boil. When the custard will coat the back of the wooden spoon strain into a bowl and allow to cool.
5. Put the gelatine over gentle heat and when clear and runny add to the custard.
6. Stand the custard in a roasting tin or bowl full of ice and stir gently until the mixture thickens.
7. Half-whip the cream, then fold 2 tablespoons of it into the custard. Pour at once into a lightly oiled plain mould. Refrigerate until set (about 3 hours).
8. Whip the rest of the cream a little stiffer. When the custard is set turn it out on to a plate and mask with the rest of the whipped cream. Cover with the meringues and sprinkle with grated chocolate.

Note: Rubbing the sugar lumps over the orange rind extracts the orange flavour, but is a little tedious. An alternative method is to pare the rind finely from the orange and infuse it in the hot milk, then strain it.

Serves 4

Coffee Cream Bavarois

7g/¼oz gelatine
225ml/8 fl.oz milk
20g/¾oz unsweetened chocolate
3 egg yolks

85g/3oz caster sugar
1 level tablespoon instant
 coffee
150ml/¼ pint double cream

For the decoration:
Grated chocolate

Double cream

1. In a very small saucepan soak the gelatine in 2 tablespoons of water.
2. Place the milk and broken-up chocolate in a saucepan and heat gently until the chocolate has completely melted.
3. Beat the egg yolks and sugar until light and fluffy. Stir in the warm milk and chocolate mixture. Beat well.
4. Dissolve the coffee in 2 tablespoons boiling water and add it to the mixture. Set the bowl over a pan of simmering water and stir continuously with a wooden spoon for 10–20 minutes. It is ready when the custard will coat the back of the spoon. Be careful not to over-heat or the mixture will curdle.
5. Cool by standing the pan in a bowl of cold water.
6. Dissolve the gelatine over a gentle heat; when melted and clear stir it into the cooling custard. Lightly whip the cream and fold it into the coffee mixture.
7. Turn into a large dish or into individual pots and leave in the refrigerator to set. Decorate with grated chocolate and whipped cream.

Serves 4

Charlotte Russe

15 sponge fingers (page 334)
150ml/¼ pint clear lemon jelly
  (pages 271–2)

For the custard:

Vanilla pod *or* ½ teaspoon
  essence
425ml/¾ pint milk
45g/1½oz caster sugar
5 egg yolks

3 tablespoons sherry
15g/½oz gelatine
4 tablespoons water
325ml/8 fl.oz double cream,
  lightly whipped

For the decoration:

A few pieces angelica

4 glacé cherries cut in half

1. Make the lemon jelly. When it is cool but not set wet a charlotte mould and pour in a thin layer (about 1cm/½in) of jelly. When it is almost set arrange sponge fingers standing up around the sides of the mould with their ends in the jelly. Decorate the base with cherries and angelica and leave to set. Pour in the rest of the jelly and refrigerate again to set.
2. Make the custard: put the vanilla in the milk and heat gently.
3. In a bowl mix the sugar and egg yolks well together. When the milk is almost boiling, remove the pod and pour on to the yolks, stirring vigorously. If it does not immediately thicken sufficiently to coat the back of a spoon set it over a pan of simmering water and stir until it does. Strain and allow to cool. Add the sherry.
4. In a small pan soak the gelatine in the water, then dissolve over gentle heat. When runny and clear stir into the cooling custard. When the custard begins to set fold in the partially whipped cream and turn the mixture into the mould, spreading it flat. Put in the refrigerator to set.
5. Trim off any biscuits sticking up above the level of the filling. Run a knife between the biscuits and the mould to make sure they are not stuck. Dip the bottom of the mould briefly into hot water to dislodge the jelly. Invert a plate over the mould, turn the two over together and lift off the mould.

Serves 4–6

Chocolate Mousse

3 eggs
30g/1oz caster sugar

170g/6oz dark unsweetened
(Bourneville) chocolate

1. Separate the eggs and beat the yolks with the sugar until you have a pale creamy mousse.
2. Put the chocolate in a saucepan with 3 tablespoons of water and melt slowly. Simmer, stirring, until you have a creamy thick consistency, as of melted chocolate. (Alternatively, melt the chocolate in a double saucepan or in a saucer over boiling water, but do not try to melt it on direct heat without any water as it will go lumpy and hard.)
3. While the chocolate is still warm, add to the yolks and sugar mixture. Whip the whites stiffly and fold them into the chocolate mixture.
4. Turn immediately into a soufflé dish or into individual pots or glasses.
5. Chill until set, preferably overnight, but for at least 4 hours.

Note: Brandy, chopped preserved ginger, rum, grated orange rind and strong coffee flavours are all delicious additions. They should be stirred into the basic mousse mixture before the whites are folded in.

Serves 4

Layered Chocolate Mousse and Ginger Syllabub

Chocolate mousse (above)
Ginger syllabub (page 261)

Chopped walnuts

1. Prepare the chocolate mousse and ginger syllabub mixtures according to the recipes, but do not dish them up.
2. In the bottom of eight tall glasses place a layer of ginger syllabub. Spoon a layer of chocolate mousse on top. Con-

tinue the layers like this until all the mixtures are used finishing with a layer of chocolate mousse. Refrigerate until set (preferably overnight).

3. Decorate the top of each glass with the chopped nuts.

Serves 8

Prune Mousse

340g/¾lb prunes soaked in weak black tea overnight

2 heaped tablespoons caster sugar

2–3 strips finely pared lemon rind

20g/¾oz gelatine

1 tablespoon lemon juice

150ml/¼ pint double cream, lightly whipped

2 egg whites

1. Bring the prunes to the boil in the tea with the sugar and pared lemon rind. Simmer until the prunes are tender.
2. Strain the prunes, removing the lemon rind, and make the liquid up to 570ml/1 pint by adding extra water. Stone the prunes and push the flesh through a sieve.
3. In a small saucepan soak the gelatine in 3 tablespoons of water until spongy. Dissolve over a gentle heat. When clear and liquid stir in the syrup. Taste for sweetness, adding more sugar if necessary. Stir the syrup into the prune purée. Add the lemon juice.
4. When the mixture is on the point of setting fold in 1 table-spoon of the cream. Whisk the egg whites until they form soft peaks and fold into the prune mixture too. Wet a ring mould and pour the mixture into this. Allow to set in the refrigerator.
5. Invert the serving dish over the ring mould and then turn both the mould and dish over together. Give a sharp shake to dislodge the mousse. Remove the mould. If the mousse won't come out, gently separate the sides of the mousse from the bowl with the fingers. If it still won't budge dip the base of the mould into hot water for 2 seconds. But take care not to overdo the dipping or the mousse will be messy.

6. Pile the remaining lightly whipped cream into the centre of the mousse.

Serves 4

Tangerine Mousse in Chocolate Case

For the chocolate case:

170g/6oz best quality plain chocolate

2 egg yolks
3 whole eggs
55g/2oz caster sugar
15g/½oz gelatine
Juice of ½ lemon

1 large macaroon (optional) (pages 333–4)

150ml/¼ pint lightly whipped cream
150ml/¼ pint tangerine juice
Finely grated rind of 4 tangerines

1. First make the chocolate case by breaking up the chocolate and placing it in a pudding basin. Set it over a saucepan of simmering water. Stir until the chocolate is smooth and melted. Do not overheat or the chocolate will lose its gloss.
2. Brush melted chocolate thinly over the inside of an 18cm/7in paper baking case and leave to cool and harden. Repeat the process until you have a fairly thick layer and you have used up all the chocolate. Crush the macaroon and sprinkle on the still soft chocolate. Leave to harden. Carefully peel away the paper.
3. Make the mousse by putting the egg yolks, whole eggs and sugar together in a basin. Set it over a saucepan of simmering water and whisk until thick and mousse-like. Remove from the heat and whisk until cool. (If using an electric whisk, there is no need to whisk over heat.)
4. In a small pan soak the gelatine with the lemon juice and 2 tablespoons of water. Leave for 2 minutes.
5. Stir the tangerine juice and rind into the egg mixture.
6. Dissolve the gelatine over a low heat until warm and clear – do not boil. Stir this into the mousse and when on the point of setting stir in the cream. Pour into the chocolate case. Chill well.

Note: The mousse may be decorated with chocolate shapes. To make these melt plain chocolate and pour it on to greaseproof paper. When just set stamp it into small crescents or rounds or cut it into triangles or squares.

Serves 6

Cold Raspberry Soufflé

3 eggs
110g/¼lb sugar
3 tablespoons water
15g/½oz gelatine
425ml/¾ pint raspberry purée
150ml/¼ pint double cream

For the decoration:
Browned chopped *or* nibbed
  almonds
150ml/¼ pint double cream
Whole raspberries

1. To prepare a soufflé dish (which should be 15cm/6in diameter), tie a double piece of greaseproof paper around the outside and secure the ends with a paper clip or pin. The paper should stick up about 3cm/1½in above the rim. Brush the inside of the projecting paper with oil.
2. Separate the eggs. Whisk the yolks with the sugar either over a gentle heat (with the bowl set over a pan of simmering water) or in an electric machine, until light and fluffy, and thick enough for the whisk to leave a 'ribbon trail' when lifted.
3. Remove from the heat and whisk again until the mixture is almost cold.
4. Put the water into a small saucepan and sprinkle over the gelatine. Leave to soak.
5. Stir the raspberry purée into the egg yolk mixture.
6. Dissolve the gelatine over a gentle heat – do not allow it to boil – and when warm and clear stir it into the raspberry mixture. Fold in the whipped cream.
7. Whisk the whites until stiff but not dry and fold them into the soufflé mixture. Pile into the dish and flatten the top neatly. The soufflé mixture should come at least 2cm/¾in above the edge of the dish. Refrigerate for at least 4 hours.

8. Remove the oiled paper carefully. Spread the exposed sides thinly with cream. Press browned chopped almonds gently on to the cream. Pipe rosettes of whipped cream round the top and garnish each with a whole raspberry.

Serves 4

DESSERT JELLIES

These are fruit juices or syrups set with gelatine. Some are clarified in a similar manner to aspic and clear soups.

You will need:
1. Jelly bag – usually made of flannel – or a large double muslin cloth.
2. Balloon whisk.
3. Large saucepan.

Points to remember:
1. All equipment must be spotlessly clean and grease-free. Scalding in boiling water will ensure this.
2. Weigh all ingredients carefully.
3. Follow the whisking and clearing methods very carefully. Short cuts will only lead to murky jelly.
4. When turning out jellies it is a good idea to wet the serving plate. If the unmoulded jelly is not dead centre you can then slide it gently to the correct position. If the plate is dry the jelly will cling to it and be difficult to budge.

Lemon Jelly

3 large *or* 4 medium lemons
425ml/¾ pint water
30g/1oz gelatine

125g/4½oz sugar
Green *or* yellow colouring
  (optional)

1. With a sharp knife or potato peeler carefully remove the rind (without any pith) from the lemons. Squeeze the fruit and measure the juice. You need 225ml/8 fl.oz.
2. Put 6 tablespoons of the water into a small pan and sprinkle on the gelatine. Do not stir, but set aside to soak and 'sponge'.
3. Put the remaining water, lemon rinds and sugar together in a pan, cover and place over gentle heat. Do not boil. Remove from the heat and keep the liquid hot for 15 minutes in order to extract all the flavour from the lemon rind. Make sure that all the sugar has dissolved, then strain, and allow to cool to lukewarm.
4. Slowly dissolve the gelatine over a gentle heat, without boiling. When clear add it to the water and sugar.
5. Add the lemon juice. Taste the mixture and add extra sugar, if necessary, stirring until it is dissolved. Add the colouring if required.
6. Wet a jelly mould. Pour in the liquid jelly and leave refrigerated until set (at least 4 hours), but preferably overnight.
7. Turn out the jelly: loosen the top edge all round with a finger. Dip the mould briefly into hot water. Place a dish over the mould and invert the two together. Give a good sharp shake and remove the mould.

Serves 4

Clear Lemon Jelly

850ml/1½ pints water
55g/2oz gelatine
225g/½lb sugar
Rind of 4 lemons, thinly pared
290ml/½ pint lemon juice

4 small sticks cinnamon
Green colouring (optional)
The white and crushed shell of 3 eggs
8 tablespoons sherry

1. Make the lemon jelly: put all the ingredients except the egg whites, egg shells and green colouring into a very clean pan

and place over a medium heat. Stir until the gelatine and sugar have dissolved. Remove the cinnamon.

2. Place the crushed shells in a bowl, add the egg whites and whisk until frothy. Pour into the warming jelly and keep whisking steadily with a balloon whisk until the mixture boils and rises. Stop whisking immediately and draw the pan off the heat. Allow the mixture to subside. Take care not to break the crust formed by the egg white.

3. Bring up to the boil again, and allow to subside. Repeat this once more (the egg white will trap the sediment in the liquid and clear the jelly). Allow to cool for 10 minutes.

4. Fix a double layer of fine muslin over a clean basin and carefully strain the jelly through it, taking care to hold the egg white crust back. When all the liquid is through (or almost all of it) allow the egg white to slip into the muslin. Then strain the jelly again – this time through both the egg white crust and cloth. Do not try to hurry the process by squeezing the cloth, or murky jelly will result. If the jelly begins to set before it is completely strained, warm it up again to melt it just enough to filter through the muslin.

5. Colour it delicately with the green colouring, if required.

6. Pour into a wet jelly mould. Leave refrigerated until set (at least 4 hours, but preferably overnight).

7. Turn out the jelly: loosen the top edge all around with a finger. Dip the mould briefly into hot water. Place a dish over the mould and invert the two together. Give a good sharp shake and remove the mould.

Serves 4

Orange Jelly and Caramel Chips

For the orange jelly:
70g/2½oz caster sugar
150ml/¼ pint water
20g/¾oz gelatine
570ml/1 pint orange juice, just
  tepid

290ml/½ pint double cream,
  whipped lightly

For the caramel:
55g/2oz granulated sugar

1. For the jelly put the caster sugar and water in a small saucepan. Sprinkle on the gelatine and allow to stand for 10 minutes. Dissolve over a very gentle heat without allowing the gelatine to boil. Do not stir.
2. When the gelatine is clear and liquid mix with the orange juice and pour into a wet plain jelly mould or pudding basin.
3. Chill in the refrigerator for 4 hours or until set.
4. Meanwhile start the caramel. Put the sugar in a heavy pan and set over a gentle heat
5. Lightly oil a baking sheet.
6. When the sugar has dissolved boil rapidly to a golden caramel. Immediately pour on to the baking sheet. Leave to harden and cool completely.
7. Break up the caramel into chips.
8. Loosen the jelly round the edges with a finger. Invert a serving plate over the jelly mould, turn the mould and plate over together, give a sharp shake and remove the mould. If the jelly won't budge dip the outside of the mould briefly in hot water to loosen it.
9. Spread over the cream to completely mask the jelly.
10. Just before serving, scatter the caramel over the jelly (do not do this in advance as the caramel softens quickly).

Serves 4

Claret Jelly

570ml/1 pint claret *or* other red wine
560ml/1 pint water
Rind of 2 lemons
170g/6oz granulated sugar
2 small sticks cinnamon
2 bay leaves
2 tablespoons redcurrant jelly
45g/1½oz gelatine
2 egg whites and the egg shells
Drop of cochineal *or* carmine colouring (optional)

For the filling:

15g/½oz gelatine	15g/½oz candied peel
2 tablespoons water	3 tablespoons sherry
15g/½oz glacé cherries	150ml/¼ pint double cream

1. First make the jelly: put all the ingredients except the egg whites and red colouring into a very clean pan and place over a medium heat. Stir until the gelatine and sugar have dissolved. Remove the bay leaves, cinnamon sticks and lemon rind.

2. Place the crushed shells in a bowl, add the egg whites and whisk until frothy. Pour into the warming jelly and keep whisking steadily with a balloon whisk until the mixture boils and rises. Stop whisking immediately and draw the pan off the heat. Allow the mixture to subside. Take care not to break the crust formed by the egg white.

3. Bring up to the boil again, and again allow to subside. Repeat this once more (the egg white will trap the sediment in the liquid and clear the jelly). Allow to cool for 10 minutes.

4. Fix a double layer of fine muslin over a clean basin and carefully strain the jelly through it, taking care to hold the egg white crust back. When all the liquid is through (or almost all of it) allow the egg white to slip into the muslin. Then strain the jelly again – this time through both egg white crust and cloth. Do not try to hurry the process by squeezing the cloth, or murky jelly will result.

5. Add a drop of red colouring if necessary. Leave to cool.

6. In a small heavy pan, soak the gelatine for the filling in the water. Chop the fruits and soak them in sherry.

7. Half whip the cream (until thick but not quite solid), and add the fruits.

8. Dissolve the gelatine over a gentle heat. When runny and clear, stir it into the cream mixture.

9. Pour a 2·5cm/1in layer of jelly into a 1¼ litre/1½ pint mould or flat-bottomed fruit bowl. Place in the refrigerator and leave to set.

10. Wet the outside of a tumbler and place it in the centre of the

mould on top of the set layer. Fill up around the glass with liquid jelly. To encourage quick setting fill the glass with ice cubes and refrigerate the jelly.

11. When set, turn out the icy water (you can turn the whole jelly over). Fill the glass with warm water to loosen it and remove.
12. Spoon the fruit filling into the centre hole left by the glass. Leave to become completely set.
13. Invert a wet plate over the mould and turn the two over together. Give a sharp shake and remove the mould.

Note: This recipe sounds, and is, rather complicated. The filling is encased in the jelly. For a simpler version set the jelly in a ring mould and once turned out pile the cream mixture (without the gelatine) into the centre.

Serves 4

Banana and Grape Chartreuse

860ml/1½ pints clear lemon jelly   170g/6oz white grapes
  (pages 271–2)   1 banana

1. Prepare the lemon jelly.
2. Rinse a ring mould out with water. Pour a layer of lemon jelly in the bottom of the mould, about 1cm/½in deep. Put into a cold place to set.
3. If using seedless grapes just wash them. If not, cut in half and take out the seeds. (If the skins are tough or spotted the grapes should be peeled: dip them into boiling water for a few seconds to make this easier.)
4. Arrange the grapes and slices of banana in the ring mould. Pour in enough cool but not quite set jelly to come half-way up the grapes and leave in the refrigerator to set. Pour the rest of the cool jelly in so that the fruit is covered and leave to set.
5. To turn out the jelly dip the outside of the mould briefly in

hot water. Invert a wet plate over the jelly mould and turn the two over together. Give a sharp shake and remove the mould.

Serves 6

St Clement's Jelly

This jelly consists of a clear lemon lake with a solid orange border.

570ml/1 pint uncleared orange
   jelly (pages 272–3)
570ml/1 pint clear lemon jelly
   (pages 271–2)

Green colouring

To serve:
English custard (page 321) *or*
   cream

1. Set the orange jelly in a 570ml/1 pint ring mould and turn out on to a flat plate. Chill very well.
2. Make the lemon jelly, adding a very little green colouring.
3. When the jelly is cold pour into the centre hollow of the orange jelly. Refrigerate again to set.
4. Serve with English custard or cream.

Note: Angelica, cut into diagonal 'leaves', or fresh mint leaves, look pretty round the orange border.

Serves 5–6

ICE CREAMS AND BOMBES

Black Cherry Frozen Dessert

1 can morello cherries
1 can raspberries
110g/¼lb meringues (page 250)
570ml/1 pint double cream *or*
   675g/1½lbs vanilla ice cream
   (page 278)

1 tablespoon brandy *or* kirsch
   (optional)
Icing sugar to taste

For the sauce:
2 teaspoons arrowroot
1 tablespoon brandy *or* kirsch

1. Drain the cherries and raspberries well, reserving the juice. Chop them into small pieces. Break up the meringues roughly.
2. Whip the cream until stiff, add the liqueur and sweeten to taste. (If using ice cream allow it to soften but not to melt.) Mix in the chopped fruit, and meringues.
3. Spoon the mixture into a bombe mould or bowl and put immediately into the freezer. It will take at least 2 hours, and probably 4, to harden. It can then be turned out on to a plate and put back in the freezer until needed.
4. Mix the arrowroot with a little water. Heat the reserved cherry and raspberry juices together in a saucepan, pour some of the hot juice on to the arrowroot, stirring, and then pour the arrowroot and juice into the saucepan. Bring to the boil, stirring. Allow to simmer 1 minute after boiling. Add the brandy or kirsch and serve hot with the bombe.

Note: This dessert can be made with fresh or frozen strawberries, pineapple or peaches, but the fruit should be chopped rather than left whole or in large pieces.

Serves 8

Vanilla Ice Cream

(made with a mousse base)

70g/2½oz caster sugar
100ml/3½ fl.oz water
1 vanilla pod *or* 1 teaspoon
  vanilla essence

425ml/¾ pint double cream
3 egg yolks, beaten

1. Put the sugar, water and vanilla pod into a saucepan and dissolve over a gentle heat.
2. Beat the egg yolks well. Half-whip the cream.
3. When the sugar has dissolved bring the syrup up to boiling point and boil 'to the thread'. Allow to cool for 1 minute.
4. Pour the sugar syrup on to the egg yolks while whisking them, and whisk until the mixture is thick and mousse-like.
5. Cool, whisking occasionally. Fold in the cream and freeze.
6. When the ice cream is half frozen, whisk again and return to the freezer.

To boil to the thread: To test, dip your finger into cold water, then into a teaspoon of the hot syrup, which should form threads between your thumb and forefinger when they are drawn apart.

Serves 4

Chocolate Ice Cream

(made with a custard base)

340g/¾lb plain chocolate, cut
  up
570ml/1 pint milk
1 egg

1 egg yolk
55g/2oz caster sugar
570ml/1 pint double cream
1 teaspoon vanilla essence

1. Dissolve the chocolate in the milk over a gentle heat.
2. Beat the egg and yolk with the sugar until light and fluffy.

3. When the chocolate has melted and the milk nearly boiled pour on to the egg mixture and whisk well. Strain and allow to cool.
4. Whip the cream lightly and fold it into the chocolate mixture with the vanilla essence. Put into a bowl and freeze.
5. When half-frozen re-whisk and re-freeze.

Note: Chocolate mint crisps or mint cracknel, crumbled up and added to the mixture at the time of the final whisking, gives a delicious flavour and crunchy texture.

Serves 4

Basic Bombe Filling

140g/5oz granulated sugar   5 egg yolks

1. Dissolve the sugar in 150ml/¼ pint water and when completely clear, boil to the thread. Allow to cool.
2. In a double saucepan or in a bowl over a pan of gently simmering water, beat the egg yolks until light. Gradually pour in the sugar syrup, whisking all the time until the mixture is thick and has doubled in bulk.
3. Remove from the heat and cool immediately by standing in a bowl of cold water while whisking until the mixture is cold.
4. Pour into the bombe and freeze for at least 12 hours.

To the thread: see page 278, *note*.

Makes about ½ litre/1 pint

Chocolate and Vanilla Bombe

For this recipe a 860ml/1½ pint bombe mould is essential.

170g/6oz plain chocolate   450g/1lb vanilla ice cream
                                   (page 278)

1. Break up the chocolate and put it in a pudding basin. Set it over a saucepan of simmering water. Stir until the chocolate is smooth and melted. Do not overheat or the chocolate will lose its gloss.
2. Brush melted chocolate over the inside of the bombe mould. Leave to cool and harden. Repeat the process until you have a fairly thick layer and you have used up all the chocolate. Again leave to harden.
3. Pack the vanilla ice cream into the middle of the bombe and spread flat. Close the mould and freeze.
4. 30 minutes before serving put the bombe into the refrigerator, to soften slightly.
5. To serve, remove the base of the mould and unscrew the top (this releases a vacuum). Invert a plate over the mould and turn the mould and plate over together. Give a sharp shake and remove the mould.

Chocolate and Praline Bombe

Chocolate ice cream (pages 278–9)

Vanilla ice cream (page 278)
Praline (page 332)

1. Read the instructions for making bombes on pages 88–9.
2. Pack the chocolate ice cream round the sides and bottom of the bombe mould or basin. Freeze.
3. Flavour the vanilla ice cream with praline and pack it into the middle of the bombe. Freeze.
4. Unmould and return to the freezer until needed.

Note I: A tablespoon or two of mincemeat, plus a tablespoon of brandy beaten into vanilla ice cream makes a good bombe filling. The outer layer of ice cream can be coffee, apricot or peach.

Note II: If you are not using a bombe mould but a pudding basin you may find that a vacuum is formed between the outer layer of ice cream and the bowl, which makes removing the bowl very difficult even if you dip it in hot water to melt the ice cream.

The best thing to do is to prick the outer layer of ice cream with a hot fork before piling in the filling. A proper bombe mould has a screw at the top which when undone releases the vacuum and enables the bombe to slide out easily.

Serves 6

Champagne Sorbet

570ml/1 pint water
450g/1lb granulated sugar
570ml/1 pint champagne

Juice of 2 lemons and 1 orange

1. Turn the freezer to coldest.
2. Put the water and sugar in a heavy pan and dissolve slowly on a gentle heat.
3. When the sugar has completely dissolved boil rapidly until the syrup is tacky and a short thread can be formed if the syrup is pulled between finger and thumb.
4. Add the Champagne and fruit juice and allow to cool.
5. Freeze for 3 hours or until the edges are icy, then whisk until smooth. Return to the freezer. The sorbet will not freeze solidly due to the high alcohol content, and should not be removed from the freezer until it is to be served. For this reason, serve in well chilled goblets.

Serves 10

Flaming Baked Alaska

1 round of whisked sponge
  cake (pages 336–7)
425ml/¾ pint vanilla ice cream
  (page 278)

3 egg whites
170g/6oz caster sugar
2 tablespoons rum

1. Put the sponge cake on an ovenproof serving dish. Place the

block of ice cream on it. Freeze at coldest temperature for at least 1 hour. Set the oven to 230°C/450°F, gas mark 8.

2. Whisk the egg whites and when they are very stiff, whisk in 2 tablespoons of the sugar. Continue to whisk until again stiff and shiny. When the whisk is lifted the meringue mixture should stand in solid peaks – not moving at all. Fold in the remaining sugar.

3. Spoon into a forcing bag fitted with a fluted pipe. Pipe the meringue mixture over the entire surface of the cake, completely covering it and the ice cream.

4. Bake in the oven for 3 minutes until the meringue is browned. Just before the Alaska is to come out of the oven heat up the rum in a small pan. Remove the Alaska. Set the rum alight, pour around the pudding and serve while flaming.

Note I: This dish is sometimes called Norwegian Omelette. The above is the simplest recipe, but variations are legion. The cake may be sprinkled with liqueur, or replaced by shortcake or almond pastry. The ice cream can be any flavour, and jam or fresh fruit are sometimes included. The meringue can be flavoured with coffee or almond essence, it may have ground hazelnuts in it, or be sprinkled with almonds before baking.

Note II: The Alaska can be kept in the freezer, with the meringue covering, until the last minute – then baked from frozen.

Serves 6

Pistachio Ice Cream in Biscuit Cups

For the biscuit mixture:
85g/3oz butter
85g/3oz caster sugar
3 egg whites
85g/3oz plain flour

For the ice cream:
570ml/1 pint milk
225g/½lb caster sugar
1 vanilla pod
290ml/½ pint single cream
8 egg yolks, beaten
110g/¼lb chopped pistachio
  nuts

For the sauce:
3 whole eggs
3 egg yolks
140g/5oz sugar
3 tablespoons Framboise
  liqueur
340g/¾lb fresh raspberries,
  sieved

1. Set the oven to 220°C/425°F, gas mark 7.
2. To make the biscuit cups melt the butter, add the sugar, stir until dissolved and allow to cool.
3. Gradually beat in the unwhisked egg whites, using a wire whisk. Fold in the sifted flour. Spread the mixture out in eight very large paper-thin rounds on a greased and floured baking sheet. (Warm the sheet for easier spreading.)
4. Bake for 4 minutes. The biscuits should be just brown at the edges and pale in the middle.
5. While still hot and pliable shape the discs of biscuit over greased upturned jam jars. Remove the jam jars when the paste has set. (If the cups are not quite crisp when cold, return them to the oven on the jam jars.)
6. Make the ice cream: bring the milk, sugar, vanilla pod and cream very slowly to the boil. Pour on to the beaten yolks, stirring well. Remove the vanilla pod.
7. If the mixture is still very thin and runny return it to a gentle heat and stir continuously until it will coat the back of the spoon. Immediately pour into a cold bowl and allow to cool. Add the nuts.

8. Freeze, either in an ice cream maker, or in ice trays in the freezer, taking it out and beating two or three times during the freezing process to prevent large ice crystals forming.

9. When ready to serve fill each biscuit cup with ice cream, stand on a platter and put back into the coldest part of the refrigerator or into the freezer while making the sauce.

10. Whisk the whole eggs, yolks, sugar and liqueur together in a bowl. Then stand over a saucepan of simmering water and keep whisking. It will thicken like zabaglione. Stir in the sieved berries and serve, lukewarm, with the biscuit cups.

Serves 8

9
Pasta, Pastries, Batters and Breads

PASTA

Green Pasta

225g/½lb fresh spinach
340g/¾lb strong flour
Pinch of salt

2 eggs
1 tablespoon cream

1. Wash the spinach well, remove the stalks and put into a pan without water. Add a sprinkling of salt. Cover and cook, shaking the pan, until tender (5–7 minutes). Drain well, pressing out all the water. Chop or liquidize it and push through a sieve to get a fairly dry paste.
2. Sift the flour and salt on to a wooden board. Make a well in the centre and in it put the eggs, spinach and cream. Using the fingers of one hand mix together the eggs, spinach and cream, gradually drawing in the flour. The mixture should be a stiff dough
3. Knead until smooth and elastic (about 15 minutes). Wrap in polythene and leave to relax in a cool place for 1 hour.
4. Roll one small piece of the dough out at a time until paper thin. Cut into the required size. Allow to dry (hanging over a chair back if long noodles, or lying on a wire rack or clean tea-towel if small) for at least 30 minutes before cooking.

Egg Pasta

450g/1lb strong flour
Pinch of salt
4 eggs

1 tablespoon oil
3–4 tablespoons water

1. Sift the flour and salt on to a wooden board. Make a well in the centre and drop in the eggs, oil and water.
2. Using the fingers of one hand mix together the eggs, oil and water and gradually draw in the flour. The mixture should be a very stiff dough.
3. Knead until smooth and elastic (about 15 minutes). Wrap in polythene and leave to relax in a cool place for 1 hour.
4. Roll one small piece of dough out at a time until paper thin. Cut into the required sized noodles.
5. Allow to dry (except ravioli) hanging over a chair back if long noodles, lying on a wire rack or dry tea-towel if small ones, for at least 30 minutes before boiling. Ravioli is dried after stuffing.

The commonest noodle shapes are:

Cannelloni: rectangles about the size of a side-plate. Generally stuffed (like a pancake) after boiling, then reheated.

Tagliatelle (fettucine): thin ribbons of pasta, usually served with a sauce.

Lasagne: wide strips usually used in alternate layers with a savoury mixture.

Ravioli: flat sheets used to form small stuffed envelopes, which are then boiled and served with or without sauce.

Spaghetti: originally made by pulling the dough into thin strands, now usually made by machine.

Macaroni: made commercially into short tube-like pieces.

PASTRY

Shortcrust Pastry

170g/6oz plain flour   30g/1oz lard
Pinch of salt   Very cold water
55g/2oz butter

286

1. Sift the flour with the salt.
2. Rub in the fats until the mixture looks like breadcrumbs.
3. Add 2 tablespoons of water to the mixture.
4. Mix to a firm dough – first with a knife and finally with one hand. It may be necessary to add more water, but the pastry should not be too damp. (Although crumbly pastry is more difficult to handle it produces a shorter, less tough result.)
5. Chill, wrapped, for 30 minutes before using; or allow to relax after rolling out but before baking.

Rich Shortcrust Pastry

170g/6oz plain flour 　　　　　1 egg yolk
Pinch of salt 　　　　　　　　　Very cold water
100g/3½oz butter

1. Sift the flour with the salt.
2. Rub in the butter until the mixture looks like breadcrumbs.
3. Mix the yolk with a tablespoon of water and add to the mixture.
4. Mix to a firm dough – first with a knife and finally with one hand. It may be necessary to add more water, but the pastry should not be too damp. (Although crumbly pastry is more difficult to handle it produces a shorter, less tough result.)
5. Chill, wrapped, for 30 minutes before using; or allow to relax after rolling out but before baking.

Wholemeal Pastry

140g/5oz butter 　　　　　　　Pinch of salt
225g/½lb wholemeal flour 　　　1 egg yolk
110g/¼lb plain flour 　　　　　Very cold water

1. Rub the butter into the flour and salt until the mixture looks like coarse breadcrumbs.

2. Mix the yolk with 2 tablespoons of water and add to the mixture.
3. Mix to a firm dough – first with a knife and then with one hand. It may be necessary to add more water, but the pastry should not be too damp. (Although crumbly pastry is more difficult to handle it produces a shorter, less tough result.)
4. Chill in the refrigerator for at least 15 minutes before using; or allow the rolled-out pastry to relax before baking.

Note I: To make sweet wholemeal pastry mix in 4 teaspoons of sugar once the fat has been rubbed into the flour.

Note II: All wholemeal flour may be used if preferred.

Choux Pastry

85g/3oz butter
220ml/7½ fl.oz water
105g/3¾oz well sifted plain
   flour

Pinch of salt
3 eggs

1. Put the butter and water together in a heavy saucepan. Bring slowly to the boil so that by the time the water boils the butter is completely melted.
2. *Immediately* the mixture is really boiling fast tip in all the flour with the salt, and draw the pan off the heat.
3. Working as fast as you can beat the mixture hard with a wooden spoon; it will soon become thick and smooth and leave the sides of the pan.
4. Stand the bottom of the saucepan in a basin or sink of cold water to speed up the cooling process.
5. When the mixture is cool beat in the eggs a little at a time until it is soft, shiny and smooth. If the eggs are large it may not be necessary to add all of them. The mixture should be of dropping consistency, falling off a spoon rather reluctantly and all in a blob. If it runs off it is too wet, if it adheres even when the spoon is slightly jerked it is too thick.
6. Use as required.

Strudel Paste (*or filo paste*)

285g/10oz plain flour
Pinch of salt
1 egg

150ml/¼ pint water
1 teaspoon oil

1. Sift the flour and salt into a bowl.
2. Beat the egg and add the water and oil. First with a knife, and then with one hand, mix the water and egg into the flour, adding more water if necessary to make a soft dough.
3. The paste now has to be beaten: lift the whole mixture up in one hand and then with a flick of the wrist throw it on to a lightly floured board. Continue doing this until the paste no longer sticks to your fingers and the whole mixture is smooth and very elastic. Put it into a clean floured bowl. Cover and leave in a warm place for 15 minutes.
4. The paste is now ready for rolling and pulling. To do this, flour a tea towel or large cloth on the table-top and roll out the pastry as thinly as you can. Now put your hand (well floured) under the pastry and, keeping your hand fairly flat, gently stretch and pull the pastry, gradually and carefully working your way round until the pastry is paper thin. (You should be able to see through it easily.) Trim off the thick edges.
5. Use immediately – strudel pastry dries out and cracks very quickly. Brushing with melted butter or oil helps to prevent this; or the pastry sheets may be kept covered with damp cloths.

Note: If the paste is not for immediate use, wrap it well and keep it refrigerated (for up to three days) or frozen. Flour the pastry surfaces before folding up. This will prevent sticking.

Makes 450g/1lb *paste*

Pâte Sucrée

170g/6oz plain flour	3 egg yolks
Pinch of salt	85g/3oz sugar
85g/3oz butter, softened	2 drops vanilla essence

1. Sift the flour on to a board with the salt. Make a large well in the centre and put the butter in it. Place the egg yolks and sugar on the butter with the vanilla essence.
2. Using the fingertips of one hand 'peck' the butter, yolks and sugar together. When mixed to a soft paste draw in the flour and knead lightly until the pastry is just smooth.
3. If the pastry is very soft chill before rolling or pressing out to the required shape. In any event the pastry must be allowed to relax for 30 minutes before baking, either before or after rolling out.

Note: This pastry can be made in an electric mixer but care must be taken not to over-mix, which would produce a too-soft paste.

Almond Pastry (*pâte frolle*)

Care must be taken when making this pastry because if it is over-kneaded the oil will run from the almonds and make it greasy.

110g/¼lb plain flour	1 egg yolk *or* ½ egg, beaten
Pinch of salt	2 drops vanilla essence
45g/1½oz ground almonds	85g/3oz butter, softened
45g/1½oz caster sugar	

1. Sift the flour with the salt on to a board or tabletop. Scatter over the ground almonds. Make a large well in the centre and put in the sugar, beaten egg or yolk and vanilla essence.
2. Using one hand only 'peck' the egg and sugar with your fingertips. When creamy add the softened butter and continue to mix, gradually drawing in the flour and almonds.

3. Knead gently to a paste and chill. Allow to relax for 30 minutes before baking.

Note: This pastry can be made in an electric mixer but great care should be taken not to over-mix.

Pâte à Paté

285g/10oz plain flour   2 egg yolks
½ teaspoon salt   Up to 3 tablespoons water
200g/7oz butter

1. Sift the flour and salt on to a board or tabletop. Make a large well in the centre and put the butter and yolks in it. 'Peck' the yolks and butter together with the fingers of one hand and gradually draw in the surrounding flour, adding the water only if required to give a soft but not sticky paste.
2. Wrap and leave to rest in the refrigerator for 30 minutes. Use as required.

Note: This paste can be made in an electric mixer but great care should be taken not to over-mix.

Flaky Pastry

225g/½lb plain flour   85g/3oz lard
Pinch of salt   150ml/¼ pint cold water
85g/3oz butter

1. Sift the flour with a pinch of salt. Rub in half the butter. Add enough cold water to mix with a knife to a doughy consistency. Turn out on to a floured board and knead until smooth.
2. Roll into an oblong about 12 × 25cm/5 × 10in. Cut the lard into tiny pieces and dot them evenly all over the top two-thirds of the pastry, leaving a good margin.

3. Fold the pastry in three, folding first the unlarded third up, then the larded top third down and pressing the edges to seal them. Give a 90° clockwise turn so that the folded, closed edge is to your right.
4. Repeat the rolling and folding process (without adding any fat) once more so that the folded, closed edge is on your right.
5. Roll out again, dot with butter, fold, seal and roll once more.
6. Roll out again, dot with lard as before, fold, seal and roll once more.
7. Fold, wrap the pastry and 'relax' (or chill) for 10–15 minutes.
8. Roll and fold once again (without adding any fat) and then use as required.

Note I: As a general rule flaky pastry is rolled out thinly, and baked at about 220°C/425°F, gas mark 7.

Note II: If the pastry becomes too warm or sticky and difficult to handle, wrap it up and chill it for 15 minutes before proceeding.

Rough Puff Pastry

225g/½lb plain flour   140g/5oz butter
Pinch of salt   Very cold water

1. Sift the flour and salt into a cold bowl. Cut the butter into knobs about the size of a sugar lump and add to the flour. Do not rub in but add enough water to just bind the paste together. Mix first with a knife, then with one hand.
2. Wrap the pastry up and leave to relax for 10 minutes in the refrigerator.
3. On a floured board, roll the pastry into a strip about 15 × 10cm/6 × 4in. This must be done carefully: with a heavy rolling pin press firmly on the pastry and give short sharp rolls until it has reached the required size. The surface of the pastry should not be over-stretched and broken.
4. Fold the strip into three and turn so that the folded closed edge is to your right.

5. Again roll out, into a strip 1cm/½in thick. Fold in three again and leave, wrapped, in the refrigerator for 15 minutes.
6. Roll and fold the pastry as before and chill again for 15 minutes.
7. Roll and fold again, by which time the pastry should be ready for use, with no signs of streakiness and of a uniform colour.
8. Roll into the required shape (pie top or whatever).
9. Chill again before baking.

Puff Pastry

225g/½lb plain flour
Pinch of salt
30g/1oz lard

150ml/¼ pint icy water
140–200g/5–7oz butter

1. If you have never made puff pastry before, use the smaller amount of butter: this will give a normal pastry. If you have some experience, more butter will produce a lighter, very rich pastry.
2. Sift the flour with a pinch of salt. Rub in the lard. Add the icy water and mix with a knife to a doughy consistency. Turn on to the table and knead quickly until smooth. Wrap in polythene or a cloth and leave in the refrigerator for 30 minutes to relax.
3. Lightly flour the table-top or board and roll the dough into a rectangle about 13 × 25cm/5 × 10in.
4. Tap the butter lightly with a floured rolling pin to get it into a flattened block about 10 × 8cm/4 × 3in. Put the butter on the rectangle of pastry and fold both ends over to enclose it. Press the sides together to prevent the butter escaping.
5. Now tap the pastry parcel with the rolling pin to flatten the butter a little: then roll out, quickly and lightly, until the pastry is three times as long as it is wide. Fold it very evenly in three, first folding the third closest to you over, then bringing the top third down. Give it a 90° clockwise

turn to the right so that the folded, closest edge is on your right. Again press the edges firmly with the rolling pin. Then roll out again to form a rectangle as before.

6. Now the pastry has had two rolls and folds, or 'turns' as they are called. It should be put to rest in a cool place for 30 minutes or so. The rolling and folding must be repeated twice more, the pastry again rested, and then again given two more 'turns'. This makes a total of six. If the butter is still very streaky, roll and fold it once more.

Bouchée Cases

225g/½lb flour-quantity puff   Beaten egg
pastry (pages 293–4)

1. Set the oven to 220°C/425°F, gas mark 7.
2. Roll out the pastry to 0·5cm/¼in. With a round pastry cutter stamp it out in rounds. With a slightly smaller cutter cut a circle in the centre of each round, but be careful not to stamp the pastry more than half-way through.
3. Brush the tops with beaten egg, taking care not to get egg on the sides which would prevent the pastry layers separating and rising.
4. Bake on a wet baking sheet until brown and crisp; about 12 minutes.
5. Take off the pastry 'lids' and scrape out any raw pastry left inside. Return the bouchée cases to the oven for 4 minutes to dry out. Cool on a wire rack.

Note: Bouchée cases, if they are to be eaten hot, should either be filled while they are still very hot with a cooked hot filling, or, if they are cooked and cold, with a cooked cold filling. Hot fillings will tend to make the pastry soggy during the reheating process. If both filling and pastry go into the oven cold the pastry will have time to become crisp again before the filling is hot.

Makes about 20 *cocktail-size bouchées*

Vol-au-vent

225g/½lb flour-quantity puff   Beaten egg
  pastry (pages 293–4)   Salt

1. Set the oven to 220°C/425°F, gas mark 7.
2. Roll the pastry to 1cm/½in thickness and cut into a round about the size of a dessert plate. Place on a baking sheet. Using a cutter half the size of the pastry round, cut into the centre of the pastry, but taking care not to cut right through to the baking tray.
3. Flour the blade of a knife and use this to 'knock up' the sides of the pastry: try to slightly separate the leaves of the pastry horizontally; this means that the edge will flake readily when cooking. (It counteracts the squashing effect of the cutter used to cut out the round, which may have pressed the edges together, making it more difficult for the pastry to rise in even layers.)
4. With the back of the knife-blade make a star pattern on the borders of the vol-au-vent case and mark a lattice pattern on the inner circle. (The back rather than the sharp edge of the blade is used as this will not cut into the pastry – the idea is to make a pattern without cutting through the surface of the pastry.)
5. Mix a pinch of salt into the beaten egg. Brush the pastry carefully with this eggwash avoiding the knocked up sides – if they are covered with egg the pastry will be prevented from rising.
6. Bake in a hot oven for 30 minutes, and carefully lift off the top of the inner circle. Keep this for the lid of the case when filled. Pull out and discard any partially cooked pastry from the centre of the case.
7. Return the case to the oven for 2 minutes to dry out. The vol-au-vent is now ready for filling.

Note I: The above quantity of pastry will make two smaller (saucer-size) vol-au-vents.

Note II: Flaky or rough-puff pastry are also suitable. But the method of cutting is different: cut the pastry into two rounds the size of a side-plate. Stamp a circle right out of the centre of one of them. Brush the uncut round with egg and place the ring of pastry on top. Bake the middle small round of pastry too, and use it as a lid.

PASTRIES

Danish Pastries

Most Danish pastries require almond filling and icing as well as the basic dough. Instructions for these are given first, with the individual instructions for Pinwheels, Almond Squares etc., following. But the icing should not be made until the pastries are baked.

Danish pastries are frequently scattered with flaked browned almonds while the icing is still wet. Sometimes sultanas or small pieces of canned pineapple, or apple purée, are included in the filling.

For the pastry:
15g/½oz fresh yeast
1 tablespoon caster sugar
5 tablespoons milk, warmed
225g/½lb plain flour
Pinch of salt
1 egg, lightly beaten
110g/¼lb unsalted butter,
    softened

For the glacé icing:
110g/¼lb icing sugar
Boiling water to mix

For the almond paste filling:
45g/1½oz butter
45g/1½oz icing sugar
30g/1oz ground almonds
2 drops vanilla essence

For the glaze:
1 egg, beaten

When rolling out Danish pastry, care should be taken to prevent the butter breaking through the paste and making the resulting pastry heavy. Use a heavy rolling pin, bring it firmly down on to the pastry and roll with short, quick, firm rolls. Do not 'push' it. Avoid using too much flour. If the paste is becoming warm and unmanageable, wrap it up and chill it well before proceeding.

1. Dissolve the yeast with 1 teaspoon of the sugar and the milk.
2. Sift the flour with a pinch of salt into a warmed bowl. Add the remaining sugar. Make a well in the centre and drop into it the egg and the yeast mixture.
3. Using a round-bladed knife mix the liquids, gradually drawing in the surrounding flour to make a soft dough. If extra liquid is required add a little more water.
4. When the dough leaves the sides of the bowl turn it on to a floured surface and beat and knead until smooth. Roll into a longish rectangle $\frac{1}{2}$cm/$\frac{1}{4}$in thick.
5. Divide the butter into hazelnut-sized pieces and dot it over the top two-thirds of the dough leaving a 1cm/$\frac{1}{2}$in clear margin round the edge. Fold the pastry in three, folding the unbuttered third up over the centre section first, and then the buttered top third down over it. You now have a thick 'parcel' of pastry. Give it a 90° turn so that the former top edge is on your right. Press the edges together.
6. Dust lightly with flour and roll into a long rectangle again. Fold in three as before. Chill for 15 minutes.
7. Roll and fold the pastry once or twice again until the butter is well worked in and the paste does not look streaky. Chill for at least 30 minutes or overnight.
8. To make the almond paste, cream the butter, add the sugar and beat well until light and soft. Mix in the ground almonds and flavour with vanilla essence. Mix well but do not overbeat or the oil will run from the almonds making the paste greasy.
9. When ready to use the glacé icing mix enough boiling water into the sugar to give an icing that will run fairly easily – about the consistency of cream.

Note: If using dried yeast use half the amount called for, mix it with 3 tablespoons of the liquid (warmed to blood temperature) and a teaspoon of sugar. Leave until frothy about 15 minutes, then proceed. If the yeast does not go frothy it is dead and unusable.

Almond Squares

1. Follow the instructions on pages 296–8, then:
2. Set the oven to 200°C/400°F, gas mark 6.
3. Roll the pastry into a rectangle 25 × 20cm/10 × 7½in. Cut into 5cm/2½in squares. Put on to a floured baking sheet.
4. Put a spoonful of the filling into the centre of each piece of pastry. Fold each corner into the middle and press it down lightly into the almond paste to stick it in position.
5. Prove for 15 minutes (put into a warm draught-free place to allow the dough to rise). Press down the middle of the squares.
6. Brush with beaten egg and bake for 15–20 minutes.
7. When cool spoon over the freshly made glacé icing.

Pinwheels

1. Follow the instructions on pages 296–8 then:
2. Set the oven to 200°C/400°F, gas mark 6.
3. Roll the pastry out thinly and cut it into 13cm/5in squares. Place on a floured baking sheet.
4. From each corner towards the centre of each square, make a cut about 3cm/1½in long. Put a blob of almond filling in the uncut centre of each square.
5. Fold alternate points of pastry (one from each corner) into the middle and press on to the filling to secure. This leaves one unfolded point at each corner, and the pastry should now resemble a child's pinwheel (see drawing).
6. Prove in a warm place for 15 minutes (allow to rise and puff up). Press down the corners.

7. Brush with beaten egg and bake for 15–20 minutes.
8. When cool spoon on the freshly made glacé icing.

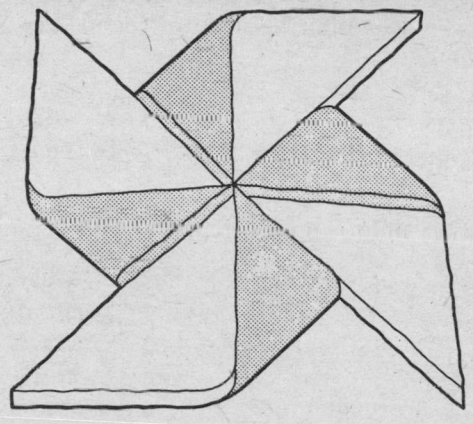

Crosses

1. Follow the instructions on pages 296–8, then:
2. Set the oven to 200°C/400°F, gas mark 6.
3. Roll the pastry out thinly and cut it into 13cm/5in squares. Place on a floured baking sheet.
4. Cut through each square as indicated in the drawing, stage 1, and then overlap the two opposite corners as shown in stages 2 and 3.

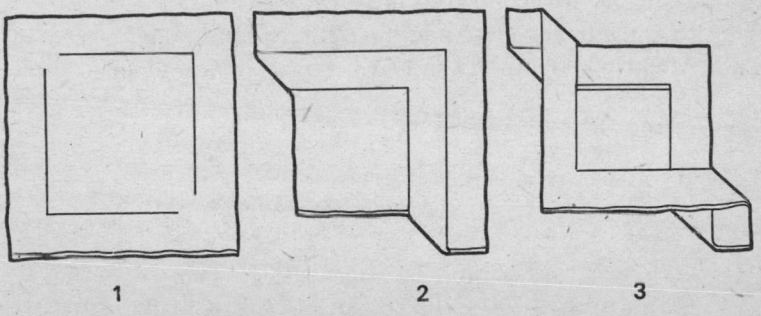

1   2   3

5. Fill the centre hole with almond paste filling or apple purée.
6. Prove for 15 minutes in a warm draught-free place.
7. Brush with beaten egg and bake for 15–20 minutes.
8. When cool dust with icing sugar or spoon over freshly-made glacé icing.

Cinnamon Wheels

In this recipe the almond paste is replaced with a cinnamon filling

55g/2oz butter
55g/2oz sugar
2 teaspoons cinnamon

Small handful of dried fruit and chopped mixed peel

1. Follow the instructions on pages 296–8, omitting the almond filling, then:
2. Cream the butter with the sugar. Add the cinnamon and mix well.
3. Set the oven to 200°C/400°F, gas mark 6.
4. Roll the pastry to a rectangle 25 × 20cm/12 × 8in. Place on a floured baking sheet.
5. Spread the butter mixture over the dough, leaving a narrow margin all round. Scatter over the dried fruit and chopped peel.
6. Roll the pastry, from one end, into a thick roll. Cut into 2·5cm/1in slices. With a lightly floured hand, flatten each slice to the size of the palm of your hand. Put somewhere warm and draught-free to rise (prove) for 15 minutes.
7. Brush with egg glaze and bake for 15 minutes.
8. Allow to cool slightly and spoon over the freshly made glacé icing.

Crescents

1. Follow the instructions on pages 296–8, then:
2. Set the oven to 200°C/400°F, gas mark 6. Roll out the pastry

into a rectangle 30 × 15cm/12 × 6in. Cut into 7·5cm/3in squares and cut each square diagonally in half. Put on a floured baking sheet.

3. Place a small piece of almond paste at the base (long side) of each triangle. Roll it up from the base to the tip and curve into a crescent shape.
4. Put into a warm, draught-free place to rise (prove) for 15 minutes.
5. Bake for 15–20 minutes or until a good brown. When cool spoon over the freshly made glacé icing.

Croissants

370g/12oz flour,
Pinch of salt
15g/½oz fresh yeast
225ml/8 fl.oz lukewarm water
  and milk mixed

225g/8oz butter at room
  temperature
Beaten egg for glazing

1. Sift the flour with the salt into a clean bowl. Rub in 55g/2oz of the butter. Cut remaining butter into small pieces.
2. Cream the yeast in a small bowl with two tablespoons of the liquid. Add the remaining liquid.
3. Make a well in the centre of the flour and pour in the yeast mixture. Mix quickly with a knife, then with your hand to a soft but firm dough.
4. Turn onto a lightly floured table top and knead for 10 minutes.
5. Roll out the dough into a rectangle three times as long as it is wide. Dot the top 2/3 of the dough with half the butter. Fold and turn as for flaky pastry pages 291–2. Roll out again into a rectangle. Dot the top 2/3 with the remaining butter. Fold, turn and roll again. Fold, then wrap loosely in a large plastic bag and refrigerate for 1 hour.
6. Roll and fold twice more. Relax for as long as possible, preferably overnight in the refrigerator.

7. Set the oven to 190°C/375°F, gas mark 5.
8. Divide the dough into two. Roll each one into a circle approximately 25cm/10in diameter. Turn over. With a sharp knife, cut each circle into six wedges. Roll up each piece from the broad end to the point. Curve slightly to form a crescent. Place on a floured tray and cover loosely with polythene.
9. Prove at room temperature till doubled in size. Brush with beaten egg and place in the oven for approximately 25 minutes until well risen and golden.

Yeast: If using dried yeast, see page 298, *note.*

Makes 12

Scotch Crescents (*Aberdeen rowies*)

225g/½lb butter
110g/¼lb lard
30g/1oz fresh yeast
1 tablespoon caster sugar

290ml/½ pint lukewarm water
450g/1lb plain flour
Salt

1. Cream the fats together.
2. Put the yeast and sugar into a jug and mix well. Add half the lukewarm water.
3. Sift the flour with a good pinch of salt into a basin and pour in the yeasty liquid. Add more water if required and mix to a soft dough. Cover the bowl and leave in a warm place until doubled in bulk. This should take about 40 minutes depending on the temperature.
4. With floured hands knead the dough briefly, then roll it out into a long rectangle. Put a third of the butter/lard mixture, in tiny blobs or dots, over the top two-thirds of the pastry strip. Fold the bottom (unbuttered) piece up over the buttered middle section, and bring the top (buttered) third down to form a parcel. Give the block of pastry a 90° turn so that the folded closed side previously furthest from you is now on your right.
5. With a rolling pin press the edges together to prevent the

fats escaping. Then roll out to a rectangle again. Again butter the top two-thirds, fold as before, turn and roll as before. Repeat the whole process once more, by which time the fat will all be used up.

6. Now divide the dough into three and roll each one into a 25cm/10in square. Cut each square into four smaller ones. Cut each square into two triangles.

7. Roll each triangle up from the broadest side to the tip. Pinch the ends together tightly, and pull gently into crescent shapes. Put on greased baking sheets, well apart. Cover with greased polythene and allow to prove in a warm place until croissant-sized (doubled in bulk).

8. While this is going on heat the oven to 220°C/425°F, gas mark 7.

9. Brush the crescents gently with beaten egg. Bake for 15 minutes or until crisp and a good brown. Cool slightly on a wire rack and serve warm.

Yeast: If using dried yeast, see page 298, *note.*

Makes 24

Palmiers

Palmiers are usually made from leftover pieces of puff pastry.

1. Set the oven to 200°C/400°F, gas mark 6.

2. Do not push the trimmings up into a ball as you would short-crust pastry – this would spoil the carefully created layers in the paste. Lay the strips or pieces flat on top of each other, folding them if necessary.

3. Using caster sugar instead of flour, roll the pastry out into an oblong ½cm/¼in thick. Sprinkle well with caster sugar. Fold each end of the pastry to the centre, and then fold the pastry in half. Cut the roll across into slices 1¼cm/½in wide.

4. Lay the slices on a wet baking sheet, far apart, and flatten well with a sugared rolling pin or your hand. Bake for 10 minutes or until pale brown, with the underside caramelized. Turn over and bake for a further 10 minutes. Cool on a wire rack.

Gaufrettes Viennoise

170g/6oz butter
225g/½lb plain flour
Pinch of salt
1 egg
85g/3oz caster sugar

85g/3oz ground almonds
Royal icing (pages 325–31)
Redcurrant jelly *or* raspberry
    jam

1. Heat the oven to 190°C/375°F, gas mark 5. Take the butter from the refrigerator and allow it to warm to room temperature.
2. Sift the flour and salt on to a pastry board or marble slab. Make a large well in the centre. Drop the egg and sugar into the well. Sprinkle the almonds on the flour. Using the thumb and fingertips of one hand only, 'peck' sugar and egg until light and creamy. Work in the butter, then gradually absorb the flour and almonds.
3. Knead until smooth, then chill for about 30 minutes. Roll the pastry into an oblong. Place on an ungreased baking sheet. Trim the edges with a floured knife and cut into squares.
4. Add a good pinch of flour to the royal icing. Fill into a paper cornet fitted with a fine plain nozzle and decorate half the squares with a lattice pattern.
5. Bake for about 7–8 minutes until just golden. When cool spread each undecorated square thinly with jelly or jam and place a decorated square on the top.

Note: Gaufrettes are waffles. These are so named because their square shape and latticed icing makes them look like waffles.

Makes 12

St Andrew's Boats

Apple marmalade (pages 332–3)   Royal icing (pages 325–31)
110g/¼lb flour-quantity pâte
  frolle (pages 290–1)

1. Allow the apple marmalade to cool before using. It should be thick – almost solid.
2. Set the oven to 190°C/375°F, gas mark 5. Line 10cm/4in boat-shaped moulds with the pâte frolle. Keep the trimmings. Bake blind.
3. When the cooked pastry cases are cold, fill with the apple marmalade.
4. Coat with royal icing. While the icing is still wet put two narrow bands of raw pastry across each boat, criss-crossed.
5. Bake again for 10 minutes or until the pastry cross is biscuit coloured. Allow to cool.

Note: If boat-shaped moulds are not available, use patty tins.

Baking blind: See page 142, *note.*

Makes 12

Goldenberry Flan

If Cape gooseberries (goldenberries) are not available apricots or golden plums can be used.

170g/6oz flour-quantity   2 tablespoons smooth apricot
  shortcrust pastry (pages   jam
  286–7)   2 level teaspoons arrowroot
2 cans Cape gooseberries
  (goldenberries)

1. Line a large flan ring or flan dish with the pastry and bake blind.
2. Drain the fruit, reserving the juice, and put the fruit into the flan.

3. Mix the arrowroot with enough of the juice to make it smooth. Put half a pint of the juice into a saucepan with the arrowroot mixture and bring to the boil, stirring all the time. Add the jam and boil to a thick syrupy consistency.
4. When tepid pour into the flan – all over the fruit – and leave to get quite cold. The glaze (the syrup and jam mixture) should set when cold but be just warm enough to run when poured on the fruit.

Baking blind: See page 142, *note.*

Serves 6

Maids of Honour

1·4 litres/2½ pints fresh milk
1 tablespoon rennet
1 egg
30g/1oz butter
55g/2oz sugar

Grated rind and juice of ½
  lemon
225g/½lb flour-quantity
  rich shortcrust pastry
  (pages 286–7)

1. Warm the milk to blood heat. Add the rennet and leave for three hours or until set into a junket.
2. Put the junket into a muslin bag (or sieve lined with muslin or flannel) and squeeze or press the curds (milk solids) gently to extract the whey (liquid). Remove the curds to a bowl.
3. Lightly beat the egg. Melt the butter without overheating it. Add both to the curds. Add the sugar, rind and juice. Mix well.
4. Set the oven to 200°C/400°F, gas mark 6.
5. Use the pastry to line tartlet tins. Prick well with a fork. Fill with the curd mixture and bake for 30 minutes.

Makes about 32 *tartlets*

Cherry Strudels

140g/5oz flour-quantity strudel paste (page 289)
340g/¾lb cherries, stoned
110g/¼lb sugar
Stick of cinnamon

290ml/½ pint water
55g/2oz butter, melted
2 tablespoons browned crumbs
Icing sugar

1. Make up the strudel paste.
2. Heat the oven to 200°C/400°F, gas mark 6. Grease a baking sheet.
3. Place the cherries with the sugar, cinnamon and water in a thick-bottomed pan and stew until just soft. Drain and allow to cool, removing the cinnamon.
4. Roll and pull the pastry into four paper-thin squares, each about 18 × 18cm/7 × 7in. (Follow the directions in the strudel paste recipe.) Put the squares on floured tea-towels.
5. Trim the edges, brush liberally with half the melted butter and sprinkle with crumbs. Put a quarter of the cherry mixture on each piece of pastry.
6. Fold the sides of the pastry over slightly to prevent the filling escaping during cooking, then, using the tea-towel to help, roll the strudels up. (See drawing overleaf.)
7. Brush with the remaining melted butter. Bake for about 15 minutes until golden brown. Remove and immediately dust with icing sugar. Serve warm.

Serves 4

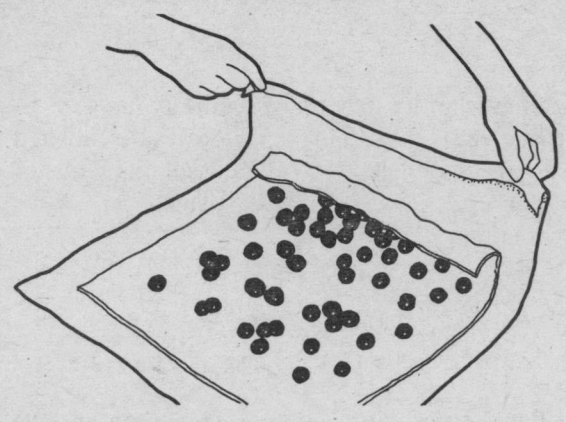

Strawberry Tartlets

170g/6oz flour-quantity
pâté sucrée (page 290)

For the filling:

225g/½lb petit Suisse cheese
55g/2oz caster sugar
450g/1lb strawberries, hulled

4 tablespoons redcurrant jelly,
melted

1. Set the oven to 190°C/375°F, gas mark 5.
2. Roll out the pastry thinly and use it to line the tartlet tins. Bake blind for about 15 minutes or until a pale biscuit colour. Remove the papers and the 'blind' beans. If the pastry is not quite cooked, return to the oven for 5 minutes. Carefully take out the pastry cases and leave to cool on a wire rack.
3. Cream the cheese with the caster sugar and place a teaspoonful of this mixture at the bottom of each case. Arrange the

strawberries, cut in half if necessary, on top of the cheese and brush lightly with warm melted redcurrant jelly.

Baking blind: See page 142, *note.*

Note: Whipped cream may be substituted for the cheese if preferred.

Makes 20

Mille Feuilles

225g/½lb flour-quantity rough puff pastry (pages 292–3) *or* puff pastry (pages 293–4)
2 tablespoons strawberry jam

290ml/½ pint double cream, whipped
225g/½lb icing sugar, sifted

1. Set the oven to 220°C/425°F, gas mark 7.
2. On a floured board roll the pastry into a large thin rectangle about 30 × 20cm/12 × 8in. Place on a wet baking sheet. Prick all over with a fork.
3. Leave to relax, covered, for 20 minutes. Bake until brown. Allow to cool.
4. Cut the pastry into three neat strips 10 × 20cm/4 × 8in. (Keep the trimmings for decoration.) Choose the piece of pastry with the smoothest base, and reserve. Spread a layer of jam on the two remaining strips and cover with cream. Place them on top of each other and cover with the third, reserved, piece of pastry, smooth side uppermost. Press down gently but firmly. (See drawing overleaf.)
5. Mix the icing sugar with boiling water until it is thick, smooth and creamy. Be careful not to add too much water. Coat the icing over the top of the pastry and while still warm sprinkle crushed pastry trimmings along the edges of the icing. Allow to cool before serving.

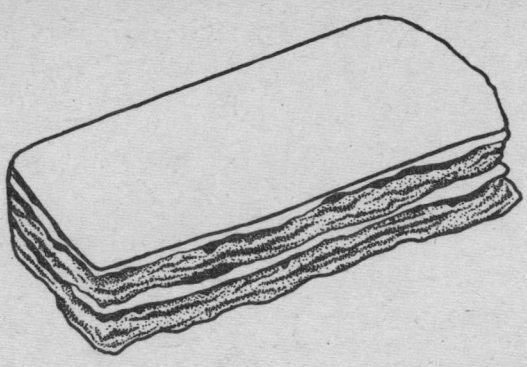

Note: To 'feather' the icing, put a tablespoon of warmed, smooth liquid jam in a piping bag with a 'writing' nozzle. Pipe parallel lines of jam down the length of the newly iced mille feuilles, about 2cm/¾in apart. Before the icing or jam is set drag the back of a knife across the lines of jam. This will pull the lines into points where the knife crosses them. Repeat this every 5cm/2in in the same direction, and then drag the back of the knife in the opposite direction between the drag-lines already made.

Serves 4–6

Gâteaux St Honoré aux Oranges

110g/¼lb flour-quantity pâte
  sucrée (page 290)
3 egg-quantity choux paste
  (page 288)
2 oranges

290ml/½ pint double cream
1 tablespoon icing sugar
110g/¼lb granulated sugar
1 tablespoon pistachio nuts,
  chopped

1. Set the oven to 200°C/400°F, gas mark 6. Have ready two baking sheets, one of them wet.
2. Make up the pâte sucrée, place it on the dry baking sheet

and shape it into a round 20cm/8in in diameter. Prick well.

3. Prepare the choux paste. Using a piping bag fitted with 1cm/½in plain nozzle, pipe a thin border of choux paste around the circle of pâte sucrée. Bake until the choux ring is brown (about 25 minutes), then make a few pea-sized holes in it to let the steam escape. Return to the oven for 5 minutes to dry out. Allow to cool. (If the pastry centre is biscuit-coloured and cooked before the outer ring is brown put a circle of foil over the pâte sucrée to prevent further browning.) Transfer to a serving plate.

4. Pipe the remaining choux paste into small profiteroles (small blobs about the size of a large gooseberry) on the wet baking sheet. Bake to a good brown (about 25 minutes).

5. While still hot make a pea-sized hole in the base of each profiterole with a skewer. Return to the oven for 5 minutes to dry out inside, then allow to cool.

6. Peel the oranges as you would apples, with a sharp knife, removing the pith. Cut out the orange segments leaving behind the membrane. Save 12 segments for decoration and cut the remainder in small pieces.

7. Whip the cream until stiff, adding the icing sugar, and fill half of it into a forcing bag fitted with a small plain nozzle. Pipe into the profiteroles through the hole made by the skewer.

8. Fold the cut-up orange segments into the remaining whipped cream. Spoon this mixture into the centre of the choux ring.

9. Slowly melt the sugar in a small heavy saucepan. Allow to melt, then to brown. Remove from the heat and, working quickly, dip each profiterole into the caramel. Dip the tops of the profiteroles (while still sticky) into the pistachio nuts, and arrange them on the orange-cream, piling them into a pyramid, and using more caramel to stick them in place if necessary.

Serves 6

Honey Boats

110g/¼lb pâté sucrée (page 290)

For the filling:

85g/3oz unsalted butter
85g/3oz caster sugar
85g/3oz ground almonds

1 tablespoon honey
Coffee essence
Coffee fondant icing (page 324)

1. Line boat moulds thinly with the pâte sucrée. Bake blind.
2. Cream the butter and sugar together until light. Stir in the almonds and honey and flavour with coffee essence. Fill the cooked cases with this coffee almond cream, shaping it to give a slightly domed surface. Leave in a cool place to set.
3. Melt the fondant icing and spoon over the boats.

Baking blind: See page 142, *note.*

Makes 9

Almond Cakes

125g/4½oz caster sugar
125g/4½oz ground almonds
25g/scant 1oz flour
2 small egg whites

55g/2oz pounded praline (page 332)
Icing sugar
Rice paper

1. Set the oven to 180°C/350°F, gas mark 4.
2. Sift together the caster sugar, almonds and flour. Add enough egg white to just bind the mixture together and stir in the praline.
3. Roll into balls the size of a walnut, brush with egg white and coat with icing sugar. Bake on rice paper for 15 minutes.

Makes 24

Printaniers

4 egg-quantity Genoise
commune mixture (page 337)
170g/6oz butter-quantity crème
au beurre mousseline
(page 333) with the lemon
rind omitted

Vanilla essence
Coffee essence
Sieved strawberry jam
White fondant icing (page 324),
warmed

1. Set the oven to 190°C/375°F, gas mark 5.
2. Brush a Swiss roll tin, lined with paper, with melted lard. Dust with caster sugar. Pile in the Genoise mixture, making sure that it is evenly distributed throughout the tin. Bake for 25 minutes, allow to cool and turn out on to a wire rack.
3. Split the cake and sandwich it with a little of the crème au beurre. Cut it into strips 3·75cm/1½in wide.
4. Divide the remaining crème au beurre into three and flavour one-third with vanilla essence, one-third with coffee essence and one-third with sieved strawberry jam.
5. Using a forcing bag fitted with a 1·75cm/⅝in plain pipe, pipe one row of coffee- and one of vanilla-flavoured crème au beurre side by side along the top of each strip of cake. Then pipe a row of strawberry crème au beurre on top of the first two strips and refrigerate to harden.
6. Using a large spoon carefully coat each strip with the warm fondant icing. Leave to set.
7. Cut each cake strip on the diagonal, into pieces about 2cm/¾in wide. Keep cool until ready to serve.

Makes 24

BATTERS

French Pancakes (*crêpes*)

110g/¼lb plain flour
Pinch of salt
1 egg
1 egg yolk

290ml/½ pint milk *or* milk and
    water mixed
1 tablespoon oil
Oil for frying

1. Sift the flour and salt into a bowl and make a well in the centre exposing the bottom of the bowl.
2. Into this well place the egg and egg yolk with a little of the milk.
3. Using a wooden spoon or whisk mix the egg and milk and then gradually draw in the flour from the sides as you mix.
4. When the mixture reaches the consistency of thick cream beat well and stir in the oil.
5. Add the rest of the milk – the consistency should now be that of thin cream. (Batter can also be made by placing all the ingredients together in a liquidizer for a few seconds, but take care not to over-whizz or the mixture will be bubbly.)
6. Cover the bowl and refrigerate for about 30 minutes. This is done so that the starch cells will swell, giving a lighter result.
7. Prepare a pancake pan or frying pan by heating well and wiping out with oil. Pancakes are not fried in fat like most foods – the purpose of the oil is simply to prevent sticking.
8. When the pan is ready pour in about 1 tablespoon of batter and swirl about the pan until it is evenly spread across the bottom.

9. Place over heat and, after 1 minute, using a palette knife and your fingers, turn the pancake over and cook again until brown. (Pancakes should be extremely thin so if the first one is too thick, add a little extra milk to the batter. The first pancake is unlikely to be perfect, and is often discarded.)

10. Make up all the pancakes, turning them out on to a tea-towel or plate.

Note I. Pancakes can be kept warm in a folded tea-towel, on a plate over a saucepan of simmering water, in the oven, or in a warmer. They reheat well with filling, or by being briefly returned to the frying pan.

Note II: Pancakes freeze well, but should be separated by pieces of greaseproof paper. They may also be refrigerated for a day or two.

Makes about 12

Fritter Batter

125g/4½oz plain flour
Pinch of salt
2 eggs

1 tablespoon oil
150ml/¼ pint milk

1. Sift the flour with the salt into a bowl.
2. Make a well in the centre, exposing the bottom of the bowl.
3. Put 1 whole egg and 1 yolk into the well and mix with a wooden spoon or whisk until smooth, gradually incorporating the surrounding flour and the milk. A thick cream consistency should be reached.
4. Add the oil. Allow to rest for 30 minutes.
5. Whisk the egg white and fold into the batter with a metal spoon just before using.

Note: This batter can be speedily made in a blender. Simply put all the ingredients, except the egg white, into the machine and whizz briefly.

BREADS

Plaited White Loaf

450g/1lb warmed plain flour
  (preferably 'strong')
1 teaspoon salt
290ml/½ pint tepid milk
15g/½oz butter

15g/½oz fresh yeast
1 teaspoon caster sugar
1 egg, beaten
Milk and poppy seeds for
  glazing

1. Sift the flour and salt into a warm mixing bowl. Make a well in the centre.
2. Heat the milk, melt the butter in it and allow to cool until tepid. Cream the yeast and sugar together. Mix the milk, egg and creamed yeast together and pour into the well.
3. Mix and knead until smooth and elastic (this should take 10–15 minutes). The dough should be soft.
4. Cover the bowl with a piece of oiled polythene and put to rise in a warm place for about an hour. It should double in bulk.
5. Heat the oven to 200°C/400°F, gas mark 6.
6. Divide the dough into three equal pieces and knead on a floured board. Form a long sausage with each piece and plait them together. Place on a greased baking sheet.
7. Cover again with the oiled polythene and prove (allow to rise) in a warm place for 15 minutes.
8. Brush with milk, sprinkle with poppy seeds and bake for about 25 minutes or until the loaf is golden and sounds hollow when tapped on the underside.

Yeast: If using dried yeast, see page 298, *note*.

French Bread

30g/1oz fresh yeast
1 teaspoon sugar
55ml/2 fl.oz warm water
345ml/12 fl.oz warm milk
110ml/4 fl.oz warm water

2 teaspoons salt
900g/2lb plain flour
1 teaspoon salt (for brushing)
110ml/4 fl.oz warm water (for
   brushing)

1. Cream the yeast and sugar with the 55ml/2 fl.oz warm water.
2. Pour the warm milk, 110ml/4 fl.oz warm water and salt into a bowl.
3. Stir in the yeast mixture and slowly add the flour, a little at a time. Mix with a wooden spoon until the mixture becomes a medium firm dough.
4. Knead well on a lightly floured surface, for at least 10 minutes. Sprinkle the surface with more flour if the dough becomes sticky.
5. Place the dough in a bowl, cover with a damp cloth and leave to rise in a warm place until doubled in size (at least 1 hour). Knock back, knead for 2 minutes, then leave to rise, covered with the cloth, for about 40 minutes.
6. Knock back again, then divide the dough into 3 equal portions. Shape into 3 loaves, as long as your baking tray. This is best achieved by rolling the dough into 3 flat rectangles and then rolling them up like tight Swiss rolls. With a sharp knife cut diagonal slashes about ½cm/¼in deep at 5cm/2in intervals on top of the loaves.
7. Dissolve the salt in the warm water and use to lightly brush the loaves. Cover again and let the loaves rise until doubled in bulk.
8. Set the oven to 220°C/425°F, gas mark 7. Put a roasting tin of hot water on the oven floor. (The steam will help to make the crust crisp.)
9. Bake the loaves for 15 minutes. Reduce the heat to 190°C/375°F, gas mark 5 and brush the loaves with more salt water. Bake for a further 25–30 minutes, brushing once or twice more

with salt water. When the loaves feel rigid and light in weight, and sound hollow when tapped on the underside, they are done. Cool on a wire rack.

Yeast: If using dried yeast, see page 298, *note.*

Brioche

225g/½lb flour
Pinch of salt
5 level teaspoons caster sugar
2 eggs, beaten

2 tablespoons warm water
55g/2oz melted butter
7g/¼oz fresh yeast

For the glaze:
1 egg mixed with 1 tablespoon
water and ¼ teaspoon sugar

1. Grease a large brioche mould or 12 small brioche tins.
2. Mix the yeast with 1 teaspoon of the sugar and the water. Leave to dissolve.
3. Sift the flour with a pinch of salt into a bowl. Sprinkle over the sugar. Make a well in the centre. Drop in the eggs, yeast mixture and melted butter and mix with the fingers of one hand to a soft but not sloppy paste. Knead on an unfloured board for 5 minutes or until smooth. Put into a clean bowl, cover with a damp cloth or greased polythene and leave to rise in a warm place until doubled in bulk (about 1 hour).
4. Turn out and knead again on an unfloured board for 2 minutes.
5. Place the dough in the brioche mould (it should not come more than half way up the mould). If making individual brioches divide the dough into 12 pieces. Using three-quarters of each piece roll them into small balls and put them in the brioche tins. Make a dip on top of each brioche. Roll the remaining paste into 12 tiny balls and press them into the prepared holes. Push a pencil, or thin spoon handle, right

through each small ball into the brioche base as this will anchor the balls in place when baking.

6. Cover with greased polythene and leave in a warm place until risen to the top of the tin(s). The individual ones will take 15 minutes, the large one about 30 minutes.

7. Set the oven to 230°C/450°F, gas mark 8.

8. Brush the egg glaze over the brioche. Bake the large one for 20–25 minutes, or small ones for 10 minutes.

Yeast: If using dried yeast, see page 298, *note*.

10
Sweet Sauces, Fillings, Cakes and Icings

SWEET SAUCES

Sugar Syrup

285g/10oz granulated sugar   Pared rind of 1 lemon
570ml/1 pint water

1. Put the sugar, water and lemon rind in a pan and heat slowly until the sugar has completely dissolved.
2. Bring to the boil and cook until the syrup feels tacky between finger and thumb. Allow to cool.
3. Strain and keep covered in a cool place until needed.

Note: Sugar syrup will keep unrefrigerated for about 5 days, and for several weeks refrigerated.

Crème Pâtissière

290ml/$\frac{1}{2}$ pint milk   20g/$\frac{3}{4}$oz flour
2 egg yolks   20g/$\frac{3}{4}$oz cornflour
55g/2oz caster sugar   Vanilla essence

1. Scald the milk.
2. Cream the egg yolks with the sugar and when pale mix in the flours. Pour on the milk and mix well.

3. Return the mixture to the pan and bring slowly up to the boil, stirring continuously. (It will go alarmingly lumpy, but don't worry, keep stirring and it will become smooth.) Allow to cool slightly and add the vanilla essence.

Crème Anglaise (*English Egg Custard*)

290ml/½ pint milk
1 tablespoon sugar
½ vanilla pod *or* few drops
  vanilla essence

2 egg yolks

1. Heat the milk with the sugar and vanilla pod and bring slowly to the boil.
2. Beat the yolks in a bowl. Remove the vanilla pod and pour the milk on to the egg yolks, stirring steadily. Mix well and return to the pan.
3. Stir over gentle heat until the mixture thickens so that it will coat the back of a spoon; do not boil.
4. Add the vanilla essence if using.

Melba Sauce

225g/½lb fresh *or* frozen
  raspberries (not canned)

Icing sugar

1. Defrost the raspberries if frozen. Push the raspberries through a nylon or stainless sieve to remove all seeds.
2. Sift in icing sugar to taste. If too thick add a few spoons of water.

Sweet Gooseberry Sauce

225g/½lb ripe gooseberries
150ml/¼ pint water

110g/¼lb sugar
Pinch ground ginger

1. Put all the ingredients in a thick-bottomed saucepan. Bring gradually to the boil and then simmer until the gooseberries pop open and change to a yellowish colour.
2. Push through a sieve and reheat.

Apple Purée

450g/1lb cooking apples
110g/¼lb sugar

4 tablespoons water

1. Peel and core the apples. Cut them into chunks. Put them with the sugar and water into a heavy saucepan and simmer gently until they are a soft pulp. Beat out any lumps with a wooden spoon.
2. If the purée is too sloppy boil it rapidly to reduce and thicken it, but leave the lid half on as it splashes dangerously.

Apple Marmalade

3 cooking apples
Strip of lemon rind

A little butter
About 85g/3oz brown sugar

1. Wash the unpeeled apples, quarter and core them. Rub the bottom and sides of a heavy saucepan with butter.
2. Slice the apples thickly into the pan and add the lemon rind. Cover and cook gently, stirring occasionally until completely soft.
3. Push through a sieve. Rinse out the pan and return the purée to it. Add at least 55g/2oz of brown sugar to 570ml/1 pint

of purée. Cook rapidly until the mixture is of dropping consistency, about 4 minutes. Allow to cool. Add more sugar if necessary.

Chocolate Sauce

55g/2oz plain chocolate
150ml/¼ pint water
2 tablespoons golden syrup

15g/½oz caster sugar
1 teaspoon brandy

1. Chop the chocolate roughly and put into a small heavy pan with the water, syrup and sugar. Allow the chocolate to melt and the sugar to dissolve over a gentle heat.
2. When completely dissolved increase the heat and boil the sauce rapidly for 30 seconds. Add the brandy. Serve hot or cold.

Makes 225ml/8 fl.oz

Apricot Glaze

3 tablespoons apricot jam
2 tablespoons water

Juice of ½ lemon

1. Place all the ingredients in a thick-bottomed pan.
2. Bring slowly to the boil stirring gently (avoid beating in bubbles) until syrupy in consistency. Strain.

Note: When using this to glaze food use when still warm, as it becomes too stiff to manage when cold. It will keep warm standing over a saucepan of very hot water.

ICINGS
AND CONFECTIONERY

Fondant Icing

220g/½lb loaf sugar
115ml/4 fl.oz water

½ teaspoon liquid glucose *or*
pinch of cream of tartar

1. Dissolve the sugar in the water over a low heat without boiling.
2. Mix the cream of tartar with a spoonful of water and add it, or the liquid glucose, to the water and sugar. Cover and bring to the boil. Boil to 'soft ball' consistency (to a temperature of 110°–115°C/230°–240°F or when, if a spoonful is dropped into a bowl of cold water, it will form a soft ball when rubbed between the fingers). Stop the sugar syrup from cooking any further by dipping the bottom of the pan into a bowl of cold water. Let it cool slightly.
3. Moisten a cold hard surface and pour the sugar syrup on to it in a steady stream. With a metal spatula fold the outsides of the mixture into the centre.
4. Continue to turn with a spatula and work until the fondant becomes fairly stiff. Knead into balls. Place in a bowl and cover with a damp cloth for 1–2 hours.
5. If the fondant is to be stored place in a screw-top jar. When ready to use put it in a bowl and stand over a pan of simmering water to melt.

Note: A sugar thermometer is almost essential. It is vital to get the syrup exactly the right consistency, not too liquid or hard.

Coffee Fondant Icing

Proceed as above but add 2 teaspoons of coffee essence to the syrup before pouring on to the work surface.

Royal Icing

Royal icing is a hard icing, traditionally used (over a layer of marzipan) for the coating and decoration of special-occasion cakes, which keeps very well. There are some important points to remember:

1. More than with any other cooking it is vital to clean up as you go along. It is almost impossible to produce delicate and neat work from a cluttered work surface. Get all the nozzles and bags lined up before you begin icing.
2. Never overfill the piping bag. This leads to the sticky icing squeezing out of the top.
3. Keep all full piping bags under a damp cloth to prevent the icing in the nozzle drying out.
4. Always keep the icing covered with a damp cloth when not in use to prevent it drying out.
5. Always clean the nozzles immediately after use using a pin to ensure that no icing is left in the tip.
6. Practise the required pattern on the table top before tackling the cake. Don't try complicated things like roses and scrolls before you have thoroughly mastered the easier decorations like trellis, shells, stars and dots.
7. Follow the instructions slavishly.

Note I: Never lick your fingers or equipment. Even a little wet icing can make you feel very sick.

Note II:
450g/1lb sugar makes enough for a 20cm/8in cake.
900g/2lb sugar makes enough for a 30cm/12in cake.

For the first coat of icing for a 20cm/8in cake:
2 egg whites
450g/1lb icing sugar

(Make up more icing for the second and third coats and for the decoration as you need it.)

Additions (optional)

A few drops blue food colouring (makes white icing very bright white)

1 teaspoon lemon juice to each 225g/½lb sugar (makes the icing a little sharper and less sickly)

½ teaspoon glycerine to each 225g/½lb sugar (produces a softer icing which will not splinter when cut. Without glycerine royal icing eventually hardens to an unbreakable cement. More glycerine can be added, but this will give a softer icing unsuitable for a tiered cake. None need be used if the cake is to be eaten within 24 hours of icing)

Mix the egg white with 3 tablespoons of the sugar, add lemon juice or glycerine if required and beat well. Gradually add the remaining sugar and beat for about 15 minutes in all until the icing is soft, very white, fluffy and will hold its shape. More sugar can be added if the mixture is too sloppy. The blue colouring, if used, is added last.

Consistency　A cake is normally covered with 2–3 coats of icing and decorated with either piping or 'run in' work. The consistency varies for each coat.

　　First coating:　Very thick; the icing should stand up in points if the beating spoon is lifted from the bowl.

　　Second coating:　A little thinner (the points should flop over at the tips, like rabbit ears).

　　Third coating:　The icing should be of pouring consistency.

　　For piping:　Consistency as for first coating.

　　For run-in-work:　As for the third coating.

Beating　The icing should be smooth and glossy. It is difficult to beat properly if the icing is too solid or too thin, so first get the consistency to that described above for the first coating. It can be thinned once beaten absolutely smooth.

Beating with an electric whisk　The machine must be robust. Use the heaviest beater rather than a wire whisk. Icing made with an electric beater will have air bubbles if beaten too quickly at the beginning, or for too long. Beat for 5 minutes at the lowest speed, then gradually turn up the speed until, after 10 minutes, the machine is at full speed. Once smooth and glossy, stop. If there are any bubbles, leave the icing, covered with a damp cloth, in the refrigerator overnight.

First coating

Make sure that the marzipan is smooth. Brush away any excess sugar or crumbly paste with a dry pastry brush. Put all the icing on top of the cake and work it across the top and down the sides with a spatula or large knife. Completely cover the cake and spread the icing smooth and free from air bubbles. Do not 'pat' the cake as this will cause air bubbles. Make sure that all the almond paste is covered.

To smooth the top You will need a long-bladed straight ham knife, palette knife or metal ruler, longer if possible than the diameter of the cake to be iced. It is used either wet and hot, or dry:

Wet: If you dip the knife in hot water it helps to smooth the surface, especially if the icing is beginning to set; the water, however, dilutes some of the icing and may cause a streaked effect.

Hot: If you heat the knife it helps to smooth the surface, especially if the icing is beginning to set, but it tends to dry out the icing and form a crust.

Dry: This is the best method for a fine finished result, but the hardest to accomplish.

Hold the knife blade or ruler at both ends and draw it in one long steady slow movement across the cake top, tilting the top edge of the ruler slightly towards you. An even pressure should be maintained. Alternatively, place the cake on an icing turntable. Hold the palette knife or ruler so that the tip or end is at the centre of the cake and the blade is just touching the surface of the icing. Keep the blade or ruler still and rotate the cake under it. Always wipe the knife clean after each attempt at smoothing.

To trim and neaten the sides of the cake If the cake is square, hold the ruler or blade upright and with an even pressure draw it along the sides of the cake. If the cake is round, place it on an icing turntable. Put the left arm as far round the cake as possible and hold the turntable. Hold the ruler or knife upright in your right hand and rotate the cake slowly anti-clockwise. An attractive pattern can be achieved by using a serrated knife.

To store Store the cake for at least 24 hours in a clean, cool, dry place. If the storage place is damp it will prevent the icing from drying and it will slowly slip down the sides of the cake. If it is too warm the cake will 'sweat' and oil from the marzipan will be drawn into the icing.

Second coating

When the icing is dry pare away any projecting edges with a sharp knife and smooth flat with sandpaper. Brush away all the dust.

Ice the cake following the rules for the first coating but using a slightly thinner icing. When dry place on a cake board 5cm/2in larger in diameter or width than the cake. Leave to dry for at least 24 hours.

Third coating (or float)

The third coating may not be necessary if the second is perfect and the cake is not to be kept for more than a few weeks before eating. If it is necessary, proceed when the second coating is dry. Prepare the surface as previously instructed. Before converting the icing into the desired pouring consistency, pile a little thick icing into an icing bag fitted with a no. 1 or 2 writing nozzle and cover it with a damp cloth.

Add a little egg white to the remaining icing and beat until smooth and of pouring consistency. Leave in a tightly covered container for 30 minutes. (Stretching a piece of polythene wrap over the bowl will do.) This is to make the air bubbles rise to the surface. If you do not do this air bubbles will break all over the surface of the cake, making little holes in the icing.

With the writing tube pipe an *unbroken* line around the top edge of the cake. Pour the runny icing into a piping bag without a nozzle and guide it over the top of the cake, flooding the surface and carefully avoiding the piped line. With the handle of a teaspoon work the flooding to the edge of the cake. The piped line will prevent the icing running off.

Decorating

You must have a clear idea of the design before you begin. If it is a geometric pattern, draw it on a piece of tracing paper and place this on the cake. Using a large pin, prick where the lines meet. Remove the paper and you will be left with guidelines made by the pin points. Join these up with a fine pencil or with more pricked holes so that the design is visible.

Half-fill the piping bags, fitted with the chosen nozzles, with the icing mixed to the correct consistency (see above). Put them under a wet cloth until needed. Get everything you will need ready on or near your work surface (e.g. more bags and extra nozzles, a large spoon, a palette knife, a small basin of hot water to wash the nozzles in).

Direct piping

Star piping: Hold the pipe upright, immediately above and almost touching the top of the cake and squeeze gently from the top of the bag. Stop pressing and lift the bag away. Always stop pressing *before* lifting the bag away.

Dot or pearl piping: Pipe as for stars. If the dots are too small, do not try to increase their size by squeezing out more icing; use a larger nozzle.

Straight lines: Press the bag as for making a dot but leave the icing attached to the cake surface – do not draw away by lifting the bag. Hold the point of the nozzle about 4cm/1½in above the surface of the cake and, pressing gently as you go, guide rather than drag the icing into place. The icing can be more easily directed into place if it is allowed to hang from the tube.

Trellis work: Pipe parallel lines ·5cm/¼in apart. Pipe a second layer over the top at right angles or at an angle of 45° to the first. Then pipe another layer as closely as possible over the first set of lines, then another set over the second layer, and so on until you have the desired height of trellis. Six layers (three in each direction) is usual for an elaborate cake.

Shells: Use a star nozzle. Hold the bag at an angle of about 45°. Pipe a shell, release the pressure on the bag and begin a new shell one-eighth of the way up the first shell, so that each new shell overlaps its predecessor.

Scrolls: Use a star nozzle. Hold the bag at an angle of about 45°. Pipe a scroll first from left to right and the second from right to left.

Run in work: Using a writing nozzle pipe the outline of a design (e.g. leaf, Father Christmas etc.) on to oiled foil or greaseproof paper. 'Float' runny icing in the centre, and leave to set. Lift off and stick on to the cake with wet icing.

Note: Variations of pressure when piping both shells and scrolls make the icing emerge in the required thicknesses. Shells and scrolls can be made into very attractive borders when combined with trellis work and edged with pearls.

Causes of failure

Broken lines	(a)	icing too stiff
	(b)	pulling rather than easing into place
	(c)	making the icing with a mixer set at too high a speed, causing air bubbles
Wobbly lines	(a)	squeezing the icing out too quickly
	(b)	icing too liquid
Flattened lines	(a)	icing too liquid
	(b)	bag held too near the surface

Indirect piping

This piping is done on to oiled moulds or waxed paper and when dry the piped shapes are stuck to the cake with a little wet icing.

Trellised shapes: Pipe as for direct piping on to waxed paper or oiled moulds (the backs of teaspoons, patty tins, cups or glasses). Leave for 24 hours then warm over a very gentle heat to dislodge them. Slide off the mould and fix to the cake with a little wet icing.

Flowers: You need confectioners' 'flower nails' and petal nozzles. The icing should be thick. The petals are piped individually on to the oiled surface of the 'flower nail', the biggest petals first and then the smaller ones. If the flower nails are covered with oiled foil, this can be removed carefully after piping so that the nail can be used for the next flower. When dry green icing leaves (piped and dried separately) can be attached to the back of the flowers with a little wet icing.

When making coloured flowers it is helpful to tint the icing to a *pale* colour first. After they have dried they can be touched up with a paint brush to give the flowers a more natural appearance. By varying the angle at which the piping bags are held, flatter petals (for daisies, violets and primroses) or thicker, more rounded petals (for roses) can be made. Sweet peas are made with 2–3 flat petals slightly overlapping each other with a smaller upright rounded petal piped on top of each flat one.

Cooked Marzipan

This recipe gives a softer, easier-to-handle paste than the more usual, uncooked marzipan.

2 eggs	340g/¾lb ground almonds
170g/6oz caster sugar	4 drops vanilla essence
170g/6oz icing sugar	1 teaspoon lemon juice

1. Lightly beat the eggs.
2. Sift the sugars together and mix with the eggs.
3. Place the bowl over a pan of boiling water and whisk until light and creamy. Remove from the heat.
4. Add the ground almonds, vanilla and lemon juice, and beat briefly with a wooden spoon. The marzipan should be a soft paste.
5. Lightly dust the working surface with icing sugar. Carefully knead the paste until just smooth. (Overworking will draw out the oil from the almonds giving a too greasy paste.) Wrap well and store in a cool place.

Chocolate Caraque

30g/1oz dark chocolate

Melt the chocolate on a plate over a pan of boiling water. Spread thinly on a hard cold surface. When just set use a long knife to shave off curls of chocolate: hold the knife horizontally with one hand on the handle and one on the tip of the blade. Scrape the chocolate surface by pulling the knife towards you.

Praline

Few drops oil   55g/2oz caster sugar
55g/2oz unblanched (with the
   skins on) almonds

1. Oil a baking sheet.
2. Put the almonds and sugar in a heavy pan, and set over a gentle heat. Stir with a metal spoon as the sugar begins to melt and brown. When thoroughly caramelized (browned) tip onto the oiled sheet.
3. Allow to cool completely, then pound to a coarse powder in a mortar or blender.
4. Store in an air-tight jar.

Note: Whole praline almonds, as sold in the streets of Paris, are made in the same way, but are not crushed to a powder. They are sometimes used for cake decoration.

Crème au Beurre Mousseline

A rich creamy cake filling.

55g/2oz granulated sugar
4 tablespoons water
2 egg yolks

Grated rind of ½ lemon
110g/¼lb unsalted butter

1. Dissolve the sugar in the water and when completely dissolved boil rapidly to about 105°C/215°F. At this point the syrup, if tested between finger and thumb, will form short threads. Take off the heat immediately.
2. Whisk the yolks and lemon rind and pour on the syrup. Keep whisking until thick.
3. Soften the butter and whisk into the mixture slowly. Allow to cool.

BISCUITS AND CAKES

Macaroons

110g/¼lb ground almonds
170g/6oz caster sugar
1 teaspoon plain flour
2 egg whites

2 drops vanilla essence
Rice paper for baking
Split almonds for decoration

1. Set the oven to 180°C/350°F, gas mark 4.
2. Mix the almonds, sugar and flour together.
3. Add the egg whites and vanilla. Beat very well.
4. Lay a sheet of rice paper or vegetable parchment on a baking sheet and with a teaspoon put on small heaps of the mixture, well apart.
5. Place a split almond on each macaroon and bake for 20 minutes. Allow to cool.

Note I: To use this recipe for petits fours the mixture must be put out in very tiny blobs on the rice paper. Two macaroons can then be sandwiched together with a little stiff apricot jam and served in petits fours paper cases.

Note II: Ratafia biscuits are tiny macaroons with added almond essence.

Makes 25

Sponge Fingers

3 eggs
85g/3oz caster sugar
Vanilla essence

85g/3oz plain flour sifted with
    pinch of salt
Extra caster sugar for glazing

1. Set the oven to 190°C/375°F, gas mark 5. Grease and flour a baking sheet and have ready a piping bag fitted with a medium-sized plain nozzle.
2. Whisk the egg yolks with the sugar until light and fluffy.
3. Add a few drops of vanilla essence.
4. Whisk the whites until stiff and fold a third of them into the yolk mixture.
5. Fold in the flour. Fold in the remaining whites very lightly with a large metal spoon.
6. Pile the mixture into a piping bag and pipe on to the baking sheet in 5cm/2in lengths.
7. Dust each finger with plenty of caster sugar. Bake for 5–6 minutes and cool on a wire rack.

Note: Special baking sheets, moulded to take sponge fingers, are available; but they are not strictly necessary.

Christmas Cake

(with rough icing)

This cake is for a 20cm/8in cake tin, 8cm/3in deep

170g/6oz butter
170g/6oz light brown sugar
4 eggs
225g/½lb plain flour
Pinch of salt
½ teaspoon mixed spice
1 tablespoon black treacle
225g/½lb currants, washed and
  dried

450g/1lb sultanas
55g/2oz chopped candied peel
110g/¼lb glacé cherries, cut in
  half
110g/¼lb chopped almonds
3 tablespoons brandy *or* stout
1 small apple grated

For the covering and icing:
450g/1lb marzipan (page 331)
About 450g/1lb icing sugar
1–2 egg whites

½ teaspoon glycerine
Few drops blue colouring

For the decoration:
Red ribbon

2 sprigs holly

1. Set the oven to 180°C/350°F, gas mark 4. Grease and line the cake tin as instructed on pages 42–3.
2. Cream the butter and sugar until light and fluffy.
3. Beat the eggs in one by one, then fold in the flour, salt and spice.
4. Stir in the remaining cake ingredients in the order in which they are listed. Beat very well.
5. Put the mixture into the greased and lined tin and bake for 1 hour. Turn the oven down to 170°C/325°F, gas mark 3 and bake for a further 2½ hours, covering the top of the cake with thick brown paper for the last hour if it seems to be browning too fast.
6. The cake is cooked when a skewer will emerge dry after being stuck into the middle.
7. Cool the cake before turning it out. Remove the paper.

8. When the cake is quite cold wrap it up in greaseproof paper and put into an air-tight container.
9. If the cake is to be iced it should be covered in marzipan at least two weeks before Christmas: follow the instructions on page 327.
10. About a week before Christmas ice the cake. Sift the icing sugar.
11. Whisk the egg whites until frothy and beat enough of the icing sugar into them to get the icing absolutely smooth but stiff enough to stand up in peaks.
12. Beat in half a teaspoon of glycerine (to prevent the icing setting like concrete) and a drop or two of colouring (to make it look less yellow and more pure-white).
13. Using a large knife or spatula spread the icing all over the cake: dip the knife in hot water to get the sides smooth, and use a fork to lift the top into spiky peaks all over.
14. Next day, when the icing is dry, wrap the ribbon round it and cover the join with one of the holly sprigs, secured with a long pin. Put the other holly sprig on top.

Note: Instructions for more sophisticated icing techniques are on pages 329–31.

Whisked Sponge

3 eggs   85g/3oz plain flour
85g/3oz caster sugar   Pinch of salt

1. Set the oven to 180°C/350°F, gas mark 4. Grease a 20cm/8in cake tin and line with greaseproof paper. Brush out with melted lard and dust with flour and sugar.
2. Place the eggs and sugar in a bowl and fit it over (not in) a saucepan of simmering water. Whisk the mixture until light, thick and fluffy. (If using an electric mixer no heat is required.)
3. Remove the bowl from the heat and continue whisking until cool. (Stand the bowl in a large basin of cold water to speed up cooling.)

4. Sift the flour and salt and with a large metal spoon fold it in to the mixture quickly and gently, being careful not to beat out any of the air.
5. Turn the mixture into the prepared tin and bake in the middle of the oven for about 30 minutes.
6. Test to see if it is cooked. When the cake is done it will shrink slightly and the edges will look crinkled. When pressed gently it will feel firm but spongy and sound 'creaky'.
7. Turn out on to a wire rack to cool.

Serves 4

Genoise Commune

4 eggs
125g/4½oz caster sugar

125g/4½oz plain flour
55g/2oz very soft but not melted butter

1. Set the oven to 190°C/375°F, gas mark 5. Prepare a moule-à-manqué or deep sandwich tin: brush with melted fat or oil; line the bottom with a round of greaseproof paper, grease again and dust out with caster sugar and flour.
2. Break the eggs into a bowl. Add the sugar. Place the bowl over a saucepan of simmering water and whisk until the mixture has doubled in bulk, and will leave a ribbon trail on the surface when the whisk is lifted. Lift the bowl off the heat and continue to whisk until the mixture has cooled slightly (about 4 minutes). (If using an electric beater whisking need not be done over heat.)
3. Sift in about half the flour and fold it in gently but thoroughly with a metal spoon.
4. Pour and fold in the very soft, but not melted, butter and sift and fold in the remaining flour.
5. Pour the mixture into the prepared tin. Bake for 30–35 minutes. Allow to cool slightly in the tin and turn out on to a wire rack.

Note: Classic cooks would not call a Genoise (which contains fat) a sponge cake (which should be made from eggs, flour and sugar only). But in everyday English the word sponge is used for both types of cake.

Genoise Fine

4 eggs
125g/4½oz caster sugar
100g/3½oz plain flour

100g/3½oz butter, runny but
    not melted

1. Prepare a moule-à-manqué or deep sandwich tin with flour, greaseproof paper and sugar. Set the oven to 190°C/375°F, gas mark 5.
2. Break the eggs into a large bowl and add the sugar. Set the bowl over (not in) a pan of simmering water and whisk until light, fluffy and doubled in bulk. Take off the heat and whisk until cool.
3. Fold in the sifted flour – be very careful not to stir at all vigorously, or this will push out all the air that has been laboriously whisked in.
4. Pour in the butter and mix it in with a large metal spoon. Do not stir for a second longer than is necessary or the light consistency will be spoiled.
5. Turn into the prepared tin and bake for 30–35 minutes. Leave to cool in the tin for a few minutes then turn on to a wire rack to cool.

Note: This is sometimes called a 'butter sponge'. However, this description is not culinarily correct, as a true sponge contains no fat.

Dobez Torte

This is a cake with five layers. The mixture will not deteriorate if all layers cannot be baked at the same time because of a lack of baking sheets or space in the oven.

For the cake:
4 eggs
170g/6oz caster sugar
140g/5oz plain flour
Pinch of salt

For the decoration:
140g/5oz sugar
2 tablespoons browned
 chopped almonds *or* ground
 browned hazelnuts
6 whole hazelnuts

For the butter cream:
85g/3oz sugar
4–5 tablespoons water
3 egg yolks
225g/½lb butter
Coffee essence
55g/2oz skinned, toasted and
 ground hazelnuts

1. Set the oven to 190°C/375°F, gas mark 5. Grease and flour five baking sheets and mark a 20cm/8in circle on each sheet (use a flan ring or saucepan lid in the floured surface).
2. Start with the cake: whisk the eggs, adding the sugar gradually. Set the bowl over (not in) a pan of simmering water and whisk until the mixture is thick and mousse-like. Remove from the heat and whisk until cold. Sift the flour and salt and fold into the egg mixture with a metal spoon. Divide the mixture between the five baking sheets and spread into circles as marked.
3. Bake for 8 minutes. Trim the edges and leave to cool on a wire rack.
4. Prepare the butter cream: dissolve the sugar in the water and when clear boil rapidly to the thread (to test, put a little sugar syrup on to a wooden spoon, dip your index finger and thumb into cold water and then into the syrup in the spoon. When you pull your finger and thumb apart there should be a thread of syrup between them). Allow to cool slightly.
5. Separate the eggs. Whisk the yolks in a bowl and then pour

the syrup slowly on to them, whisking all the time. Keep whisking until you have a thick, mousse-like mixture. Cream the butter well and beat in the egg and sugar mixture. Flavour 2 tablespoons of the butter cream with coffee essence and keep for decoration. Mix the ground hazelnuts and coffee essence into the remaining mixture.

6. Lay one piece of cake on a wire rack over an oiled tray. Melt the sugar for the caramel in a little water and when dissolved boil fiercely until a good caramel colour and pour immediately over the piece of cake, covering it completely.

7. Allow to harden *slightly* and mark into six portions with an oiled knife. (The idea is to cut through the setting caramel but not through the cake.) Trim the edges of excess caramel.

8. Sandwich the cake layers together with the coffee and hazelnut butter cream, placing the one with caramel on top. Spread the coffee and hazelnut butter cream thinly around the sides and press on the nuts.

9. Using a forcing bag with a large fluted nozzle pipe a rosette with the remaining plain butter cream on top of each portion of cake. Decorate each rosette with a whole hazelnut.

Serves 6

Gateau Nougatine

For the cake:
110g/¼lb hazelnuts
4 eggs
117g/4¼oz sugar
117g/4¼oz plain flour
55g/2oz butter, well softened

For the royal icing:
1 small egg white
170g/6oz icing sugar
Squeeze of lemon juice

For the crème au beurre mousseline:
85g/3oz lump or granulated sugar
3 tablespoons water
2 egg yolks
110–140g/4–5oz unsalted butter

For the nougat:
45g/1½oz finely chopped
  almonds
85g/3oz caster sugar
½ teaspoon glucose
1 lemon

For the chocolate fondant icing:
225g/½lb loaf sugar
115ml/4 fl.oz water
½ teaspoon liquid glucose *or*
  pinch of cream of tartar
30g/1oz unsweetened chocolate
7g/¼oz sweetened chocolate
1 drop vanilla essence

1. Set the oven to 180°C/350°F, gas mark 4. Lightly butter a moule-à-manqué or deep sandwich tin and dust out with flour.
2. Start with the cake: bake the nuts in the oven until brown. Rub the skins off in a dry cloth. Grind the nuts until fine.
3. Separate the eggs. Beat the yolks thoroughly with the sugar until white and creamy.
4. Whisk the whites until stiff but not dry and fold them into the yolk mixture alternately with the flour, butter and hazelnuts.
5. Pile into the prepared tin and bake for 40–45 minutes. (The edges of the cake will look slightly shrunken and the top will feel firm to the touch when the cake is cooked.) Turn on to a wire rack to cool.
6. For the royal icing whisk the egg white until frothy. Beat the icing sugar into it with the lemon juice until very smooth, white and stiff. Cover with a damp cloth until ready for use.
7. For the nougat bake the chopped almonds until pale brown. Keep warm. Put the sugar and glucose into a heavy pan and place over moderate heat. When golden add the warmed almonds and continue to cook gently for 1 minute.
8. Turn on to an oiled baking sheet to cool. As it cools keep turning it over with a palette knife using a half-mixing half kneading motion. When still warm and pliable roll as thinly as possible with an oiled orange or lemon. When cold and brittle break up and store in an air-tight bag, jar or tin.
9. For the crème au beurre mousseline dissolve the sugar in water. Boil until the syrup will form short threads when stretched between finger and thumb. Whisk the yolks as you

pour on the sugar syrup in a steady stream. Whisk until thick and mousse-like. Cream the butter and when soft gradually stir it into the mousse.

10. For the chocolate fondant icing dissolve the sugar over a low heat in the water without boiling. Mix the cream of tartar with a spoonful of water and add it, or the liquid glucose, to the water and sugar. Cover and bring to the boil. Boil to 'soft ball' consistency (to a temperature of 110°–115°C/ 230°–240°F or when, if a spoonful is dropped into a bowl of cold water, it will form a soft ball when rubbed between the fingers). Stop the sugar syrup from cooking any further by dipping the bottom of the pan into a bowl of very cold water. Let it cool slightly.

11. Meanwhile melt the chocolate on a plate over a pan of simmering water. Moisten a cold hard surface and pour the sugar syrup on to it slowly. With a metal spatula fold the outsides of the mixture into the centre. Add the melted chocolate and vanilla essence and continue to turn with a spatula and work until the fondant becomes fairly stiff. Put in a bowl and stand over a pan of simmering water to soften.

12. To assemble, split the cake into three layers. Crush the nougat with a rolling pin and mix half of it with the butter cream (crème au beurre mousseline). Sandwich the cake together with this. Pour melted chocolate fondant over the top of the cake. Spread butter cream around the sides and press on the remaining crushed nougat.

13. When the chocolate has set fill a piping bag fitted with a writing nozzle with the royal icing and pipe the word 'nougatine' across the cake top.

Note I: To store fondant icing, knead into balls with one hand and store in a screw-top jar. Warm over a pan of hot water when needed.

Note II: A lemon or orange is used in place of a rolling pin because the nougat sticks less to its surface.

Note III: A sugar thermometer for fondant icing is almost essential. It is vital to get the syrup to exactly the right temperature to ensure a workable consistency, not too liquid or hard.

Chocolate Meringue Cake

For the meringue:
4 egg whites
255g/9oz caster sugar

For the filling:
100g/3½oz dark chocolate
2 egg whites
110g/¼lb icing sugar
225g/½lb unsalted butter

For the decoration:
Browned chopped *or* nibbed
  almonds
Icing sugar

1. Set the oven to 100°C/200°F, gas mark ½. Line two large (or four small) baking sheets with greaseproof paper or foil, brush lightly with oil and dust with flour.
2. First make the meringue: whisk the egg whites until stiff but not dry. Add 2 tablespoons of the sugar and keep whisking until very stiff and shiny. Fold in the remaining sugar.
3. Divide the mixture into four and spread thinly into equal-sized circles about 18cm/7in across.
4. Bake until crisp and dry (about 1½ hours). Immediately peel off the paper or foil and leave to cool on a wire rack.
5. Meanwhile prepare the filling: melt the chocolate on a plate over a pan of hot water. Whip the egg whites with the sugar in a bowl set over a pan of simmering water until the mixture is stiff, smooth and shiny.
6. Beat the butter until light and creamy. Gradually beat in the meringue mixture. Stir in the chocolate.
7. Sandwich the meringue discs with chocolate filling and spread the top and sides with the same mixture. Completely cover the sides with browned chopped almonds. Chill.
8. Place three thin strips of greaseproof paper over the gateau in parallel lines. Dust the cake with icing sugar. Carefully remove the greaseproof paper strips, leaving a pretty stripy pattern.

Pain de Gênes (rich almond cake)

110g/¼lb blanched almonds
3 eggs
140g/5oz caster sugar
55g/2oz potato starch *or* plain
  flour
½ teaspoon baking powder

Good pinch of salt
85g/3oz butter
1 tablespoon Amaretto *or*
  kirsch
Icing sugar

1. Set the oven at 180°C/350°F, gas mark 4. Brush a moule-à-manqué or 20cm/8in cake tin with butter, line the bottom with a circle of greaseproof paper and brush it again.
2. Grind the almonds finely and put them into a bowl. Add the eggs one at a time, beating thoroughly between each addition until the mixture is pale and thick. Add the sugar.
3. Sift the potato starch or flour, baking powder and salt into the mixture, folding as lightly as possible with a large metal spoon.
4. Melt the butter and carefully fold it in with the minimum of stirring. Add the kirsch or Amaretto. Pour the mixture into the cake tin.
5. Bake for 30–35 minutes or until the cake is brown on top and springs back when lightly pressed with a finger.
6. Allow the cake to cool for 5 minutes in the tin, then loosen the sides with a knife and turn out on to a wire rack to cool. When cold sift a thin layer of icing sugar over the top.

Index

Index

Aberdeen rowies (Scotch crescents) 302 3
Accompaniments, traditional British 28
Aioli sauce, general information 58
Almond cake, rich 344
Almond cakes 312
Almond pastry:
  method 52
  recipe 290–1
Anchovy sauce, general information 55
Andalouse sauce, general information 59
Apple fritters, Chinese 260–1
Apple marmalade 322 3
Apple purée (sweet) 322
Apple sauce:
  general information 59
  recipe 239
Apricot glaze 323
Artichokes with clarified butter (starter) 120
Aspic 229–30
  setting capacity of packeted 16
Aurore sauce, general information 56

Bacon, general information:
  preparing gammon steaks or bacon chops 77

Baked Alaska, flaming 281–2
Baking, general information 34, 37–54
  cakes 40–3
  pastries 49–54
  raising agents 38–40
Baking blind 142
Baking powder 39
Baking with yeast, general information 43–9
  baking process 48
  bran 45
  cooling bread 48
  fat 46
  flour 43–4
  functions and forms of yeast 45
  glazes 49
  kneading 47
  knocking down (knocking back) 47
  leavening 45
  liquid 46
  mixing and sponging 46
  'oven spring' 48
  proving 47–8
  rising 47
  using sugar or molasses 46
Banana and grape chartreuse 275–6
Basting roasting meat 33
Bâtarde sauce, general information 58

Batters 314–15
  French pancakes (*crêpes*)
    314–15
  fritter 315
Bavarois:
  coffee cream 264
  orange, with meringues 262–
    264
Beans:
  bean and bean salad 130–1
  bean and salami casserole
    (starter) 116–17
  broad beans and bacon 133
  lima beans with dill and to-
    matoes 132–3
  whole broad beans in water-
    cress sauce 134
Béarnaise sauce, general information 58
Béchamel sauce:
  general information 55
  recipe 240
Beef, general information:
  catering quantities 91
  cooking times for steaks 69–
    70
  cutting meat for stewing 73
  cutting meat for stroganoff
    73
  cutting steaks 73
  preparing lean meat for
    roasting 73
  roasting 68–9
Beef, main dishes 170–9
  boeuf à la mode 176–8
  boeuf à la mode en gelée 178–
    179
  boeuf Philippe 171

  filet de boeuf à la Stroganoff
    172
  fillet *en croûte* 175–6
  green peppercorn steaks 173
  spiced beef 170
  steak Wellington 173–4
Beef bouillon (broth) 233–4
Beef consommé 97
Beurre à l'Anglaise see Butter
  sauce
Beurre blanc 236
Beurre manié 55
Bicarbonate of soda 39
Bigarade sauce, general infor-
  mation 59
Biscuits 333–4
  macaroons 333–4
  sponge fingers 334
Black cherry frozen dessert 277
Boiling 37
Bombes, general information
  88–9
Bombes, recipes *see Ice creams*
  and bombes
Boned stuffed chicken 209–10
Boned stuffed poussin 206–7
Boning:
  meat 70–1
  poultry 83
Bordelaise sauce:
  general information 57
  recipe 245
Borscht, iced creamy 96–7
Bouchée cases 294
Bouillons:
  beef 233–4
  court 233
Braising 36

Bran 45
Brawn 197–8
Bread sauce, general information 60
Breads 316–19
  brioche 318–19
  French 317
  plaited white loaf 316
Brioche 318–19
Broad beans and bacon 133
Broad beans in watercress sauce, whole 134
Broiling 33
Brown flour 44
Brown rice pilaff with sesame seeds 138
Brown sauces, general information 56–8
Brown stock 230–1
Brussels sprouts, creamed 132
Butchery 70–7
  beef 73–4
  boning 70–1, *71*
  lamb 74–6
  larding 72–3
  pork and bacon 77
  rolling and tying 72
  sewing up joints after stuffing 72, *72*
Butter sauce, general information 58
Butters 235–6
  beurre blanc 236
  clarified 236
  maître d'hôtel 235
  mint and mustard 235

Cabbage, spring, with cream

and nutmeg 134–5
Cake tins, preparation 42–3
  for buns 42
  for fruit cakes 42–3
  for melting- and creaming-method cakes 42
  for whisking-method cakes 42
Cakes, methods 40–3
  creaming 40–1
  melting 40
  rubbing-in 40
  whisking 41
Cakes, recipes 335–44
  chocolate meringue 343
  Christmas 335–6
  Dobez torte 339–40
  gâteau nougatine 340–2
  Genoise commune 337–8
  Genoise fine 338
  pain de Gênes (rich almond) 344
  whisked sponge 336–7
Cannelloni (starter) 111–12
Cannelloni with spinach and mushroom filling (starter) 117–18
Câpre (caper) sauce, general information 58
Caramel custard, pear 262
Caraque, chocolate 332
Cardinale sauce, general information 55
Catering quantities 89–95
  cocktail parties 94–5
  fish 91–2
  game 90
  meat 90–1

Catering quantities – *cont.*
  miscellaneous 93
  poultry 90
  salads 94
  vegetables 92
Ceviche 140
Champagne sorbet 281
Charlotte russe 265
Chasseur sauce, general information 56
Cheese and sorrel soufflé (starter) 127
Cherry sauce for duck 245
Cherry strudels 307–8
Chicken, general information (*see also Poultry and game birds*):
  catering quantities 90
  roasting times 84
Chicken and beanshoot salad (starter) 108
Chicken and turkey, main dishes 201–15
  boned stuffed chicken 209–210
  boned stuffed poussin 206–207
  chicken *à la King* 201—2
  chicken chaudfroid 210–13
  chicken Maryland 203–4
  chicken St Menehould 204–5
  Christmas stuffed turkey with ham 214–15
  jambonneaux de poulet 208
  poussins with Pernod 205–6
  tarragon chicken 202–3
  vinegar chicken 213–14
Chicken filling for *gougère* 107–8
Chicken liver pâté 101
Chinese apple fritters 260–1
Chocolate and praline bombe 280–1
Chocolate and vanilla bombe 279–80
Chocolate *caraque* 332
Chocolate ice cream 278–9
Chocolate meringue cake 343
Chocolate mousse 266
Chocolate mousse and ginger syllabub, layered 266–7
Chocolate sauce 323
Choron sauce, general information 58
Choux pastry:
  method 53
  recipe 288
Christmas cake 335–6
Christmas stuffed turkey with ham 214–16
Claret jelly 273–5
Clarified butter 236
Cocktail parties, catering quantities 94–5
Coffee cream *bavarois* 264
Coffee fondant icing 324
Confit d'oie 221–2
Consommé:
  beef 97
  garnishes 98
  royale 99
Conversion tables 13–16
Cooking methods 28–37
Cooking times *see Beef, Chicken etc*
Court bouillon 233

Crab or lobster sauce 243

Cranberry sauce, general information 59

Crayfish flan 141–2

Cream desserts *see Puddings and desserts*

Crème Anglaise (English egg custard) 321

Crème au beurre mousseline 333

Crème pâtissière 320–1

Crème sauce, general information 55

Crêpes 314–15

Crêpes Suzette 249–50

Croissants 301–2

Cucumber *à la crème*, hot 135

Cucumber with soured cream (starter) 121–2

Cumberland sauce:
general information 60
recipe 237

Curry, lamb 181–2

Custards *see Puddings and desserts*

Danish pastries:
almond squares 298
basic recipe 296–8
cinnamon wheels 300
crescents 300–1
crosses 299–300
pinwheels 298–9

Deep frying 30–3
dealing with fat fire 32
reasons for coating food 30–1
safety precautions 32–3

technique 31–2
temperatures 31

Demi-glace sauce, long method:
general information 57–8
recipe 244

Demi-glace sauce (*sauce espagnole*), short method:
general information 56–7
recipe 244

Desserts *see Puddings and desserts*

Diane sauce, general information 57

Dobez torte 339–40

Duck, general information (*see also Poultry and game birds*):
catering quantities 90
cooking time (wild) 85

Duck and goose, main dishes 216–22
cold boned goose with aspic 219–21
confit d'oie 221–2
pressed duck 216–17
roast duck with cherry or apple sauce 218

Duck pâté with aspic, smooth 103–4

Eel, to skin 64–5

Eel pie 168–9

Egg and prawn mousse with aspic (starter) 125–6

Egg custard, English (crème Anglaise) 321

Egg pasta 285–6

Egg sauce, general information 56
Espagnole (easy demi-glace) sauce:
  general information 56–7
  recipe 244

Fats for pastries 49
Fennel sauce, general information 58
Filet de boeuf à la Stroganoff 172
Fillet of beef *en croûte* 175–7
Filo pastry *see Strudel pastry*
Fish, general information 60–5
  catering quantities 91–2
  filleting and skinning round fish 63–4, *63, 64*
  gutting and cleaning 62
  removing scales 61
  skinning and filleting flat fish 62–3, *63*
  skinning eel 64–5
  slicing smoked salmon 65
  stuffing 65
Fish, main dishes 140–69
  baked turbot with cheese and shrimp sauce 162
  ceviche 140
  chaudfroid of sole 158–61
  crayfish flan 141–2
  deep-fried seafood envelopes 142–3
  deep-fried whitebait 163
  easy quenelles 166–7
  eel pie 168–9
  flat salmon pie 150

fritto misto 167–8
  grilled sardines 141
  inkfish (squid) stew 145–6
  lemon sole with burnt hollandaise 155
  lobster thermidor 146–7
  pain de poisson 144–5
  prawn pilaff 147–8
  salmon *en croûte* 151–2
  salmon mayonnaise 148–9
  sea trout *en papillote* 153–4
  sole Colbert 157–8
  sole Véronique 156–7
  trout with hazelnuts 161
  turbot and scallop moulds 164–6
Fish, starters:
  haddock pudding 128–9
  Italian seafood salad 105–6
Fish stock 231
Flaky pastry:
  method 51–2
  recipe 291–2
Flaming baked Alaska 281–2
Flour:
  brown 44
  for pastries 49
  for yeast baking 43–4
  plain household 44
  self-raising 39, 44
  stoneground 44
  strong 43
  wheat 37–8, 43
  white 43
  wholemeal (wholewheat) 44
Fondant icing 324
Fond brun 232
French bread 317–18

French dressing (vinaigrette):
general information 60
recipe 237
Fritter batter 315
Fritters:
Chinese apple 260–1
pineapple 259–60
sweetcorn 138
Fritto misto 167–8
Frogs' legs (starter) 109–10
Fruit puddings and desserts *see
Puddings and desserts*
Fruit starters:
jellied grape and mint ring
121
pears with Stilton and poppy
seed dressing 118–19
pineapple *japonais* 122–3
Frying 30–3
deep 30–3
shallow 30

Game, general information:
catering quantities 90
Game, main dishes 223–8
cold game pie 224–6
galantine of pheasant 226–8
partridge baked with cab-
bage 223–4
Game birds *see Poultry and
game birds*
Game chip baskets filled with
chestnuts 136
Garnishes:
classic 25–7
for consommé 98
Gâteau nougatine 340–2

Gâteau St Honoré aux oranges
310–11
Gaufrettes Viennoise 304
Gelatine, setting capacity of 16
Genoise commune 337–8
Genoise fine 338
Ginger roll, spiced 255–6
Ginger syllabub 261
Ginger syllabub and chocolate
mousse, layered 266–7
Glace de viande 232
Glaze, apricot 323
Glazes for yeast breads 49
Glossary of cooking terms 17–
25
Gluten 38
Gnocchi, fried (starter) 110–11
Goldenberry flan 305–6
Goose, general information
(*see also Poultry and game
birds*):
catering quantities 90
Goose, main dishes *see Duck
and goose*
Gooseberry sauce, sweet 322
Gougères (starter) 107–8
Goulash, Hungarian veal
191–2
Grape and banana chartreuse
275–6
Grape and mint ring, jellied 121
Green peppercorn steaks 173
Grilling 29–30
grilling steaks 69–70
Grouse, general information
(*see also Poultry and game
birds*):
catering quantities 90

Grouse – *cont.*
  cooking time 85

Haddock pudding (starter)
  128–9
Ham dishes *see Pork and ham*
Hare terrine 102–3
Hearts, braised lambs' 199–200
Hollandaise sauce:
  general information 58
  recipe 242–3
Honey boats 312
Hot water crust pastry, general
  information 52–3
Hungarian veal goulash 191–2

Ice cream, general information
  86–9
  bombes 88–9
  methods of making 86–8
  water ices 88
Ice cream and bombes, recipes
  277–84
  basic bombe filling 279
  black cherry frozen dessert
    277
  Champagne sorbet 281
  chocolate and praline bombe
    280–1
  chocolate and vanilla bombe
    279–80
  chocolate ice cream 278–9
  flaming baked Alaska 281–2
  pistachio ice cream in biscuit
    cups 283–4
  vanilla ice cream 278
Icing, techniques 325–31

Icings and confectionery 324–
  333
  chocolate caraque 332
  coffee fondant icing 324
  crème au beurre mousseline
    333
  fondant icing 324
  marzipan, cooked 331
  praline 332
  royal icing 325–31
Inkfish (squid) stew 145

Jalousie 248–9
Jambalaya 189–90
Jambon persillé 186–8
Jambonneaux de poulet 208
Jellies, dessert *see Puddings and
  desserts*

Kidneys Robert, veal 198
Kneading yeast dough 47
Knocking down (knocking
  back) yeast dough 47

Lamb, general information:
  catering quantities 90–1
  preparing crown roast 76
  preparing French trimmed
    best end cutlets 74–5
  preparing guard of honour
    76
  preparing noisettes 75, *75*
  preparing saddle 74
  roasting 69
Lamb, main dishes 179–86
  curry 181–2
  cutlets in pastry 184–5

Lamb, main dishes – *cont.*
  cutlets soubise 182–3
  daube 180–1
  noisettes with onion and
    mint purée 183–4
  steak *à la Catalane* 179–80
  with dill sauce 185–6
Lasagne verde bolognese
  (starter) 114–15
Leeks mimosa vinaigrette
  (starter) 119
Lemon jelly 270–1
Lemon jelly, clear 271–2
Lemon sole *see Sole*
Lima beans with dill and tomatoes 132–3
Lobster or crab sauce 243
Lobster thermidor 146–7

Macaroons 333–4
Madeira sauce, general information 57
Maids of Honour 306
Maître d'hôtel butter 235
Marrow with garlic and tomato
  136–7
Marzipan, cooked 331
Mayonnaise:
  general information 58–9
  recipe 241–2
Measurements, useful 16
Meat, general information 65–
  77
  butchery 70–7
  catering quantities 90–1
  factors affecting tenderness
    65–8

hanging 66–7
  roasting 68–9
Meat, main dishes 170–200
  beef 170–9
  lamb 179–86
  offal 197–200
  pork and ham 186–91
  veal 191–6
Melba sauce 321
Meringues 250
  floating islands 253–4
  floating islands with caramel
    254
  floating islands with coffee
    custard 254
  floating islands with orange
    254–5
  meringue Mont Blanc 251–2
  Pavlova 252
Methods of cooking 28–37
Metric conversion tables 13–16
  American/European meas-
    ures 15
  lengths 15
  liquid measures 14
  oven temperatures 16
  useful measurements 16
  weights 13–14
  wine quantities 14
Mille feuilles 309–10
Mint and mustard butter 235
Mint sauce:
  general information 60
Mornay sauce:
  general information 56
  recipe 240
Mousseline sauce, general information 58

Mousses, savoury:
  egg and prawn with aspic (starter) 125–6
Mousses, sweet *see Puddings and desserts*
Moutarde sauce, general information 58
Mushroom sauce, general information 56

Noisettes, preparation of 74, *75*
Noisettes of lamb with onion and mint sauce purée 183–4

Offal, main dishes 197–200
  braised lambs' hearts 199–200
  brawn 197–8
  veal kidneys Robert 198
Onion and mint sauce, thick 238
Orange *bavarois* with meringues 262–4
Orange jelly and caramel chips 272–3
Oven roasting 33
'Oven spring' 48
Oven temperatures 16

Pain de Gênes 344
Pain de poisson 144–5
Palmiers 303–4
Pancakes, French (*crêpes*) 314–15
Parsley, fried 139
Partridge, general information (*see also Poultry and game birds*):

catering quantities 90
cooking time 85
Partridge, main dishes:
  baked with cabbage 223–4
Pasta 285–6
  egg 285–6
  green 285
Pasta, starters:
  cannelloni 111–12
  cannelloni with spinach and mushroom filling 117–18
  lasagne verde bolognese 114–15
  Prue's easy party pasta 115–116
  ravioli 112–13
Pastries 296–313
  almond cakes 312
  cherry strudels 307–8
  croissants 301–2
  Danish 296–301
  gâteau St Honoré aux oranges 310–11
  gaufrettes Viennoise 304
  goldenberry flan 305–6
  honey boats 312
  Maids of Honour 306
  mille feuilles 309–10
  palmiers 303–4
  printaniers 313
  Scotch crescents (Aberdeen rowies) 302–3
  strawberry tartlets 308–9
Pastry, general information 49–54
  addition of water 50
  choux 53
  fats 49

Pastry – *cont.*
  flaky and puff 51–2
  flours 49
  hot water crust 52–3
  pâte sucrée, almond pastry
    and pâte à paté 52
  shortcrust 50–1
  strudel 54
  suet crust 51
Pastry, recipes 286–96
  almond (pâte frolle) 290–1
  bouchée cases 294
  choux 288
  flaky 291–2
  pâte à paté 291
  pâte sucrée 290
  puff 293–4
  rich shortcrust 287
  rough puff 292–3
  shortcrust 286–7
  strudel paste (filo paste) 289
  vol-au-vent 295–6
  wholemeal 287–8
Pastry starter:
  gougères 107–8
Pâte à paté:
  method 52
  recipe 291
Pâte frolle *see Almond pastry*
Pâte sucrée:
  method 52
  recipe 290
Pâtés and terrines 101–4
  chicken liver pâté 101
  hare terrine 102–3
  smooth duck pâté with aspic
    103–4
Pavlova 252

Peaches:
  pêches Cardinales 257
  stuffed with praline cream
    258
Pear caramel custard 262
Pears with Stilton and poppy
  seed dressing (starter) 118
  119
Perigueux sauce, general infor-
  mation 57
Pesto sauce for pasta 238–9
Pheasant, general information
    (*see also Poultry and game
    birds*):
  catering quantities 90
  cooking time 85
Pheasant, main dishes:
  galantine of 226–8
Pigeon, general information
    (*see also Poultry and game
    birds*):
  catering quantities 90
  cooking time 85
Pineapple fritters 259–60
Pineapple *japonais* (starter)
  122–3
Pistachio ice cream in biscuit
  cups 283–4
Plain household flour 44
Plaited white loaf 316
Poaching 37
Poivrade sauce:
  general information 57
  recipe 246
Pork, general information:
  catering quantities 91
  preparing American or
    Chinese spare ribs 77

Pork – *cont.*
  preparing chops 77
  roasting 69
Pork and ham, main dishes 186–91
  jambalaya 189–90
  jambon persillé 186–8
  spiced cherry pork with tarragon dressing 188–9
  sweet and sour pork 190–1
Pork jelly 233
Pot roasting 36
Potatoes:
  new, vinaigrette 129
  pommes Parisienne 137
Poulette sauce, general information 56
Poultry and game, main dishes 201–28
  chicken and turkey 201–15
  duck and goose 216–22
  game 223–8
Poultry and game birds, general information 77–85
  barding 83
  boning and stuffing 83
  catering quantities 90
  cleaning and drawing 77–8
  giblets, etc 78–9
  jointing 80–2, *80–2*
  roasting times 84–5
  trussing 79–80, *79*
Poussins:
  boned, stuffed 206–7
  with Pernod 205–6
Praline 332
Praline and chocolate bombe 280–1

Prawn and egg mousse with aspic (starter) 125–6
Prawn pilaff 147–8
Pressed duck 216–17
Printaniers 313
Proving yeast dough 47–8
Prune mousse 267–8
Prue's easy party pasta 115
Puddings and desserts 247–284
  banana and grape chartreuse 275–6
  charlotte russe 265
  Chinese apple fritters 260–1
  chocolate mousse 266
  claret jelly 273–5
  clear lemon jelly 271–2
  coffee cream *bavarois* 264
  cold raspberry soufflé 269–270
  crêpes Suzette 249
  floating islands 253–4
  floating islands with caramel 254
  floating islands with coffee custard 254
  floating islands with orange 254–5
  ginger syllabub 261
  Greek iced fruit salad 256–7
  ice creams and bombes 277–284
  jalousie 248–9
  layered chocolate mousse and ginger syllabub 266–7
  lemon jelly 270–1
  meringue Mont Blanc 251–2
  meringues 250

orange *bavarois* with meringues 262–4
orange jelly and caramel chips 272–3
Pavlova 252
peaches stuffed with praline cream 258
pear caramel custard 262
pêches Cardinales 257
pineapple fritters 259–60
prune mousse 267–8
rhubarb lattice flan 247–8
St Clement's jelly 276
spiced ginger roll 255–6
summer pudding 258–9
tangerine mousse in chocolate case 268–9
Puff pastry:
method 51–2
recipe 293–4

Quail, general information (*see also Poultry and game birds*):
catering quantities 90
cooking time 85
Quantities, catering 89–95
Quenelles, easy fish 166–7

Raising agents:
air 38
baking powder 39
bicarbonate of soda 39
self-raising flour 39
steam 38
yeast 40
Raspberry soufflé, cold 269–70
Ravioli (starter) 112–13

Reforme sauce, general information 57
Remoulade sauce, general information 59
Rhubarb lattice 247–8
Rice:
brown rice pilaff with sesame seeds 138
catering quantities 92
Rich shortcrust pastry 287
Roasting 33–4
basting 33
game 85
in bag, etc 33–4
meat 68–9
oven 33
poultry 84
spit 33
Robert sauce, general information 57
Rough puff pastry, recipe 292–3
Roux, general information 54
blond 54
brown 54
white 54
Rowies, Aberdeen 302–3
Royal icing 325–31

Salads, catering quantities 94
Salads:
bean and bean 130–1
chicken and beanshoot 108
Italian seafood 105–6
new potatoes vinaigrette 129
watercress with croutons 130

Salami and bean casserole (starter) 116–17
Salmon, smoked, to slice 65
Salmon *en croûte* 151–2
Salmon mayonnaise 148–9
Salmon pie, flat 150
Sardines, grilled 141
Sauces, savoury, general information 54–60
  adding egg yolks 55
  aioli 58
  anchovy 55
  andalouse 59
  apple 59
  aurore 56
  bâtarde 58
  béarnaise 58
  béchamel 55
  beurre manié 55
  bigarade 59
  blond (velouté) 56
  bordelaise 57
  bread 60
  brown 56–8
  butter 58
  câpre (caper) 58
  cardinale 55
  chasseur 56
  choron 58
  cornflour or arrowroot (*fécule*) 54
  cranberry 59
  crème 55
  Cumberland 60
  demi-glace 57–8
  Diane 57
  egg 56
  espagnole 56–7
  fennel 58
  French dressing (vinaigrette) 60
  hollandaise 58
  Madeira 57
  mayonnaise 58–9
  mint 60
  mornay 56
  mousseline 58
  moutarde 58
  mushroom 56
  Perigueux 57
  poivrade 57
  poulette 56
  reforme 57
  remoulade 59
  Robert 57
  roux 54
  soubise 56
  suprême 56
  tartare 59
  tomato 60
  white 55–6
Sauces, savoury, recipes 237–246
  apple 239
  béchamel 240
  bordelaise 245
  cherry (for duck) 245
  crab or lobster 243
  Cumberland 237
  demi-glace (long method) 244
  demi-glace (*sauce espagnole*) (short method) 244
  French dressing (vinaigrette) 237
  hollandaise 242–3

mayonnaise 241–2
mornay 240
pesto (for pasta) 238–9
poivrade 246
soubise 241
tartare 242
thick onion and mint 238
tomato 238
white 239
Sauces, sweet, recipes 320–3
apple marmalade 322–3
apple purée 322
apricot glaze 323
chocolate 323
crème Anglaise (English egg custard) 321
crème pâtissière 320–1
gooseberry 322
Melba 321
sugar syrup 320
Scotch crescents (Aberdeen rowies) 302–3
Sea trout en papillote 153–4
Seafood envelopes, deep-fried 142–3
Seafood salad, Italian (starter) 105–6
Self-raising flour 44
Shallow frying 30
Shellfish, catering quantities 92
Shellfish, recipes see Fish
Shortcrust pastry:
method 50–1
recipe 286–7
Shortcrust pastry, rich, recipe 287
Smoked salmon, to slice 65

Snails à la bourguignonne (starter) 108–9
Snipe, general information (see also Poultry and game birds):
cooking time 85
Sole:
chaudfroid of 158–61
lemon, with burnt hollandaise 155
Colbert 157–8
Véronique 156–7
Sorrel and cheese soufflé (starter) 127
Soubise sauce:
general information 56
recipe 241
Soufflés, savoury:
sorrel and cheese (starter) 127
Soufflés, sweet see Puddings and desserts
Soups 96–100
beef consommé 97
consommé royale 99
iced creamy borscht 96–7
soupe au pistou 99–100
Spiced beef 170
Spiced cherry pork with tarragon dressing 188–9
Spiced ginger roll 255–6
Spinch mould (starter) 124–5
Spinach (green) pasta 285
Spinach roulade (starter) 123–124
Spit roasting 33
Sponge, whisked 336–7
Sponge fingers 334

'Sponging' yeast 46
Spring cabbage with cream and nutmeg 134–5
Squid:
  inkfish stew 145
Starters 96–131
  eggs, savoury soufflés and mousses 125–9
  fruit and vegetable 118–25
  pasta and other miscellaneous 105–18
  pâtés and terrines 101–4
  salads 129–31
  soups 96–100
Steaks, general information:
  catering quantities 90
  cooking times 69–70
Steaks, main dishes:
  green peppercorn 173
  Wellington 173–4
Steaming 34–5
  in pudding basin 34–5
  in two-tier steamer 34
Stewing 35–6
  fruit 35–6
  to avoid discoloration of fruit 36
Stocks 229–34
  aspic 229–30
  beef bouillon (broth) 233–4
  brown 230–1
  court bouillon 233
  fish 231
  fond brun 232
  glace de viande 232
  pork jelly 233
  white 229
Stoneground flour 44

Strawberry tartlets 308–9
Stroganoff, beef 172
Strong flour 43
Strudel pastry:
  method 54
  recipe 289
Strudels, cherry 307–8
Suet crust pastry, method 51
Sugar syrup 320
Summer pudding 258–9
Suprême sauce, general information 56
Sweet and sour pork 190–1
Sweetcorn fritters 138
Sweets see Puddings and desserts
Syllabub, ginger 261

Tangerine mousse in chocolate case 268–9
Tarragon chicken 202–3
Tartare sauce:
  general information 59
  recipe 242
Teal, general information (see also Poultry and game birds);
  cooking time 85
Terrine, hare 102–3
Tomato sauce:
  general information 60
  recipe 238
Trout with hazelnuts 161
Turbot, baked, with cheese and shrimp sauce 162
Turbot and scallop moulds 164–6

Turkey, general information (*see also Poultry and game birds*):
  catering quantities 90
  thawing and cooking 84–5
Turkey, main dishes *see Chicken and turkey*

Vanilla and chocolate bombe 279–80
Vanilla ice cream 278
Veal, general information:
  catering quantities 91
  roasting 69
Veal kidneys Robert 198
Veal, main dishes 191–6
  cordon bleu 193–4
  escalopes with *ragoût fin* 194–5
  escalopes with rosemary 192
  Hungarian goulash 191–2
  Marsala 193
  vitello tonnato 195–6
Vegetables 132–9
  broad beans and bacon 133
  brown rice pilaff with sesame seeds 138
  creamed Brussels sprouts 132
  fried parsley 139
  game chip baskets filled with chestnuts 136
  hot cucumber *à la crème* 135
  lima beans with dill and tomatoes 132–3
  marrow with garlic and tomato 136–7
  pommes Parisienne 137
  spring cabbage with cream and nutmeg 134–5
  sweetcorn fritters 138
  whole broad beans in watercress sauce 134
Vegetables, general information:
  catering quantities 92
Vegetables, starters:
  artichokes with clarified butter 120
  cucumber with soured cream 121–2
  leeks mimosa vinaigrette 119
  spinach mould 124–5
  spinach roulade 123–4
Venison, catering quantities 90
Vinaigrette 237
Vinegar chicken 213–14
Vitello tonnato 195–6
Vol-au-vent case 295–6

Water ices, general information 88
Watercress salad with croutons 130
Whisked sponge 336–7
White bread, plaited 316
White flour 43
White sauce, savoury:
  general information 55–6
  recipe 239
White stock 229
Whitebait, deep-fried 163
Wholemeal (wholewheat) flour 44
Wholemeal pastry, recipe 287–8

Wine quantities, imperial/
  metric equivalents 14
Woodcock, general information (*see also Poultry and
  game birds*):

cooking time 85
Yeast (*see also Baking*) 45
  compressed or fresh 45
  cooking with yeast 43–9
  dried 45